July 18/22

Presented to Kayla,
a very special
niece ☺

Steven Kodruba

TO WAR SURVIVE

A STORY OF BETRAYAL, ETHNIC CLEANSINGS, DEPORTATIONS, AND REPATRIATIONS.

STEVEN KASHUBA

Also by the author:

Once Lived a Village   **Destination Gulag**

Order this book online at www.trafford.com
or email orders@trafford.com

Most Trafford titles are also available at major online book retailers.

Print information available on the last page.

ISBN: 978-1-4907-8752-7 (sc)
ISBN: 978-1-4907-8753-4 (hc)
ISBN: 978-1-4907-9559-1 (e)

Library of Congress Control Number: 2019907357

Trafford rev. 06/29/2019

 www.trafford.com

North America & international
toll-free: 1 888 232 4444 (USA & Canada)
fax: 812 355 4082

CONTENTS

STALIN'S CONSPIRACY

ROOTS

IN SEARCH OF FAMILY

Communism, The Equal Sharing Of Misery

Against All Odds

About the Book

Steven Kashuba formulates his literary family saga on the backdrop of the most complex and emotional issues still being debated today by historians and government research agencies. His story provokes shock and emotion, moving readers to want to learn more and construct a better future.

Dr. Roman Petryshyn, *Trustee, Ukrainian Foundation for College Education.*

***

Readers will find much to stimulate their thinking in this book. The stark nature of presentation will provoke both thought and emotion and help us think more clearly about important issues.

Lyle Abraham, *sports enthusiast and entrepreneur in the petroleum services industry.*

***

To War Survive takes the reader not only on a dark and twisted journey into the perils of world conflict but also into ethnic cleansings and population transfers. A must read!

John Wronko, *businessman and staunch supporter of the Ukrainian Community.*

***

Steven Kashuba deals with the complexities of national and international conflict in a way to immediately capture your interest.

Dr. Bohdan Medwidsky, *Professor Emeritus,*
Modern Languages and Cultural Studies, University of Alberta.

***

To *War Survive* is a riveting drama based on historical truths that were initiated by man's avarice and lust for power. The story takes us to that devastating place where history itself fears to tread, but that is precisely where master story-teller Steven Kashuba takes us on his decades-long trek to find his ancestral roots. *To War Survive* is a *must read* for anyone who has ever wondered about their own ancestry and what happened to their relatives before, during, or after two world wars. *Thank you*, Steven, *for having lit that wick of wonder in me and my family through this great book!*

The Honourable Gene Zwozdesky,
Former Speaker, Legislative Assembly of Alberta,
author of Bill 37, The Ukrainian Famine and
Genocide (Holodomor) Memorial Day Act.

DEDICATION TO ORPHANS

Orphans have become the innocent victims of the world's worst calamities. Without parents and the support of an extended family, vulnerable orphans face the world without the comfort and assurance of belonging and connection. Many nations suffered at the hands of Nazis and Soviets during World War II. However, no group suffered as much as did the orphans left behind. Two orphans, thanks to their adoptive family, not only survived the war but also found a warm and loving home in Poland. Although it is too late to seek justice for the orphans of war, the least we can do is recognize their suffering and do all we can to make certain that such atrocities do not happen again.

About The Author

Steven Kashuba is a first-generation Canadian whose parents immigrated to Canada from Poland. He started his professional career as a teacher in a small rural community, soon moved to Edmonton, and sought degrees in educational administration, culminating with a PhD from Oregon State University. He has a wide range of teaching and educational administration experiences in secondary and post-secondary schools. Upon retiring from Alberta Education as an education manager, he undertook several business consulting assignments in Europe, served on several quasi-judicial boards, and managed a home building company.

Over the years, Steven wondered why his parents referred to their place of birth as the *Old Country*. While serving with the Department of National Defense in Germany, he set out in search of family in the *Old Country*—an interest that remains with him to this day. After completing several trips to Europe, he uncovered something that perhaps even his parents did not know. The aftermath of World War II left behind millions of orphans. He was shocked to discover that in 1944 his father's cousin and wife were murdered leaving behind two infant children. This raised important questions: *Were those two orphans living today? If so, would he be able to find them?* The answers to these perplexing questions are found in this story.

Steven, the author of *Once Lived a Village*, and *Destination Gulag*, continues to be involved in uncovering the rich tapestry of his heritage. Aside from research and writing, much of his time is spent in volunteerism and real estate. As an avid sports enthusiast, you will often find him out on the golf links trying to discover the elusive secrets of the game.

ACKNOWLEDGEMENTS

This story takes place over time and in several East European countries—among them Poland, Ukraine, and Russia. Without travel to these countries and access to genealogical and historical records, the telling of this story would not be possible. And yet, perhaps the most important source of information came not from national archives but from the first-hand experiences of those who had been directly impacted by and survived the horrors of war.

I want to extend my appreciation to the Central State Historical Archives of Ukraine and the State Archive of Lviv Oblast for providing me with information relating to population transfers at the end of World War II and to the State Archives in Przemysl, Poland, for their assistance in accessing civil and church records for the Subcarpathian Voivodeship.

Thank you, Franek Zaborniak, for sharing the story of the events which led to the loss of your birth parents and your adoption by a Polish family. Your story has captured the indomitable spirit of orphans of world conflict and inspired me to write this book.

From numerous cousins in Europe, I came to understand the horrors of war and the needless loss of life. I listened to a tearful aunt who told me about working in Nazi Germany during the war as an Ostarbeiter and to a cousin who served the Nazi Regime in Austria as an Eastern Worker. I was especially saddened to hear of the peculiar circumstances which led to the loss of an uncle shortly after his family safely arrived in Soviet Ukraine from Poland.

My special thanks go to Shellie Gray for putting me in touch with PolishOrigins.com and Rooted in Eastern Europe, and to Fr. Henry Licznerski of the St. Joan of Arc Catholic Diocese in Blythe, California, for blessing the initial manuscript of the book with copious amounts of Holy Water. Thank you, Izzacc Rosas of Blythe, California, and Maryana

Medvid-Yurkiv of Lviv, Ukraine, for improving the quality of the images used in this manuscript.

Every author needs a good illustrator, a competent editor, and the support of many. With these thoughts in mind, I want to thank Dr. Roman Petryshyn, Trustee of the Ukrainian Foundation for College Education, Dr. Bohdan Medwidsky, Professor Emeritus, University of Alberta, and the Honourable Gene Zwozkesky, former Speaker, Legislative Assembly, Governement of Alberta for their input and support. Perhaps the most important person in getting this story into print is my wife, Sharon, who spent countless hours reviewing and editing the story. *Without your help*, Sharon, *this book would not have seen the light of day!*

MAIN CHARACTERS

Many of the characters in this story are members of my extended family and are presented as such. However, in some cases it was necessary to use a pseudonym or a code name in order to protect the identity of a particular group, person, or family member.

1. Clan Kaszub

    1.1 Johannes Kaszuba and his sons, Jakub and Ivan, freed from serfdom, are among the first to settle in the village of Grochi, Galicia.

    1.2 Mariia Kaszuba, daughter of Johannes Kaszuba, marries a Pole (Mareusz Zaborniak), leaves the Greek Catholic Church in favour of the Roman Catholic Church.

    1.3 Adam Kaszuba, (great grandson of Johannes Kaszuba) and hs wife Katarzyna are murdered, leaving behind two infants, Franek and Sofija.

    1.4 Franek and Sofija are adopted by Franciszek and Bronislawa Zaborniak (Bronislawa is the descendant of Mareusz and Mariia-Kaszuba Zaborniak).

2. Brygada Salon

    2.1 Kapitan Bartek Kawa, code name: *Kon/Horse*, Commander.

    2.2 Wiktor Wozniak, code name: *Wilk/Wolf.*

    2.3 Igor Kawa, code name: *Kula/Bullet,* Corporal.

    2.4 Myron Mora, code name: *Puma/Cougar.*

    2.5 Adam Krawczyk, code name: *Lew/Lion.*

    2.6 Michal Komarski, code name: *Karabin/Rifle.*

3. Wozniak Family (Polish military colonists)

3.1 Filip and Marta Wozniak and their children, Wiktor, Donek, Monika, and Agata.

4. Konenko Family (Ukrainian military colonists)

4.1 Jan and Danuta Konenko and their children, Tanja, Juli, and Janko.

5. Kawa Family

5.1 Kapitan Bartek Kawa, Polish Cavalry, leader of Brygada Salon.
5.2 Corporal Igor Kawa (nephew of Kapitan Bartek Kawa).

IMPORTANT DATES

The partitions of Poland came to have considerable political impact upon my ancestors, particularly in Austrian Galicia, a province dominated by Polish aristocracy. After World War I, most of Galicia was ceded to the re-emergent nation of Poland. As a result, frictions between Ukrainians and Poles increased, leading to ethnic cleansings.

1772	First Partition of Poland to Austria, Prussia, and Russia
1793	Second Partition of Poland to Russia and Prussia
1795	Third Partition of Poland
1815	Poland falls under the control of Russia
1848	Austria emancipates the serf
1861	Russian Empire emancipates the serf
1863	Ukrainian language officially prohibited in the Russian Empire
1864	Emancipation of the serf in Congress Poland
1890	First Ukrainian political party, Halytska, is formed
1897	Marxist Social Democratic Party is founded in Russia
1905	Restrictions on the use of the Ukrainian language in the Russian Empire lifted
1914	Russian-Austrian rivalry leads to World War I
1917	Tsar Nicholas abdicates throne in Russia; Bolsheviks take over the government

1918	Poland becomes a Republic; Ukrainian People's Republic exists briefly
1922	USSR is formed, includes Soviet Socialist Republic of Ukraine
1932	Man-made famine occurs in Ukraine (Holodomor)
1939	Stalin concludes non-aggression pact with Germany
1941	Operation Barbarossa; Germany attacks the Soviet Union
1941	Germany occupies Ukraine
1945	East European borders are redrawn
1991	December 26, the Soviet hammer and sickle flag lowered over the Kremlin

Common Acronyms Used In The Story

1. AK; Armija Krajowa; Polish Home Army
2. Cheka, Federal Security Service of Russia, later becoming the NKVD
3. NKVD, Soviet Secret Police
4. NKVD Troika, three-member special courts martial in the Soviet Union
5. OGPU, Soviet state security agency
6. NKGB, Russian State Security
7. MVD, Ministry of Internal Affairs in Russia
8. GPU, State Political Directorate in Russia
9. KGB, Committee for State Security in the Soviet Union, from 1954 to breakup of Soviet Union
10. OUN, Organization of Ukrainian Nationalists
11. UPA, Ukrainian Partisan Army (Ukrayins'ka Povstans'ka Armiya)
12. Wołyń and Volhynia both refer to the same province

PROLOGUE

As a young boy growing up in Northern Alberta I became interested in family history, especially at times when I heard my dad talk about his service in the Austrian Infantry during World War I. Immediately, he became my hero. I learned how he dealt with tough situations brought on by world conflict and crippling economic conditions. There was, however, one thing he never talked about—his childhood and the family he left behind. I wondered why.

It would not be until I served with the Canadian Department of National Defence in Germany that I would take up the challenge of uncovering more information about my heritage. What made the challenge all the more difficult was the realization that the birthplace of my father occurred in a region of the world that did not welcome researchers with open arms. I persevered and during my final year in Germany, I received a telegram from the Prime Minister's Office in Ottawa, Canada, permitting me to travel to the Soviet Union.

My experiences, while in Russia and Soviet Ukraine, are documented in my first book, *Once Lived a Village,* a story about my search for my ancestral village which was burned to the ground in 1945 by zealous Polish nationalists. Expelled by the KGB for visiting family in Soviet Ukraine without permission, I was not able to return to any Soviet Union satellite country until after the dissolution of the Soviet Union.

Setting out in search of family once again in 1997, I was able to find all of my first cousins and their families living in Ukraine, Latvia, Russia, and Poland. However, there was one exception. When I examined my genealogical chart starting with my great-great grandfather, I was able to account for every descendant with one exception—I could not account for the descendants of Jan Kaszuba. Yes, I do understand that many church records were lost during World War II. And, yes, I was also aware that state records might have held the answer. Unfortunately, there was one problem. During this period in the history of Galicia, which was then a part of the Austrian Empire until the end of World War I, all state records had their origin with church records. Sadly, the records of Jan Kaszuba's descendants did not survive the war.

My attempts to discover what happened to all members of this one family proved fruitless until 2012. It was during one particular visit to a region of Poland, home to my ancestors, that I uncovered a startling fact.

"*Yes,*" said a very elderly woman in Ruda Różaniecka, a village near Płazów, "*Jan Kaszuba's great-grandson did live in this village. But,*" she added, pointing to a home across the street, "*Adam and his wife were murdered in 1945, leaving behind two little toddlers.*"

Her shocking revelation gave me further encouragement to research and write, *To War Survive.* Although the main tenet of the story may be about how two little orphans survived the war, the full impact of their survival cannot be told without first examining the historical events which occurred in this region of Poland during the 19th and 20th centuries. As I pieced together the story, I was not surprised to learn that even the two orphans were not completely aware of their humble beginnings. Important questions arose, *why and by whom were their parents killed? Are the two orphans living today? If they are living today, what are their names and where do they live?*

Come aboard! I hope that you will enjoy reading this story as much as I did researching and writing it.

INTRODUCTION

With invasions by the Nazis from the west and the Red Army from the east, World War II began in Poland in 1939. For many Poles, the Soviet invasion and occupation in eastern Poland was just as disastrous as was the Nazi attack on Poland in the west. The Soviets had the same goal of wiping out the Polish nationality as did the Nazis. When the Soviets occupied eastern Poland in 1939, they set about moving large numbers of Poles to Central Asia and Kazakhstan in an effort to Russify the region. At the same time, the Nazis set about occupying western Poland. As a result of the invasions by the Nazis and the Soviets, large numbers of Polish and Ukrainian children were orphaned.

When the tide of World War II began to turn in favour of the Soviet Union in 1943, the Soviets forcibly moved thousands of ethnic Poles out of the province of Volhynia to Poland. Earlier, Volhynia was part of Poland but became part of Soviet Ukraine as a result of the Molotov-Ribbentrop Pact. As a corollary, ethnic Ukrainians living in the border region of Poland were forcibly transferred to Soviet Ukraine after the war. Once again, these actions led to unintended consequences.

The human toll of population transfers is but one aspect of this story. Beyond the official statistics compiled once the war was over is another important story. Behind every soldier, father, or mother killed or missing on the battlefield lived a family who had to cope with an infant left behind—young girls and boys forced to proceed through life without the care and guidance of at least one of their parents. Orphans left behind had much to contend with. Some were referred to as *bastards* because they did not have a living father. Others said that an orphan would *not amount to anything because their parents were gone.* In postwar schools of Poland and Ukraine, many orphans said that they were shunned by classmates.

Though society seemed to discourage keeping alive the memories of their fathers, war orphans nevertheless maintained a place in their hearts for the parents they never knew or only vaguely remembered. The maelstrom of emotions surrounding the absence of their fathers and the public's reaction to it created a variety of responses among war orphans. Many of the stories of war orphans are poignant and heart wrenching. One cannot help but be deeply affected by the profound impact that losing a parent had on orphans during those chaotic times. Many orphans would rather not think or talk about their experiences.

The *World Day of War Orphans, SOS Enfants en Detresses,* was initiated by a French organization soon after World War II ended. Held on the sixth of January every year, this special day enables the International Community to recognize the plight of this particularly vulnerable group. Statistics show that World War II left behind 300,000 orphans in Poland alone. Tragically, there were many thousands of children who remained in orphanages or continued to live as street children. Most had little hope of ever achieving what they were capable of. At the end of the war in eastern Poland, thousands of people were still without proper shelter, fuel, clothing, and food. Worse yet, the border region between Poland and Soviet Ukraine was being cleared of all ethnic Ukrainians. Children, especially, were suffering untold hardships. Half the babies born in 1944 were dying before their first birthday.

This situation demanded that nations become more engaged in many areas of human activity. It certainly involved the creation of services to help children directly through the provision of maternal and child health, early childhood care, and primary education. The main objective was to reduce the rates of mortality and disease, malnutrition, and illiteracy. For years after the war, posters were going up soliciting clues about the identity of thousands of orphans cast up by World War II. Helped by the Red Cross, many orphans were located by their parents, their families, or their relatives.

To War Survive is written so that we might understand and remember their fate and light a candle for those precious orphans who survived the aftermath of World War II and who deserved a future that would have enabled them to fulfil their dreams.

During the interwar period, the Lutsk region (Volhynia) belonged to Poland. During the final stages of WWII, Volhynian Poles were forced to vacate the Lutsk region in favour of Lublin. After the war, the province of Volhynia was ceded to Soviet Ukraine.

PART 1

STALIN'S
CONSPIRACY

1

A Most Unholy Pact

A secret agreement that resulted in bitter disputes which continue to this day

September 1, 1939, turned out to be a day engraved in the memory of millions of ethnic Poles and Ukrainians. It was a day when all hell broke loose in the sleepy little village of Grochi, Poland. By prior arrangement, it was on that day that Misha Kaszuba was to help his brother with the construction of his new home. Bursting into Dima's home, which was nearing completion, it was obvious that something was terribly wrong.

"*Dima,*" stammered Misha, completely out of breath, "*have you heard the news?*"

"*Calm down, Misha. What news do you have for me?*"

"*Synowie suk, those murdering Nazi sons of bitches have attacked Poland. They destroyed the town of Mokra. The rumour is that the German Luftwaffe is headed towards Krakow and Warsaw. It looks like an all-out war.*"

Just over a week earlier, Adolf Hitler had a military plan on his mind when he addressed his Wehrmacht commanders in the Berghof, his place of residence in Obersalzberg, Bavaria.

"*The object of the war,*" announced Adolf Hitler, Reich Chancellor and leader of the Nazi Party, "*is to physically destroy the enemy and kill without pity or mercy all men, women, and children of Polish descent or language. Only in this way can we obtain the living space that Germany needs.*"

Relying on his knowledge of military history, Hitler believed that the strength of the German Wehrmacht was about to be displayed through its speed and brutality, a method similar to that used by Genghis Khan who led millions of women and children to slaughter some seven hundred years earlier.

"*Genghis Khan,*" bragged a confident Hitler, "*led them with premeditation and a happy heart. After all, history sees Genghis Khan as the leader who united many of the nomadic tribes of Northeast Asia and as the founder of the Mongolian Empire. It's a matter of indifference to me what a weak western European civilization will say about me.*"

"Yes, Dima," excitedly continued Misha, "*the rumour I heard this morning is true. No one seems to know for certain what the hell is happening. The Nazis are attacking Poland from the west. I heard that there is some sort of a secret agreement between Hitler and Stalin.*"

"*You heard of an agreement between Germany and Russia? How can that be when the two countries have been throwing shit on each others' heads for years? How is it possible for them to agree on anything?*"

"*There is a rumour that Hitler and Stalin have an agreement to occupy all of Poland. They have secretly agreed not attack one another.*"

Sadly, what Misha had to say was no longer a rumour. It turned out to be the day that Germany attacked Poland. In the small village of Grochi, the rumour spread like wildfire. Villagers gathered at the home of Andriy Kaszuba, the assumed leader of the pioneering village by virtue of his age, service in the Austrian Army during World War I, and knowledge of Polish politics. Those in attendance were suddenly aware that they had much more to contend with than tensions between Poles and Ukrainians. For them, their vision of building a free and independent Ukrainian nation had to be set aside. With the Nazi attack on Poland and the sceptre of an all-out war before them, the conversations moved quickly from Polish nationalism and the appearance of zealous Poles in their midst intent upon punishing them to talk of the Nazis and their attack on Poland.

Even as the war broke out, many Ukrainians in the region were not willing to completely abandon the notion of a free and independent Ukraine. They were well aware of the fact that ethnic Ukrainians constituted a majority of the population. It was for this reason that they had a vision of what the future might hold for Ukrainians, a position in direct opposition to that held by Polish leaders. Members of the Ukrayins'ka Povstans'ka Armiya (*Ukrainian Insurgent Army*) and regular ethnic Ukrainians were ready to confront those Poles who stood in their way.

"Yes," confirmed Ivan Klymus, a resident of Grochi, *"I heard that just before dawn German tanks, infantry units, and cavalry entered Polish territory with five armies and over one million troops. Those warmongering bastards attacked Poland without even first declaring war. Skurwysyn. Bastards."*

Under attack by the Nazi Wehrmacht, Poland immediately declared war on Germany. Three days later, the United Kingdom and France declared war on Germany. Unfortunately for Poland, by mid-September the formidable German Army controlled nearly half of Poland. To everyone's surprise, the Soviet Union attacked Poland from the east on September 17. Just two days later, on September 19, thanks to their secret pact, the German and Soviet armies linked up at Brest-Litovsk, Belarus. By the end of October, all of Poland was occupied by Germany in the west and by Russia in the east. *How did all of this come about so suddenly and without warning?*

Long before the outbreak of World War II, the European balance of power was being eroded step by step. Nazi Germany and the Soviet Union aspired to regain territories lost in the aftermath of World War I. Stalin feared that the Western nations were encouraging Hitler to attack the Soviet Union.

With this fear in mind, the defenders of the Soviet position argued that it was necessary to enter into a non-aggression pact in order to buy time. Stalin recognized that the Soviet Union was not in a position to fight a war in 1939 and needed at least three years to prepare. He was of the opinion that a non-intervention pact would secure the Soviet Union some breathing space of immunity from a German attack. Further to this, Stalin concluded that in light of a secret pact, Germany would be reluctant to attack the Soviet Union because they would already be involved in a war against the Western Powers. Stalin was confident that the time was right for a secret pact.

Enter the Molotov-Ribbentrop Pact, named after the former Soviet Minister Vyacheslav Molotov and the German Foreign Minister Joachim von Ribbentrop. The secret pact, officially known as the Treaty of Non-Aggression between Germany and the Union of Soviet Socialist Republics, was a guarantee that neither party would ally itself to or aid any enemy of the other party. This secret protocol explains why Poland was attacked by Germany from the west and by Russia from the east, thereby dividing vast territories of central Europe, including all of Poland, into German and Soviet spheres of influence. No other international agreement, act, or pact had a greater impact upon Polish-Ukrainian relationships during or after the war than did the Molotov-Ribbentrop Accord.

The Molotov–Ribbentrop Pact was signed by Nazi Germany and the Soviet Union in Moscow on August 23, 1939. Vyacheslav Molotov, Soviet Foreign Minister and Joseph Stalin, General Secretary, Soviet Union.

When Adolf Hitler, Chancellor of the Reich, addressed the Reichstag on September 1, 1939, he stated that, *"Russia and Germany are governed by two different doctrines. Germany has no intention of exporting its doctrine to Russia. Soviet Russia has no intention of exporting its doctrine to Germany. We have, therefore, resolved to conclude a pact which rules out forever any use of violence between us."*

What the German Reichstag did not know at that moment was that the pact between Germany and Russia, signed in Moscow on August 23, 1939, was already fait accompli.

In occupying Poland from 1939 to 1941, Germany and Russia worked hard to control their respective regions of influence. Things would not change dramatically during this period until Germany attacked the Soviet Union in 1941. Suddenly, the horrors of World War II would unfold with all of the attendant tragic events. Somehow, the village of Grochi, situated so close to a massive Polish national forest, would escape most of the major military battles.

Thanks to the duplicity of Stalin's secret pact with Hitler, which established the *Curzon Line* as the border between the two nations, Poles had little alternative but to concede the loss of eastern Poland to the Soviet Union and western Poland to Germany. But this did not mean that Poles would not seek to establish an independent Poland west of the Curzon Line once the Nazis were routed. For this reason the Curzon Line took on a new and significant meaning.

The Curzon Line, named after the British Foreign Secretary, Lord Curzon of Kedleston, was put forward by the Supreme War Council in 1919 as the demarcation line between the Second Polish Republic and Bolshevik Russia and was supposed to serve as the basis for a future border. The Allies forwarded it as an armistice line during World War I. However, both parties disregarded the line when the military situation lay in their favour, and it did not play a role in establishing the Polish-Soviet border in 1921. Instead, the final Treaty of Riga signed in 1921 provided Poland with almost 135,000 square kilometres of land that was, on average, about 250 kilometres east of the Curzon Line. The Nazis and Soviets, under the proposed provisions of the Pact, wanted to resurrect the original Curzon Line.

The Curzon Line, first proposed after World War I, was recognized as the Polish-Soviet border after WWII. The region below the notation, 1945 Curzon Line "A" was subject to the transfer of Ukrainians from Poland to Soviet Ukraine.

With minor variations, the northern half of the Curzon line lay approximately along the border which had been established between the Prussian Kingdom and the Russian Empire in 1797. Along most of its length, the line also followed an ethnic boundary. Areas west of the line contained an overall Polish majority while areas to its east were mostly inhabited by Ukrainians, Belorussians, Poles, Jews, and Lithuanians. The secret protocol divided territories into German and Soviet spheres of influence.

To the shock of the residents of Grochi, the border of the German and Soviet occupational zones followed the Curzon Line and ran right through their county, the County of Lubaczow. Gmina Narol, including the village of Grochi, fell under the control of Germany. Residents living in the southern sector of the county fell under the control of the Soviet Union and immediately experienced occupational terrors. Stalin initiated numerous arrests in 1939-1940 and deported all local intellectuals to Siberia. Although future events would unfold in different ways in the two jurisdictions, the end game of the two belligerent super powers was quite similar; complete control of all Poland.

Just before the Soviet invasion of Poland in 1939, the province of Volhynia was part of the Second Polish Republic and the site of one of Eastern Europe's most ambitious policies of toleration. This was being accomplished by supporting Ukrainian culture, religious autonomy, and Ukrainization of the Orthodox Church between 1928 and 1938. It was the aim of Józef Klemens Piłsudski and his allies to achieve Ukrainian loyalty to the Polish state and to minimize Soviet influences in the borderline region. This approach was gradually abandoned after Piłsudski's death in 1935.

In an effort to pacify civil unrest in the Galician countryside, the Poles demolished Ukrainian community centres and libraries, confiscating property and produce, and beating protesters. To prevent them from participating in elections, Ukrainian parliamentarians were placed under house arrest and their constituents terrorized into voting for Polish candidates. The ongoing policies of the Polish state led to the deepening of ethnic cleavages in the area.

Beginning in 1937, the Polish government in Volhynia initiated an active campaign to use religion as a tool for Polonization and to forcibly convert the Orthodox population to Roman Catholicism. Over 190 Orthodox churches were destroyed and another 150 were converted to Roman Catholic cathedrals. The remaining Orthodox churches were forced to use the Polish language in their sermons. In August, 1939, the last remaining Orthodox Church in the Volhynian capital of Lutsk was converted to a Roman Catholic cathedral by decree of the Polish government.

By late 1939, the German Third Reich had already begun annexing significant portions of Eastern Europe in order to fulfil its policy of *Lebensraum*, a core component of Nazi ideology calling for new *Living Space* in the East for German people.

The annexation of eight eastern provinces (*referred to as the Eastern Borderlands or Kresy Wschodnie*) by the Soviet Union resulted in the state gaining 50,600 square miles of territory and increasing its population by over seven million people. In losing these provinces, Polish leaders were well aware that this territory was ceded to Poland in 1921 under the provisions of the Treaty of Riga. Stalin, by virtue of the *Molotov-Ribbentrop Accord*, felt justified in returning the territory to Ukraine, Belarus, and Lithuania.

Most Ukrainians welcomed the Soviet intervention, believing that the new political alignment would free them from Polish domination. At the same time, many Ukrainians remembered the Soviet man-made *Holodomor* which occurred in Ukraine in 1932-1933. They, in particular, resisted Soviet involvement. But, that seemed not to matter. Under the direct order of Josef Stalin, Nikita Khrushchev accompanied the Soviet troops when they attacked Eastern Poland in 1939. Once under Soviet control and under the leadership of Nikita Khrushchev, a law was passed making the former eastern Polish territories a part of the Ukrainian Soviet Socialist Republic.

The Molotov-Ribbentrop secret pact had dire consequences for Poland. Within a matter of days of the announcement of the non-aggression treaty, Germany launched its planned invasion of Poland. As the Third Reich expanded into the new territories, the Soviet Union did not stay inactive. The Red Army began its own advance into Poland on September 17, 1939. Russia and Germany had secretly agreed to divide their expansion into Poland along the Narew, Vistula, and San Rivers.

The Soviet Union created six new oblasts in the newly acquired territories, one of which was Volhynia. Most of the factories, including the almost-finished radio station in Lutsk, were dismantled and shipped east to Russia. The Polish language was eliminated from public life and Ukrainian became the language of government and the courts. All Polish institutions were abolished, and all Polish officials, civil servants, and police were deported to Siberia or Central Asia. Stalin wanted to deport all prominent Polish and Ukrainian civilians who might one day oppose the Communist way of life. With the elimination of individuals, organizations, and parties that represented moderate or liberal political tendencies, the extremist underground Organization of Ukrainian Nationalists (*OUN*) was left as the only political party with a significant organizational presence in Western Ukraine.

Due to the sensitive location of Western Ukraine along the border with the German-held territory, the Soviet administration made attempts to gain the loyalty and respect of the Ukrainian population. They did not want Ukrainians to support the Nazi regime and create problems for the Soviet Union. As a result, health care, after being drastically reduced by the Poles during the inter-war period, improved, and the Ukrainian language began to flourish once again. Although the Russian language became a mandatory foreign language course, academic subjects in the schools were taught in Ukrainian.

In the annexed territories, over fifty percent of the land belonged to Polish landlords. Seventy five percent of the Ukrainian peasants owned less than two hectares of land. In 1939, lands not owned by the peasants were seized and re-distributed to landless peasants. However, the Soviet government soon seized all of this land for incorporation into collective farms. This caused the peasants to turn against the Soviet regime.

The publicly-stated intentions of the Pact were a guarantee of non-belligerence by either party towards the other and a *commitment that neither party would ally itself to or aid an enemy of the other party*. What Stalin's propaganda machine did not tell Soviet citizens was that the treaty included a secret protocol which divided Poland into *spheres of influence* between Germany and the Soviet Union.

Following the launch of Barbarossa and the German attack on the Soviet Union in June, 1941, Germany already controlled and occupied all of western Poland. It was now time for Germany to begin its attack and occupation of eastern Poland. The attack, in particular, brought intensified terror to thousands of Jews who were rounded up and transported to the extermination camp in Bełżec. It also led to the arrest of numerous Poles, many of whom were transported as Eastern Workers to concentration camps and forced labour in Germany.

As events unfolded, there was no other country in Europe where the Nazis were so cruel and consistently hostile towards the local population as was the case in Poland. Millions were suddenly deported by the Nazis to German concentration camps. Caught between two warring combatants, Polish citizens were killed by both the Nazis and the Soviets.

The population of Poland was divided on both sides of the Curzon Line. The entire northwestern part of Poland and a portion of central Poland were incorporated directly into the Reich and became an integral part of Germany. Many young Poles were arrested and conscripted into the Wehrmacht. In turn, the Soviets divided their spoils between Soviet Belorussia and Soviet Ukraine.

1942: Many young people in the Narol region of Poland were arrested by the Gestapo, shipped to Germany, forced into labour, and required to wear an OST badge signifying that they were Eastern Workers.

According to the Nazis, the Slavs were a non-Aryan group of people referred to as the *Untermenschen*, the subhumans, largely destined to be labourers for the Reich. The exceptions were those who were considered by the Nazis as being suitable for Germanization. The Soviets also built a similar social ladder. On its top were Soviet people sent to the newly incorporated areas from the prewar Soviet territories. Next were the native communists and the lower classes of the local population, mostly representatives of the non-Polish people, including Jews, who, at least initially, were happy that the Polish state had appeared.

The Soviets and the Germans did their best to deepen the abyss between the various groups within the local population. This contributed greatly to conflicts between Poles and Ukrainians. The elite of Polish society were savagely attacked by the Nazis on one side and by the Soviets on the other. Both the Germans and the Soviets were determined to kill the best and the brightest in Polish society. As the conflict escalated, the most promising youth, the most patriotic intelligentsia, and the most outstanding Polish intellectuals were killed.

Perhaps the most atrocious attack occurred in March, 1940, when Stalin decided to execute twenty-two thousand Polish war prisoners, including over fifteen thousand military officers in what became known as the Katyn Forest Massacre near the city of Kharkiv. Most of the victims were reserve officers, the elite of the Polish nation. At the same time, about 18 percent of Poland's clergy were eliminated.

Photo from the 1943 exhumation of a mass grave of Polish officers killed by NKVD in the Katyń Forest in 1940.

In the territory under German control, all Polish scientific, artistic, and educational institutions were closed and many historical buildings, scientific and art collections, and libraries were destroyed. The Nazi struggle against Polish heritage included a carefully planned destruction of the monuments to Polish kings, heroes, writers, and scholars. Nazi authorities ordered the removal of all public notices and inscriptions in Polish, Germanized Polish place names, and banished the Polish language from public use. In order to lower the intellectual and moral level of Polish society, the Nazis tried to deprive the Poles of education and culture, and promoted drunkenness and collaboration as a means to corrupt and demoralize Polish citizens.

In a similar campaign, the Soviets destroyed Polish monuments, removed Polish street signs, and closed Polish bookstores, publishing houses, and newspapers. Ukrainian and Belorussian became the languages of instruction in schools and universities. The Russian language became compulsory and Polish textbooks were removed. A campaign against Polish culture was presented as a rebuilding of Ukrainian culture unfairly suppressed by the Poles. Soviet propaganda portrayed the Polish population in the former eastern Polish provinces as consisting of a group of colonizers and exploiters.

Mass deportations became the means through which the Soviets began to de-Polonize the territories incorporated into the Soviet Union. The deportations started immediately after September 1939 and lasted until the very day of the German attack on the Soviet Union in 1941. During this campaign, the Soviets deported about 1.6 million people, mostly Poles, to Siberia. Of this number, 30 percent would die in the Soviet Union.

During the occupation of Kresy in WWII, Polish families were loaded onto trains for transport to Siberia. The first wave of mass deportations began on February 9, 1940, the second on April 13, 1940, and the third on June 29, 1940. In all, 1.6 million Poles were deported to Siberia.

A similar deportation and de-Polonization plan was implemented by the Germans. In the winter of 1939-1940, about one million Poles were brutally deported, under extremely harsh conditions, to the *general gouvernement polen,* the Polish territories which had been incorporated into the Reich. Expelled and their property confiscated by the Nazis, the deportees were allowed to take with them only a little cash and a few possessions. Transported in unheated freight cars, thousands of them died. Also caught in the dragnet were over two hundred thousand Polish children, hundreds of them from Gmina Zamosc, and taken to the Reich for Germanization.

Had it not been for the secret agreement between Germany and the Soviet Union, it is unlikely that the most obvious atrocities would have occurred. These atrocities occurred because two superpowers wanted to establish complete control over their territories by eliminating all opposition. German and Soviet occupation authorities began street roundups in November, 1939, sending captives to concentration and forced-labour camps in Germany or Siberia.

The Pact opened the gates of aggression in Europe. Poland was divided when Nazi troops occupied western Poland and Soviet troops occupied eastern Poland. Without doubt, the Pact is one of the greatest tragedies of the *Old Continent.* It formed scars on the body of Europe and represents a subsequent gravitation to international law which supports the principles of the coexistence of people.

Even today, it would be difficult to find a person living in Poland or Ukraine whose family had not been touched by the provisions of the Molotov-Ribbentrop Accord.

Blame the secret pact which led to World War II, accelerated ethnic cleansings, and tore apart countless families. Most tragically, these events left countless orphans in their wake, four of whom belonged to my extended family.

What was the source of the discord between Ukrainians and Poles? Why were Polish villages attacked in Volhynia? Did Poles retaliate by torching Ukrainian villages in Poland? Why did Stalin deport so many citizens to Siberia? Who masterminded the population transfer program?

To unravel how all of this, I must first take you back in the recent history of my family. Only then will the answers to these questions make any sense.

PART 2

ROOTS

2

Clan Kaszub

Peasant unrest leads to the emancipation of the serf and freedom

When I consider the nature of my heritage, I immediately conjure up images of Austrian Galicia, Polish aristocracy, and serfdom. After all, both of my parents were born in Galicia, the northernmost and most populous province of the Austrian Empire, a province annexed by the Kingdom of Poland in 1352 as the Ruthenian Voivodeship and becoming a part of the Austrian Empire following the partition of the Polish-Lithuanian Commonwealth in 1772. Populated by Ukrainians and Poles, the region was contested between Poland and Ukraine in the 20th century. This factor had dire consequences for my extended family.

When I think about the structure of my family, I think about the nature of a tree, a perennial plant with an elongated stem supporting branches and leaves. We see the tree but we do not see what goes on underground. Trees must develop deep *roots* in order to grow strong. But we don't see the roots. In much the same way, what goes on inside us is like the roots of a tree.

The elongated stem of my family tree is my father. He personified the very nature of and the importance of work. For him work, or *robota* as he called it, was not only the means to success but also necessary for the very survival of the family. After all, the word *robota* has a special ring to it; a Slavic word meaning *serf, slave,* or *forced labour.* Throughout the Austro-Hungarian Empire, a system of *robota* was in force to extract labour from peasants, similar to obligatory work systems elsewhere in Europe. All of this is part and parcel of my heritage.

My earliest recollection of life on an isolated homestead in Northern Alberta had to do with the excitement of watching a steam locomotive spewing billows of smoke as it coursed its way from one water stop to another. In the late 1930s, steam locomotives devoured huge amounts of water and coal. This is why, on average, these water and coal stops were located about ten miles apart. One of those water stops happened to be near our homestead.

In the mid-1920s, the Government of Alberta recognized that the Peace Country offered endless opportunities for new immigrants. With this in mind, the government took ownership of the Northern Alberta Railways and set out to extend the steel rails all the way from Edmonton to Dawson Creek, British Columbia. My dad, an immigrant to Canada in 1928, found employment with Northern Alberta Railways at just about the time that the rails reached the small village of High Prairie. It was here that he would set down permanent roots.

Drawn to Canada under the provisions of the Dominion Lands Act, it was my father's plan to work on the railway system in order to earn sufficient funds to improve the homestead, a requirement consistent with legislative guidelines before seeking title to the land. He needed money to buy farm implements, seed grain, and work horses. Each time that he left home for work on the nearby Northern Alberta Railway system, he would declare to my mother that he was about to undertake some important *'robota.'* That is why I always associated the word *robota* with work, hard work. Years later I discovered that the word *robota* was not only a concept embraced by my father but that it had a most interesting history of its own, a history surrounding my ancestors in Eastern Europe.

In time and with sufficient land under cultivation, my dad would organize a threshing crew in order to take in the crops each fall. He referred to the workers as his *robotniki,* and I was one of them. Little wonder that I began to associate *robota* with subservience and a form of punishment—a reflection of my heritage in the Austrian province of the Kingdom of Galicia. After all, it was during this period in history that serfdom was a form of peasant servitude and dependence on the upper land-owning classes. The degree of subservience and the prevalence of the serf-lord relations differed with time and country according to natural, economic, social, and political conditions and sometimes by the very nature of the lord himself.

During the 19th century, several members of clan kaszub were indentured as *robotniki* to Polish nobles. The concept of nobility, an aristocratic social class in Poland during the 19th century, was an important social structure. Polish kings rewarded subjects who distinguished themselves in battle, performed a heroic deed, or held a prominent position. Once obtained, an armorial shield was handed down to the family through the generations.

Vienna counted on the Polish nobility as allies in a complex political calculus of its multinational realm. In return for loyalty, Austrian Poland received considerable administrative and cultural autonomy. However, and even though Galicia did gain a reputation as an oasis of toleration in the midst of oppression from Germans and Russians, ethnic Ukrainians felt that they were completely left out of the political loop.

Under feudalism, serfdom was the status of most peasants—they were the *robotniki*. Most *robotniki* served the country's agricultural needs. In exchange for their labour the serfs were entitled to protection, justice, and the right to cultivate certain fields within the manor in order to maintain their own subsistence. Unfortunately, agricultural productivity of Galician peasants was one of the lowest in Europe. The situation was compounded by the lack of good land and a growing population resulting in the steadily diminishing size of an individual peasant's plot. In the 19th century, most of the plots had less than five acres. Many peasants were not able to grow enough food on their plots to support their large families. Little wonder that all of this led to peasant unrest. Many serfs began to look for better work opportunities, going so far as to demand to be paid for their services.

Under the Polish system of serfdom, serfs were bound by law to their plots of land which were owned by the lord. The amount of obligatory labour owed by the peasant to the lord depended on the size and quality of the peasant's plot.

By contrast, the Russian system of serfdom which was established in most Ukrainian territories under Russian rule at the end of the 18th century was based on the principle that the lord owned the peasant under his control. He could dispose of his serfs as he wished; he could even separate them from their land. The amount of labour owed by the peasants and the size of their allotments depended on the number of adult males in their families.

Unpaid labour was limited to a fixed number of days depending on the size of the land allotment. Over time the peasant acquired the right to sell his products freely. Village communities were given new powers of self-government. The peasants were divided according to the amount of property and number of obligations into married serfs, single serfs, and landless serfs. On average, a peasant household had to till two hectares of the lord's land and perform 78 days of labour per year on state lands and 133 days and sometimes as much as 300 days on private estates. Obligations consisted of labour, monetary payments, and other services and fees. The lord sometimes made further exactions from the peasants by imposing various fines or forcing them to buy a certain amount of alcohol.

During the final days of serfdom in the region under the control of Austria, every farmer had first to complete his dues at the manor house, whether with his team of horses or by hand. Only then could he work his own land, sowing and reaping at night. No excuse of pressing needs at home was of any use. If one did not appear as ordered, the overseer would come at once. If he found the wife busy cooking, he might throw a pail of water on the fire. Or in winter the overseer would carry off the windows or the doors of the dwelling. In case that this did not work, and men were needed for service, the overseer would come with his foremen and eject the farmer from their homestead and another put in his place. Nor was there any appeal anywhere. The lord of the manor was owner of everything. His was both land and water, and even the wind, since only he was allowed to build a windmill to grind corn.

Even though the lord was esteemed as being kindly and humane, no one dared to go to the manor with any complaint about the servants of the manor. Should a complaint be lodged, the servants would find excuses and then make trouble for the complainants. The result was that all gave up the thought of *just* dealing. Running away would have done no good, for elsewhere it was no better, maybe even worse.

Serfdom in Russia was abolished in 1861.

To make matters worse for the peasant, the Austrians decided that Galicia should not develop industrially but remain an agricultural area that would serve as a supplier of food products and raw materials to other Habsburg provinces. New taxes were instituted, investments were discouraged, and cities and towns were neglected. Galicia was described as the poorest province of Austria-Hungary. With but a couple of exceptions, Austria-Hungary failed to create transportation networks necessary for the development of industries and markets throughout the empire.

The legally-privileged class of Poles, the *Szlachta,* had complete control over their serfs. They owned landed property, often in the form of *manor farms,* and frequently developed a sense of distinction which led to practices that in later periods could be classified as *racism.* Ruled by an iron fist, the burden placed upon serfs was extremely high. Simply put, serfs were no more than work animals and feudal superiors took great joy in referring to them as *robots.* As a result of the actions of Polish nobles, frictions developed not only between Ukrainian serfs and Polish nobles but also between Ukrainians and Poles. The less-privileged Ukrainian peasants wanted to bring to an end their subservience. In an effort to improve their economic and political status in the community, many serfs began to look elsewhere for employment.

New industries came into existence and farming operations became increasingly mechanized. From being indentured to a land baron as serfs to surviving the destructiveness of two world wars, my ancestors had much to contend with. They faced the horrors of armed warfare, ethnic cleansing, and religious conflicts, while at the same time providing for themselves and their families. Having survived abuse at the hands of Polish nobility, their next challenge came from poor economic conditions which challenged the best of them. Those challenges, in effect, were a prelude to the destructiveness of two world wars.

It was also a time in history when Poland had gone through three partitions in 1772, 1793, and 1795. The partitioned territories came under the control of Prussia to the west, Russia to the east, and Austria to the south. Prior to 1772, Poland existed as part of the Polish-Lithuanian Commonwealth. However, as a result of pressure from Prussia, Russia, and Austria, the First Partition of Poland occurred in 1772.

Under the pretext of protecting the rights of the Polish nobles, Russia invaded Poland in 1792 and carried out the Second Partition of Poland, placing the country under the occupation of Russian troops. In 1794, soon after the first and second partitions of Poland, a Polish revolt was thwarted by Russia, Prussia, and Austria—resulting in the third and final partition of Poland-Lithuania in 1795. For Poles, the third partition began a period of continuous foreign rule that would endure for the next 123 years. Poland would not emerge as a nation until 1918.

For many years and especially during the 19th century, the Vistula River which drains most of eastern Poland into the Baltic Sea was one of the main trading arteries of a partitioned Poland. Salt, timber, grain, and building stone were among the goods shipped via this route to the seaport of Gdansk. As a result, Gdansk gained great importance in the Baltic area as a centre of merchants, trade, and as a port city. Knowing that they could be bought, sold, traded, or abused with no rights over their own bodies, two members of clan kaszub decided to abandon their Polish landlord and join the *Zamoyski Family Enterprise*. They became Zamoyski's *robotniki* on Poland's river transport system.

At the turn of the 19th century and with main centers around Zamosc, the Zamosc State consisted of 23 towns and 816 villages. By mid-19th century, the estate had a collection of folwarks, mills, breweries, distilleries, and a direct involvement in the transportation of goods, by barge, from the Austro-Hungarian Empire to Gdansk. To improve the company's transportation enterprise, Zamoyski founded the Steam Navigation Company which soon monopolized transport on the Vistula River. In need of workers, Zamoyski recruited serfs from the Prussian, Austrian, and the Russian territories who soon manned river barges and steamships on the Vistula River and its tributaries, the San and Bug rivers.

For two members of clan kaszub, the change in their status came at a most opportune time. Farming operations were becoming more mechanized and the demand for slave labour using primitive agricultural techniques began to dry up. Suddenly, Polish nobles began to release many of their serfs from bondage. At the same time, Count Zamoyski began to recruit serfs for his business enterprises, many of whom were already indentured to one of his associates. In other cases, and against the law, serfs abandoned the lord to whom they were indentured. They were on the run hoping to join a Polish noble who valued and treated them with more respect; a noble who would make certain that they were safe, content, and healthy.

By the middle of the 19th century, new railway systems began to compete with Zamoyski's river-shipping enterprises. With less demand for serfs coupled with increased demands for pay, Count Zamoyski released many of his serfs. However, he felt duty bound to find other work opportunities for those serfs about to be released from his transportation company.

During the same period in history, Count Andrzej Artur Zamoyski took a special interest in the Zamosc region of Poland. With the decreasing need for workers in the transportation industry and having other enterprises, Count Zamoyski enticed several of his serfs to take up residence at Gmina Narol, among them my great-great-grandfather, Johannes Kaszuba. As a hard-working twenty-three year old serf, Johannes accepted the Count's invitation and, in 1848, travelled to the Narol region, taking up residence in Ruda Różaniecka. Zamoyski assured Johannes that his large company required the services of several men in the logging industry.

For the youthful Johannes Kaszuba, 1848 turned out to be a pivotal year. Released from bondage and now a free man, Johannes took his first paying job with Baron Brunicki, an associate of Count Zamoyski who was in the process of constructing a palace in Ruda Różaniecka. Within a short period of time, Johannes met and married Joannis Zukh. In 1850, the couple gave birth to a daughter, Mariia, followed by two sons, Ivan in 1852 and Jakub in 1854.

It would be at this point in the history of clan kaszub that a schism developed; one faction embraced the Ukrainian language and Greek Catholicism while the other faction embraced the Polish language and Roman Catholicism. This decision would soon result in unforeseen consequences.

As the controlling relationship between lord and servant came to a screeching halt, serfs found liberty and freedom from robota. The little village of Grochi was about to take flight.

3

A Village Is Born

A village that is soon earmarked for annihilation

During the mid-19th century, the emancipation of the serf in the Austrian Empire was accelerated when Polish demands for Galician autonomy increased. As a multi-national empire, the Austrian Imperial Council under Franz Joseph I, Emperor of Austria from 1848 to 1916, often played the Poles against the Ruthenians[1] who also demanded national equality. The Austrian Imperial Council believed that by releasing the serfs from bondage would placate both the Poles and Ukrainians and result in political stability.

It was also during the decade of the 1850s that the Polish industrialist and landowner, Count Zamoyski, granted permission to land-hungry peasants to create a small settlement on the River Plazivka near the villages of Ruda Różaniecka and Płazów. He felt duty-bound to grant an audience to several indentured families under his control, including members of clan kaszub.

Freed from bondage, Jakubus Groch spearheaded the development of a settlement next to River Plazivka. Count Zamoyski had set aside sufficient land for their homes, farm buildings, agriculture, and

---

1   In 1843, the term *Ruthenian* became the official name for Rusyns and Ukrainians living within the Austrian Empire. By 1900, Ruthenians living along the borderlands of the Austro-Hungarian Empire and the Russian Empire referred to themselves as *Ukrainians*. After World War II, Soviet policy disallowed Ruthenian ethnicity, considering them to be a part of the Ukrainian ethnic group and language.

pastureland for their cattle and horses. Jakub and Ivan Kaszuba, the sons of Johannes and Joannis Kaszuba, gained permission from Baron Brunicki, Count Zamoyski's associate, to build on the designated site just two kilometres north of the village of Płazów. In honour of Jakubus Groch, the budding village came to be named as the village of Grochi.

As was the practice in those days, there wasn't a great need for the development of an infrastructure in the village. With the guidance of Count Zamoyski and under the supervision of Baron Brunicki, the first settlers began the construction of their log houses and barns for hogs and cattle. Soon, with their frontages facing eastward, a row of houses stood by a dirt roadside. Set against a forest of pine and deciduous trees, the village took on an unusually serene characteristic. Made of splints from pine or spruce, most of the farmyards were soon enclosed with a fence, several of them artfully constructed of willow branches commonly known as a willow-wattle fence.

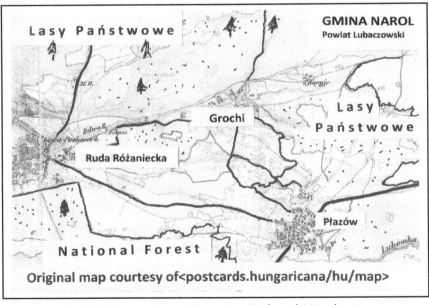

A 19th Century Austro-Hungarian Cadastral Map showing the extent and ownership of land for taxation purposes.

In exchange for permission to build a small village, the villagers consented to tend to Baron Brunicki's manor house and grounds in Ruda Różaniecka. The villagers took great care to annually trim to a height of five feet the hedgerow of planted oak and beech trees which surrounded the manor house and park. In order to improve the appearance of the property, the villagers soon replaced the hedgerow with a brick wall and iron pickets.

The original 19th century castle at Ruda Różaniecka, Poland.

With the emancipation of the serf, the demand for agricultural land increased and many worried about their ability to survive in tough economic conditions. However, this factor did not deter Jakub and Ivan Kaszuba from improving their economic standing. Married in 1877, Ivan set out to construct a typical log home in the newly created village.

By the end of the 1880s, the total number of log houses in Grochi grew to over two dozen. Of this group of settlers, sixteen occupants were owners and the remainder were tenants and day-labourers. Baron Brunicki granted the head of each household sufficient land for their gardens. In recognition of this, each was required to work for the lord with a team of horses or yoke of oxen and with such implements as a wagons, ploughs, harrows, and discs.

Although the serfs were freed from bondage did not mean that Count Zamoyski lost the use of labourers. He did retain the help of tenants under the tutelage of masters in several of his estates. In these situations, the tenants each had four morgens of land and did their dues three days a week with hand tools such as flail, sickle, hoe, or spade. The labourers had only huts and were not bound to any dues or taxes. The master in each case would give directions for the morrow's work, appointing a foreman under whom each hired helper was to work.

Initially, the log house of each villager was made of a single living room. Beside the house, most villagers had a large shed, store room, and a barn for horses, cows, hens, and pigs. The more enterprising of the villagers soon had a granary. All such buildings were built of round logs, laid almost as they grew, and with little trimming. At the corners the ends projected a couple of feet in order to provide fuel when wood was scarce. Many, however, were built this way in order to get a better appearance.

The log houses were almost all smoke-ones where the fire was built on a broad drum made of packed clay called an *old woman*. The smoke went through the whole room and out through the door to the shed and then out the roof. The door had to be open when cooking and everybody had to sit on the ground or go about stooped in order not to be choked. Saturated with smoke, the walls would soon be covered with soot, making it necessary to improve their appearance by periodically using whitewash, a low-cost type of paint made from slaked line or calcimine.

With time, improvements came to the village. Made of clay mixed with straw, the chimneys of newer homes were built through the roof. Here and there were chimneys made of a hollowed-out tree trunk, and then lined with clay. Not until about 1870 did the peasants begin to build proper brick chimneys. It was also during this decade that iron cooking stoves came into use.

For cooking, an open hearth was used on which the pots with food were set either close to or on the fire. Some cottagers used tripods or other iron fixtures to hold the pot in place. In addition to the open hearth, every house had a bake-oven, big enough so that one could bake the bread from the dough of a half a sack of flour at one time. There was also a heater into which the fuel was put from an outside passage through an opening called the shoot. Built of raw brick, these ovens took up a lot of room. The top surface of the oven and the heater were faced with stucco, big enough so that four people could sleep on it. It was not unusual to find that the children slept on the surface of the oven throughout the winter. A member of the family who felt miserable or got a chill would crawl up on the oven to stretch and toast himself.

House furnishings consisted of a table, a couple of benches, and a chest which took the place of drawers. Beds or bunks in the sleeping area were made of the simplest construction. In addition, the house had a hand-mill for grinding, a mortar for cracking meal for porridge or linseed for oil, and a block for splitting wood. The walls were hung with religious icons, paintings of a wedding, or wood carvings—something that everyone loved. Once a year all the walls of the house would be whitewashed, mostly before Easter.

In every living room, just under the ceiling, there would be two beams. The home-owner would often place a variety of items on these two beams—including loaves of bread, wood, flax, hemp, bunches of onions, and garlic braids. In place of earthen floors, some of the houses soon introduced floors made of wood.

Most of the villagers used earthenware pots for their cooking needs. Only in the late 1800s, with the coming of iron stoves, did iron utensils and kettles come into being. Dishes, jugs, and bowls were also made of earthenware. For utinsels families used wooden spoons, much larger than the metal ones in use today. During mealtime, it was not unusual to find all members of a family eating from one large cookpot.

When the cow was ready to calve in the winter, the villager would often bring her into the house so that she would be warmer. This unusual procedure confirmed the importance and value of having a milk-cow as close as possible to the family home.

Rumour had it that there wasn't a single clock in the village of Grochi. However, the villagers liked to brag about their roosters, saying that their shrill crowing would tell a villager when to get up, especially in winter months. One villager went so far as to say that his rooster would crow with the greatest regularity, the first time at midnight, the second about three in the morning, and the third at daybreak! It was not until about 1880 that the first clock appeared in the village of Grochi.

In those days, feather ticks and pillows were seen only in the better-situated and kept peasant homes. The poor did not have them at all, using instead sheepskin coats, cloaks or jackets—the same things they wore during the daytime. The children, or servants who slept on the oven or behind it in a warm place, needed only a sheet or a jacket. The beds for the most part lay in a state of confusion during the day. Only the more diligent wives made them up for the day. Fair bed linen became one of the aims of all the best housewives who would put out the bedding on the line during the day, both to air it and to show it to the neighbours.

With increased economic and political stability in Grochi, the new settlers set about doing their domestic chores and thinking about raising their families. No longer under the direct control of nobility, Mariia Kaszuba reached the age of 20 in 1870. Her father, Johannes Kaszuba, urged her to select a mate and start a family. Unfortunately for Johannes, the strong-headed girl insisted on marrying a young man who was neither a member of the Ukrainian community nor the Ukrainian Greek Catholic Church. Mareusz Zaborniak, a strapping young Pole and a member of the Roman Catholic Church, swept the impressionable Mariia completely off her feet! Breaking with tradition and upon the urging of the Zaborniak family, Mariia reluctantly left the Ukrainian Greek Catholic Church in favour of the Roman Catholic Church.

The inter-faith marriage caused a stir in family relations. For, as was the custom, membership in a particular parish determined who your friends and acquaintances would be in the future. Suddenly, more and more of Mariia's family and friends came from the Polish community, even though her parents and brothers were ethnic Ukrainians who lived in the same locale. In contrast, Jakub and Ivan Kaszuba continued to have close relationships within the Ukrainian community and membership in the Greek Catholic Church. Time passed quickly but the schism within the family would not heal. It took a tragic event during the latter stages of World War II to once again bring the families together.

In the meantime, Mariia's two brothers, Ivan and Jakub, inherited seven morgens of land (*seven morgens of land is equivalent to about 15 acres*) from their father, Johannes. Although not a very large inheritance, it was sufficient for a small farming operation during a period in history when primitive agricultural techniques continued to be employed. It was not until the 1860s that the kaszubs would begin the use of iron ploughs in place of the wooden ones. To add to their subsistence problems, the brothers used a three-fold system for putting their cultivated land into production where two portions were planted while one portion was set aside for summer fallow.

Their daily diet consisted of potatoes, turnip, and cabbage. Grain yields were exceptionally low and the family was often forced to eat different types of weeds, grass, and leaves from beech trees. The poor diet led to malnutrition, unrelenting hunger, starvation, and disease. In particular, the potato blight of 1850 accelerated the rate of starvation. To add to these problems, the ravages of cholera, typhus, smallpox, and syphilis decimated the population.

In military uniform, Dmytro Vitovsky, first Commander of the Ukrainian Galician Army, flanked by two officers, 1918.

Poor economic conditions in Gmina Narol continued to challenge members of clan kaszub throughout the balance of the 19th century and well into the 20th century. Andrij Kaszuba, my father and the grandson of Ivan Kaszuba, must have had this in mind when, as a fifteen year-old, he volunteered to serve in the Austrian Infantry during World War I. In 1918, Andrij returned home to a hero's welcome. However, his joy at having survived the war while serving with the Austrian infantry at the Serbian front was short-lived. The tensions between Ukrainians and Poles would not go away. Perhaps it was a question from his cousin, Jan Tychan, which put a damper on the joy of his return.

Ukrainian Sichovi Striltsi (Ukrainian Sharpshooters)—reminiscent of Andrij Kaszuba's service in the Austrian Infantry, Carpathian Mountains, 1915.

"*Have you heard, Andrij,*" was Jan's question, "*that Marshal Piłsudski is leading a group of Poles seeking the creation of an independent Poland?*"

"*Are you serious? What kind of bullshit is this? I volunteered to serve Austria with the belief that Ukraine would gain its independence.*"

"*Well, Andrij, the matter is even worse. Not only do those monkeys in Warsaw want to create a new Polish state but they also want to take away many democratic rights from all minority groups.*"

"*What kind of democratic rights are they thinking about clawing back, Jan?*"

"*The democratic rights granted Ukrainians by Austria. Piłsudski wants to take away our language and religious rights.*"

"*Do you believe that the Ukrainian, Jewish, Belorussian, and German minority groups will support this kind of dictatorship?*"

"*I know that Ukrainians are hostile to the creation of a Polish state.*"

During this period of history, Galicia was a part of the Austro-Hungarian Empire under Austrian control. Most residents of the region showed their preference for and considered themselves to be proud subjects of Austria. This is why Poland's dream of independence did not sit well with Ukrainians living in Poland. Like so many other youthful Ukrainian boys who served in the Austrian military, there was a common understanding that their military service would contribute to the creation of an independent Ukrainian state.

Unfortunately, the Austro-Hungarian heir to the throne, Archduke Franz Ferdinand, was assassinated on June 28, 1914, in Sarajevo, Serbia. On July 28, 1914, Austro-Hungary declared war on Serbia. Not long after, Russia declared its support for Serbia and its wartime opposition to Austria-Hungary. With much bloodshed on both sides, the offensive against Serbia soon ground to a halt.

In Russia, losses were incredibly high on both sides. In the Battle of Gorlice-Tarnow, the Russians lost nearly one million men. As well, the disparate languages and cultures of the Empire created confusion in the ranks of all branches of the armed forces. Russia took itself out of the war in 1917. However, Austrian losses in the eastern campaign were so heavy that the Dual Monarchy failed to recover. Eventually, Russia and Austria admitted defeat. With the end of World War I came the end of the Austro-Hungarian Empire.

At the conclusion of World War I and by virtue of the Treaty of Versailles, Poland became an independent nation in 1919. Since Poland did not exist as a nation at the outbreak of World War I, the citizens of the Austro-Hungarian Empire were directed to join the Russian, German, or Austrian armies, often forced to fight against one another. Poland, devastated by the war, lost over one million of its citizens. Although Poland did regain its independence after 123 years of partitions, its institutions had to be rebuilt. To secure its borders, Poland immediately moved to form a national army from soldiers and officers who had fought in the First World War.

Marshal Józef Klemens Piłsudski, Chief of State, Poland, 1918-1922, and the de facto leader of Poland, 1926-1935.

Young Ukrainian war veterans returning from military duty had few options at their disposal. In an attempt to advance the interests of the fledgling Ukrainian People's Republic, Andrij Kaszuba joined Symon Petliura's forces. For Petliura, this was the final chance to preserve Ukrainian statehood and the theoretical independence of the Ukrainian heartlands. However, defeated by the Bolsheviks, Symon Petliura sought asylum in Poland and on April 21, 1920, signed an alliance with Poland. Petliura accepted the Polish territorial gains in Western Ukraine and joined Piłsudski's forces with the promise of independence for Ukraine and Polish military assistance in reinstalling a Ukrainian government in Kyiv.

Unfortunately, in June of 1920, the Polish army, along with Petliura's Ukrainian troops, abandoned Kyiv to the Red Army. By July, Polish forces were in full retreat and the Red Army captured Brody, Lwow, and Zamosc. In short order, five Soviet armies approached Warsaw. In the end, Marshal Piłsudski's promise to help Petliura gain independence for Ukraine was never fulfilled. Piłsudski had all he could do to save Poland's very independence.

These were the circumstances under which Andrij Kaszuba, as a citizen of Poland after World War I, came to serve in the Polish army, even though the army was both the symbol and the guarantor of Poland's independence and unity. After serving in the Legions of Poland for a short period of time, Andrij returned to the small village of Grochi to spend a weekend with his parents, his brothers Fedjko, Mikhailo, and Dmetro, and his sisters Anna and Oksana. Andrij's father, Andriy Kaszuba, who had also served in the Austrian Infantry during the war, saw himself as the patriarch of the family. Maybe he had this in mind when he called Andrij aside. He wanted to have an important conversation with his eldest son.

"Andrijchyk," is the way the senior kaszub liked to address his son, *"do you realize you are now 21 years of age? Is it not time that you got married and started a family of your own?"*

"But, father," Andrij replied, *"I'm not ready for marriage. I don't even have a girlfriend."*

"That's all right, son. I have picked the ideal wife for you."

"You have, father? Who would that be?"

"The girl's name is Pavlina. I think that you already know her. She is from the neighbouring village. I talked to Pavlina's father, a successful farmer. He said that he would approve of the marriage."

"Yes, father. I know the girl. She's not for me. I don't even like her. She is most ugly."

"What the hell does liking a girl got to do with it? She comes from a wealthy family. Besides, I don't have sufficient land for all of my sons."

"Father, I must tell you this. Pavlina is not for me. She is not very pretty. One of her legs is shorter than the other and she walks with a limp. Her eyesight is bad, very bad. How is it possible for me to marry Pavlina?"

As a result of this confrontation, nothing more was said between father and son for nearly one year. When Andrij returned home from duty with Piłsudski's Polish army for another family visit, it was his turn to call his father aside with some news of his own.

"Father, I just proposed to a beautiful young woman. I want to marry this girl."

"You proposed to a woman? Tell me that it is Pavlina."

"No, father, it is not Pavlina. Her name is Ewa Groszko."

"Son, you are a short-sighted, stupid, and a stubborn good-for-nothing. I will not approve of such a marriage. If you insist on marrying this woman, I will dispossess you of any land that I own. You will have to make it on your own."

With this pronouncement, the gulf between the two developed into a deep chasm. In fact, the tension between father and son got so bad that they rarely talked to one another. Time passed quickly and in 1926, after Poland had experienced several years of political uncertainty and weak leadership, **Piłsudski** took over the state in a military coup, assuming the posts of minister of defence and general inspector of the army.

When in 1926 Andrij heard that Marshal **Piłsudski** would soon initiate a program to pacify ethnic Ukrainians living in Poland, he decided to retire his military uniform. It was also a time when he courted and soon married, against the expressed wishes of his father, Ewa Groszko, a girl from the nearby village of Płazów, just a couple of kilometres south of Grochi.

Deep in thought, Andrij had to admit that Piłsudski, as promised, did launch a program to completely change the language of instruction in all schools of Poland. Where in the past schools were permitted to offer language instruction in Polish and Ukrainian, they were suddenly forced to teach Polish only. Grochi did not have a school of its own. Children had to walk two kilometres to a school in Płazów where Polish was the language of instruction and ethnic Ukrainians were discouraged from seeking any instruction in Ukrainian. Polonization of all ethnic groups became the policy of government. In fact, Polish replaced German as the language of instruction in secondary schools and the funding of schools and cultural institutions followed this policy.

Much like the rest of Poland, Płazów was just recovering from more than a century of partitions by Austria-Hungary, Germany, and Russia. The political scene in Poland, although democratic, was chaotic until Józef Piłsudski seized power in 1926, bringing to an end all democratic freedoms. A third of the population consisted of minorities who were hostile towards the existence of the Polish state. They were of the opinion that the ruling Poles provided them with a lack of privileges and frequently discriminated against them as they faced Polonization. There were treaties that supposedly protected the minorities; however, the government in Warsaw wasn't interested in their enforcement.

For most villagers, life in Austrian-administered Galicia was one of eternal hope. Most were subjected to a low standard of living in a region where the mortality rate was high, disease was prevalent, and access to medical care was difficult, if not impossible. Although it was true that the women of the village knew which medical herbs should be grown in the garden, picked and dried, and properly stored to ensure the best curative properties, this did not guarantee success. Even more troublesome was the knowledge that a broken bone would be set by a village bone-setter, the very same person who might also be the village blacksmith.

Harsh policies implemented by the ruling Poles contributed to a further deterioration of relations between the two ethnic groups. New policies resulted in the suppression of the Ukrainian language, culture, and religion. Although about two-thirds of the local population spoke Ukrainian as their first language, practically all government and administrative positions in the region, including the police, were assigned to Poles. This, in part, became the reason for Andrij's dilemma.

With the rise of nationalism in the 19th century, the ethnicity of citizens became an issue, and the conflicts erupted anew after the First World War. Both Poles and Ukrainians claimed the territories of the Oblast of Volhynia and Eastern Galicia. During the inter-war period, political conflicts escalated.

On November 21, 1919, the Paris Peace Conference granted Eastern Galicia to Poland. The lost war left a generation of frustrated Ukrainian veterans convinced that Poland was Ukraine's principal enemy. Although Polish statehood was established by the Treaty of Versailles, the borders between Poland and Soviet Russia were not established until a later date. After a long series of negotiations, the League of Nations decided that Eastern Galicia would be incorporated into Poland, with the understanding that Poland would recognize that ethnographic conditions fully deserve an autonomous status in Eastern Galicia.

Unfortunately, this promise to grant Ukrainians living in Eastern Galicia some measure of autonomy was never fulfilled by the Polish government. In the following years, the historical discourse between Polish and Ukrainian researchers was often based on historical stereotypes stemming from ethnic conflicts during the First World War and the interwar period, thus making it difficult to draw any objective account of historical Polish-Ukrainian relations during World War II.

During this period of Poland's history, most Poles lived in the countryside where their existence depended on a very productive and fertile land. Farmers made up two-thirds of the population while only one percent of them were landowners. Agriculture was most backward and primitive with a large number of small farms unable to succeed on either the domestic or international markets. At the same time, Poland faced another serious problem, over-population in the countryside and chronic unemployment. Living conditions were so bad that residents in several regions in Eastern Poland faced permanent starvation.

"*Ewa,*" declared a pensive Andrij Kaszuba in 1927, "*I have decided that we shall leave Poland. I heard that Canada is looking for hard-working farmers. With the political situation the way it is currently in this country, I do not see any future for our family in Poland.*"

In those days, the man of the house did not consult with his wife before making a decision. On the surface, it looked as though Andrij was making a decision that so many others were making in Poland. He wanted to seek new challenges in a new land, a land that would welcome those hard-working sheepskin-wearing peasants. To drive the final nail in his decision to immigrate, Andrij was well aware of the tensions between ethnic Ukrainians and the Polish minority in Gmina Narol. These tensions were not new. They dated back several hundred years with territorial, religious, and social dimensions.

Disappointed that a stronger Poland would not provide any support for an independent Ukrainian state, Andrij decided to travel to Lwow. In the provincial capital of Lwow, he confirmed his Polish citizenship, obtained his certificate of birth and baptism from the Greek Catholic Church, a passport photo from a professional photographer, a passport from the Polish Consulate, and a passage ticket to Canada. There was no turning back now. As the 1928 spring days of summer descended upon Grochi, Andrij would say goodbye to Ewa, his two-year-old daughter, Maria, and to Poland, a country to which he would never return.

"Yes, Ewa, I know that I have served in the Polish army. I love this land but the Poles are starting to suppress the Ukrainians in the ranks of the military. I see no opportunity for advancement."

"It's not just the Ukrainians. It's the Jews and Belorussians as well. All minority groups are being persecuted," pointed out Ewa.

"What worries me most is the amount of discrimination, even terror and murder, inflicted upon members of our Ukrainian community. I feel as though I am a second-class citizen. What happened to the Treaty of 1919? The Treaty of Riga passed in 1921? What about the Polish Constitution of 1921 that promised the protection of the rights of minorities?"

As Andrij reflected on his reasons to leave Grochi, he could not put aside the images of the din of guns during the war. *What did the war solve* was the question. *Was the conflict a natural phenomenon amongst men or was it as a result of the lack of effective leadership? Did great nations feel it necessary to go to war to secure their borders?* The thought of having risked his life for the Austrian Monarchy seemed to have little meaning. After all, what did the Monarchy do for ethnic Ukrainians? What did the Monarchy do for Andrij and his family?

In defence of their emerging political policies and persecution of Ukrainians, Polish leaders liked to recall the Khmelnytsky Uprising of the 17th century. It was this particular Ukrainian uprising that continued to smoulder in the national memories of both groups. While relations were not always harmonious, Poles and Ukrainians interacted with each other on every civic, economic, and political level throughout hundreds of years. Indeed, it was not uncommon for a Ukrainian girl to marry a Pole or a Polish girl to marry a Ukrainian boy, thus bringing the two ethnic groups even closer together.

Now safely in Canada, Andrij tried to reconstruct the reasons for leaving Poland. Perhaps the first source of discord came to him from Grochi, the village of his birth. The surrounding forest was a source of aggravation for many Ukrainians living in the area. The Polish land barons ruled the region, even though Ukrainians formed the majority. Access to the forests was limited to Poles and entry by Ukrainians without the permission of a baron was forbidden and punishable under Polish law. This is why the feelings of so many who left Poland might have been different had Austria continued to rule Galicia. And yet, the major reason for Andrij's decision to immigrate to Canada came from his decision to marry a girl that he loved as opposed to what he thought would be an arranged marriage to a girl he did not love.

Three years later, Ewa and five-year-old Maria would get their affairs in order in Poland and join Andrij in Canada. Once in Canada, Andrij and Ewa would not have to contend with the tragedies that were about to visit upon Ukrainians living in Eastern Poland.

Andrij and Ewa Kaszuba were among the lucky ones. Long before the dark clouds of world conflict would descend upon the *Old Country* in 1939, they found new freedoms and an opportunity for economic independence in Canada. As fate would have it, however, those who remained behind in the *Old Country* would not be so lucky. Tragic events would soon come to visit upon Polish villages in the Oblast of Volhynia. In retaliation, Ukrainian villages in Gmina Narol would soon be destroyed.

"That," as Andrij noted, *"will now be left up to those left behind."*

In the months and years following the departure of Andrij and Ewa for Canada, there would be no shortage of political machinations and intrigue, all of which would have a direct impact upon Poland, Ukraine, and Russia. Neither would the members of clan kaszub living in Gmina Narol escape the maelstrom. The remaining descendants of Joannis Kaszuba living in Gmina Narol would soon have a rude awakening.

*1947: Andrij and Ewa Kaszuba immigrated to
Canada in 1928 and 1931 respectively.*

There was one other thing that Ewa Groszko-Kaszuba did not know at that time of her arrival in Canada. Her cousin, Jan Konenko and his family, living in the nearby Gmina of Tomaszów Lubelski, had taken up residence in a village near the small city of Lutsk in the neighboring province of Volhynia.

All of this came about when, in 1923, the government of Poland urged more Poles to help colonize the newly acquired but sparsely occupied region of Volhynia. Those released from duty in the Polish Legions (*Polish Army*) as veterans of World War I were offered free agricultural land in the Volhynian Voivodeship. By a quirk of fate, two of the soldiers from the Lublin Voivodeship who would take up the offer of the Polish government for free land in the Volhynian Oblast as military colonists would soon play a pivotal role in this story. Filip Wozniak, an ethnic Pole, had earlier served Poland in World War I in the Second Brigade of the Polish Legions, while Jan Konenko, an ethnic Ukrainian, briefly served Poland after World War I in the First Brigade of the Polish Legions.

Even as World War II raged on, Ukrainians and Poles continued to struggle for nationhood. Polish nationalistic bands from the Chelm Voivodeship roamed the countryside with the objective of removing Ukrainians from what they envisioned would soon be a free and independent nation of Poland. In a similar move and in an effort to cleanse Volhynia of all Poles, Ukrainian nationalists began their attacks on Polish villages. Unfortunately, the small village of Grochi would soon be earmarked for destruction.

What follows is the story of how and why these ethnic cleansings occurred. To make sense of all of this, I must first take you back to my first and second visits to the Soviet Union.

PART 3

IN SEARCH OF FAMILY

4

The Intrigue of The Soviet Union

"Comrade, you are expelled from the Soviet Union…"

My adventures, or more correctly my misadventures to the Soviet Union in search of family, began in the spring of 1967. However, my deep and abiding interest in the Soviet Union was triggered one year earlier with the release of the movie entitled Dr. Zhivago, a story about the Russian Revolution. Written by Boris Pasternak, the story dealt with Russian society and class. It presented all kinds of philosophical viewpoints, different takes on the world, and expressions of personal freedom. As a consequence, I was bound and determined to travel to the Soviet Union, *the Old Country,* even though I knew that approval and travel to Soviet Bloc countries was restricted.

I made my case to the Canadian Consulate and, in early April, I received a telegram from the Prime Minister's Office in Ottawa informing me that I had the approval of the Canadian Government to travel to the Soviet Union. *Yes,* I could do so, the telegram read, *but only after being briefed by the Royal Canadian Air Force Security Office.*

Of course, I could not leave for the Soviet Union the very next day. Since I served in the Canadian Department of National Defence in Germany, and in accordance with the directive from the Prime Minister's Office, I was obligated to spend some time with Royal Canadian Air Force officials. They wanted to tell me about the inherent dangers of travel to any Soviet Bloc Country. Perhaps they wanted to dissuade me from going there in the first place.

"The KGB," stated Colonel Townsend of the Security Department, *"is the world's most effective information-gathering organization. They operate legal and illegal espionage residences in target countries, including West Germany. Perhaps by infiltrating Intourist they are already aware of your travel plans to the Soviet Union. They steal, photograph documents, and infiltrate organizations throughout the western world."*

Colonel Townsend impressed upon me that Canada was fully aware of the clandestine activities of the KGB. *"Their techniques,"* he continued, *"may have varied over the years but their end game has always been the same. Recently, the Khrushchev period was marked by relative tolerance toward dissent. However, last year President Leonid Brezhnev once again reinstituted harsh policies. As a consequence, arrests of political dissidents have risen."*

I accepted that travel to the Soviet Union was dangerous and that the penalties can be severe. *"Many political dissidents who are arrested,"* explained Colonel Townsend, *"face forcible confinement in a prison or admission to a psychiatric hospital where debilitating drugs are administered. In carrying out its task of ensuring state security, the KGB is empowered to uncover and investigate certain political crimes set forth in the Russian Republic's Code of Criminal Procedure"*

If nothing else, Colonel Townsend reinforced the notion that any political dissent in the Soviet Union was strictly forbidden. After what seemed to be a whole day of briefings, the security detachment of the Air Force must have felt that I was ready for the challenge. The only other important task remaining was the matter of getting all of my paperwork in order with Intourist, the official Soviet Union Travel Agent founded by Josef Stalin in 1929, and staffed by NKVD and KGB agents for obvious reasons. In accordance with Intourist policy, I had to purchase, in advance and in American dollars, my accommodation needs for travel to Soviet Bloc Countries.

Crossing into any Soviet Bloc country in those days was a new and frightening experience for me. Security was tight and entry closely monitored by remote cameras and armed guards. The number of vehicles entering Poland was small, but this did not seem to hasten my entry. Looking at my credentials and my readily recognizable German-made car, it seemed as though they were struggling with a question, *why would a person with a Slavic surname want to drive a German automobile into Poland? Has he no regard for the history between the two peoples?* It seemed to me as though the memories of World War II were uppermost in their minds. The fact that my car carried Canadian Armed Forces plates did not seem to matter.

As I approached the city of Warsaw, I recalled how in 1939 Hitler had given his Generals their secret orders to organize a fictitious attack on a German radio station, immediately to be used as an excuse for an attack on Poland. It was then that the tanks and motorized infantry crashed through the Polish lines. Hitler unveiled a new kind of warfare called the *blitzkrieg.* The Nazi blitzkrieg, coupled with Hitler's special arrangement with Russia wherein Poland was partitioned between the two powers, facilitated a simultaneous Russian invasion from the east and an attack by the German armies from the west.

As a tourist to any Soviet Bloc country, I was compelled to stay on a pre-planned route and on major highways. The highway from Warsaw to Moscow was full of surprises. It seemed that danger lurked at every corner and in plain view of the notorious Soviet police, the KGB. Although I did not know it at the time, I drove through the city of Smolensk and near the location of the Katyn Forest massacre where the NKVD carried out a series of mass executions of Polish nationals in the spring of 1940. The dream of setting foot in Ukraine had been with me for a very long time and even the sub-machine wielding border guards and the vision of barb wire fences at border crossings could not dampen my spirits. My parents had often talked about the *Old Country. Well,* I thought, *this is it. This is where it all began for my parents.*

En route from Moscow to Kyiv, I drove through the historic city of Kursk. It was here that the world-famous Tank Battle of Kursk occurred in August, 1943, a tank battle that would have a profound impact upon the outcome of the war. My Intourist map told me that the distance from Kyiv to Lviv was 544 kilometres. I felt excited and nervous as I took out a letter from my uncle addressed to my father. The return address confirmed that the letter came from Buzk, Soviet Ukraine. In turn, the village of Buzk was shown on my map as being just a couple of kilometres distance off the main highway. The road sign pointing in the direction of the village of Buzk was large and inviting, perhaps put into place by kolkhoz workers in competition with other kolkhozes. As I wound my way into the village on a narrow dirt road, it seemed as though every villager took an interest in me and in my car. I stopped to make an enquiry about the location of my uncle's home. A resident was most accommodating, pointing in the direction of what he believed to be my uncle's home.

Unfortunately, when I knocked on the door, I discovered that the family was not related to me at all. That evening as the sun was setting, seemingly forming a halo over the local Ukrainian Greek Catholic Church, I did meet my Uncle Fedjko Kaszuba and his family. Following a brief visit, I immediately left for the city of Lviv and my Intourist Hotel. Check-in time was regulated and I was anxious to arrive at the Intourist Hotel in a timely fashion.

In retrospect and knowing something about the work of the KGB, I might have been far more careful about where I went and what I said. In particular, I should have realized that several residents in Buzk were aware that I was a foreign visitor. As well, I should have known that it was a common practice in a Soviet Bloc country to immediately report any suspicious activity to the KGB. Soon, the fact that I visited the wrong family under the direction of a complete stranger would play itself out in the strangest of ways and lead to dire consequences.

In the meantime, I did return to Buzk the very next day to pay my Uncle another visit. As is the custom with Ukrainian families, I was invited to stay for a noonday lunch of homemade borsch and dark rye bread. As I looked out the window, I was shocked to see two Soviet military vehicles entering Uncle Fedjko's front yard. Several military police wearing Soviet military uniforms took their positions near the residence.

Without even knocking on the door, two military officers entered my uncle's home. Cool and collected, they were not in a hurry. The first question they raised of my Aunt had nothing to do with my presence. *"Do you have enough soup,"* asked one of the KGB agents, *"for me and my comrade?"*

Only after they had eaten all the bread set before them washed down with the borsch were they prepared to ask questions. And, I dare say, they knew how to interrogate a foreigner. Had the farm animals been able to talk, I am certain that the KGB would have interrogated them as well.

"We have reviewed your itinerary. We checked with Moscow about your approved route. Lieutenant Kaszuba, you have broken the laws of the Union of Soviet Socialist Republics. What you have done is contrary to the laws of the Soviet Union."

After some bantering back and forth, I could see that to argue with the KGB agents was useless. Finally, the lead officer had a decision.

"Lieutenant Kaszuba, by the authority of the Soviet Union under Article 54 of the Constitution, you are placed under house arrest. We will take you to

Lviv under military escort. Do not try to escape our authority. You will follow our lead military vehicle. One military vehicle will follow you."

Arriving in the city of Lviv, I was escorted, under guard, to my Intourist Hotel. I knew that to fabricate any kind of a story would not help my case. So, I told the KGB how proud I was of my Ukrainian family and how thrilled I was to meet them. I also thanked them for their anticipated understanding. With tongue in cheek, I even went further, telling the arresting officer that their system of government made a lot of sense to me.

The next day, I realized that my positive but contrived words about Communism had not fallen on deaf ears. This was borne out when one of the Soviet officers came to the Intourist Hotel with some surprising news.

"Lieutenant Kaszuba, the local office of the KGB has informed me that the state is prepared to bring several members of your family from Buzk and Kamianka-Buzk to Lviv for a short visit with you."

True to their word, the very next morning a small bus arrived with several members of my family. The Soviet authorities provided me with sufficient time to visit with members of my family in a meeting room in our Intourist Hotel. At no time was I left alone with family but always in the presence of at least one KGB agent. Throughout, I could not get out of my mind that the KGB was aware of family living in villages other than Buzk, family members that even I did not know about.

That afternoon, I left Lviv for the small international city of Uzhhorod and the border crossing that would take me into Czechoslovakia. However, something terrible happened at that juncture. To my horror, missing was my briefcase containing my passport, currency, and all other travel documents. What made the situation more critical is that I distinctly remembered placing the briefcase in the rear seat of my vehicle. *Those damn KGB agents,* I concluded, *they removed my briefcase from my car. I'd like to strangle a couple of those ugly bastards with my own hands!*

Without the briefcase which contained my passport, I could not leave Soviet Ukraine. I had no alternative but to report this to the border authorities who once again placed me under house arrest and booked me into the Intourist Hotel in Uzhhorod near the Czechoslovakian border. Following several telephone calls by the KGB to Moscow and Lviv, the authorities said that they would have my briefcase back in my hands the very next day.

While under house arrest in Uzhhorod, I had plenty of time to think about my time in the Soviet Union. I thought long and hard about a common question whispered to me in Moscow, *do you have any American dollars to sell?* I was also aware that it might well have been a Soviet teenager who approached me on behalf of a Communist official who was seeking American dollars. After all, what Communist official wouldn't want a pocketful of American currency in advance of travel to a western country? It really bothered me to realize that the official exchange rate of American to Russian roubles was nearly one-to-one while the black market commanded at least 25 roubles for every American dollar. Little wonder that so many tourists to the Soviet Union were so willing to break the law and exchange American dollars for Russian roubles without regard for any consequences.

During my time in the Soviet Union, the new Communist collective leadership was headed by Leonid Brezhnev, General Secretary of the Communist Party from 1964-1982, a post held by Josef Stalin from 1922-1953 and Nikita Khrushchev from 1959-1964. Once again under house arrest, I had to admit that Colonel Townsend correctly characterized the Brezhnev regime as being more militant than was Khrushchev's regime.

As promised, the KGB had my briefcase back in my hands the very next day. At this point, the KGB agents subjected me to more intensive interrogation. They wanted to know why I was involved in the black market; the marketing of select western goods. At this point I tried to make the best of a bad situation and admitted to selling a couple of t-shirts, some cigarettes, and a pen and pencil set. Not fully satisfied with my explanation, they practically tore apart the inside of my car looking for more evidence. They confiscated my American, Soviet, and Canadian currency; leaving me with only sufficient gas coupons and funds to find my way back to the Canadian Air Force base in Germany. Having exhausted all of their questions, they finally had a decision for me.

"Comrade, to prosecute you would be a great expense to the Soviet Government. However, before we release you from custody, you must sign this document."

At this point, the danger signals went up, way up. I wanted to know the precise nature of the document they wanted me to sign.

"This document states that you committed a petty crime. You entered a village without permission and you had more roubles in your possession than you declared upon entry into the Soviet Union. This means that you must

have sold western goods on the black market. You must agree not to return to the Soviet Union for twenty-five years."

Even as the KGB made reference to any perceived misdemeanor committed by me, I well knew that they were far more interested in the fact that I was stationed in Zweibrucken, Germany, a Canadian military base close to Ramstein, Germany. They would have been aware that the Americans were working on the development of strategic technologies in the face of emerging nuclear threats. I recalled that a KGB operative in Moscow had asked me about my knowledge of the Minuteman intercontinental ballistic missile weapon system, a topic about which I knew very little. It would not be until I returned to Zweibrucken that I would learn that the remotely-controlled Minuteman weapon system was conceived and put into place in the late 1950s. Maybe the KGB felt that I had knowledge of a weapons system developed in order to keep pace with technological change and any new threat environments. Were that the case, they would have been very disappointed; very wrong.

As I crossed the border into Czechoslovakia, I suddenly realized that any effort to search for my ancestral village in the county of Lubaczow, Poland, had suddenly vanished. But, never mind, having met several relatives in Buzk and in Lviv provided me with invaluable information about my family and heritage. I took some comfort in recalling the words of General MacArthur, spoken in Australia in 1942, when he said, *"I came through and I shall return."* Perhaps as an antidote, he also said, *"You are remembered for the rules you break."* Even as I bid farewell to the Soviet Ukraine, I also knew that one day I would return.

With one last and haunting look at Soviet Ukraine in my rear-view mirror, I felt that I was the luckiest person in the world. But for the seeming generosity of the KGB, it all might have turned out very differently. The road ahead seemed long and winding, much like my ancestral flowchart. Every turn in the road provided me with a new vision and another challenge. Still, I had to admit that for the first time since leaving Vienna, I tasted democracy and freedom.

5

My Return To The Soviet Union

Convinced that my family tree was missing a branch

"**E**xcuse me, sir," was the pointed question from the Auto Europe agent, "*you want to take this rental car into Ukraine? Don't you realize that you would have to drive through Poland to get to Ukraine? Are you out of your mind? Are you not aware of the dangers?*"

To say that I was taken aback by the agent's remarks would be an understatement. I was under the impression that a trip to a satellite Soviet Bloc country should not be a problem. After all, wasn't the Soviet Union on the side of the Allies during World War II? And this being 1997, didn't the Soviet Union disintegrate in 1991?

Twenty-five years earlier, we did rent a car from this very same agency in Frankfurt, Germany, to attend the 1972 Summer Olympic Games in Munich. Friendly and most accommodating, the German agent at that time had no difficulty in making a car available for our use. However, our destination this time was not Munich but an East European country, a country that had just emerged from the claws of a Communist dictator, a place where the rule of law did not necessarily prevail.

As I awaited the decision of the car rental agency, I recalled how, thirty years earlier, I had travelled to the Soviet Union from a Canadian Air Force Base in Zweibrucken, Germany. During that journey, I came face to face with a KGB operative in Soviet Ukraine; a most unpleasant experience. The words of the KGB agent, even though they were spoken so many years earlier, sent shivers throughout my whole body.

"Comrade," was the manner in which the KGB agent addressed me, *"you are under arrest for straying from your approved route. We will escort you to the Intourist Hotel in Lviv."*

Why, I thought, *would a KGB agent refer to me as comrade when that term was most commonly used in Russia between colleagues serving in the military and not between strangers?* Suddenly, it occurred to me that they must have been aware that I possessed the honorary rank of Flight Lieutenant in the Royal Canadian Air Force. Perhaps this would explain why they, out of respect for military ranks, referred to me as *comrade.* I concluded that it would not hurt my cause to be called a *comrade.*

A lot of things happened during my term of banishment from the Soviet Union. Looking at the calendar, I could see that the Soviets did not want to see me again until at least 1992. Coincidentally, and as fate would have it, the Soviet Union disintegrated in 1991, making it possible for me to consider a return to the land of my ancestors. Most unexpectedly, it turned out to be a time when independent East European countries sought and attained a path to democracy. However, it would not be until 1996 that I received clearance to travel to former Soviet Union countries and not until 1997 that my wife and I would finally get our visas in place for travel to Poland and Ukraine. This made it possible for me to plan the journey with the objective of resuming my search for family. Somehow, I sensed that finding family members after the destruction of World War II would not be easy.

In making plans to travel to Europe, I noted that the status of Poland and Ukraine, as Communist countries, had been relatively static from 1920 to 1991. Things, however, were about to change very rapidly in 1989. Poland gained its independence from the Soviet Union in the spring of 1989, soon followed by Soviet Ukraine in 1991.

On August 24, 1991, millions of Ukrainians the world over awoke as if from a dream. On that day Ukraine declared itself an independent state taking its rightful place among the nations of the world. Travel to and within Ukraine had been restricted for many years and little was written about its rich history and culture. Ukrainian politicians taking up the challenge of leading Ukraine out of the darkness soon discovered that centuries of economic and political dependence upon Moscow had sufficiently crippled the new nation to such a degree as to render it incapable of full and meaningful nationhood. Emerging from three centuries of colonialism and seventy years of totalitarianism, Ukrainians faced severe economic, ecological, transportation, communication, and energy challenges.

The dictator most identified with Poland and Soviet Ukraine during the inter-war years was Josef Stalin. When he died in 1953, an era of tyranny also came to an end. However, millions of Poles and Ukrainians minimized his crimes and emphasized his achievements. In this way, they could still embrace everything they had been taught while continuing to believe that although he made mistakes, he had turned the Soviet Union from a rural backwater to an industrial giant and a military superpower.

What the Soviet Union leaders soon discovered after World War II was that the removal of political activists did not solve the Soviet Union's problems. Even the Greek Catholic Church, with its abolition in 1940, continued to function underground. In fact, one can advance the argument that the Soviet Union had given up in its attempts to Russify the Ukrainian population despite the increasing dominance of Russian firms in the political, social, and political life of Ukraine. All of this highlights one important phenomenon and that is that a nation's hopes and aspirations for independence are very difficult to suppress.

The time had come for me to uncover some of the truths about Ukraine, Poland, and my family. In planning the journey to Europe in search of family, it saddened me to think that my parents refused to talk about their childhood or the family they left behind. Whatever the explanation, my parents never wanted to talk about their childhood in the presence of their children, not even in the presence of their adult children. Yet, they loved to talk about the *Old Country,* but only when they met up with other immigrants from the same region of Europe.

In this day and age the response to a question directed to one's parents about the extended family would be easy. All you would have to do is ask them about their childhood and it is virtually certain that they would have an answer to most of your questions. Not so, however, in my family when I was a youngster. *Why not,* that was the question. *Was it because the memories of growing up during WWI were too painful to recall or were they trying to keep something from their children?*

Perhaps it was an unwritten code or in the least a tradition of families coming to Canada from Eastern Europe to keep information away from their children. Maybe something happened in their families that they wanted to hide or forget. Perhaps they had information that would discredit or bring shame to various members of the families left behind. Maybe it had something to do with legal matters.

Although my parents are no longer living, I know what their answer would have been if I had asked either of them a question about their childhood or their ancestors. *"Why do you want to know about my childhood? Are you some kind of a policeman? Are you an agent of the NKVD? Is it any of your business?"*

Heaven forbid that I should have asked a question that might have been of a sensitive nature. Their response would always have been the same. *"Learn to listen, that is your role as a child. That is what I want from my children. Do not ask questions about my childhood. I will tell you what I think you should know about the families we left behind."*

Yes, it would have been so much easier were I able to ask these questions of my parents when they were still living and get a thoughtful response. Were that the case, it would have been easier to understand why my parents did not want to talk about the Old Country. Even more puzzling was the depth of their resolve never to return to their ancestral homeland. Responses to my questions about their childhood seemed always to be the same; there was no response. If I were to quench my curiosity about my parents' past, I would have to find the answers to my questions on my own.

Curiously, when I first met my cousins in Ukraine and Poland, it was as if each had signed a pact of silence about the history of their families as well. Obviously, this reflected the attitude held by their parents. Their parents must have impressed upon them that idle talk could result in dire consequences. Many had lived through a stressful time when their families had been forcibly transferred from Poland to Soviet Ukraine or from Soviet Ukraine to Poland. Facing survival in the midst of conflict, they had precious little time to deal with family and genealogy. The Communists made sure of that.

Above all else, I wanted to know more about the path that my father travelled when he was a young boy growing up in the small village of Grochi. I wanted to learn more about the circumstances which led to the torching of Grochi and how was it that so many members of my family survived ethnic conflict and World War II. *Did the Polish national forest reserve surrounding the villages of Płazów and Ruda Różaniecka play a significant role in the survival of members of my family? Was the region a breeding ground for the operation of partisans and nationalistic bands?*

Arriving in Lviv, Ukraine, in the fall of 1997, my first challenge was to meet all of my surviving aunts and uncles. Even as I put my plan into place, I had the suspicion that the KGB would have monitored those members of my family I met in 1967. This brought to mind a very important question—*what happened to the six members of my family I met in 1967? Were any of them persecuted by the KGB?*

The first person I wanted to meet once again was my Aunt Anna Kaszuba-Grokh. Although I did meet her in Edmonton in 1991 when she was my mother's guest, I also recalled that she refused to divulge any information about her family at that time. Maybe she feared that the Communist regime had listening devices installed in every corner of my mother's apartment. Perhaps Aunt Anna repressed memories that had been unconsciously blocked due to the memory being associated with a high level of stress or trauma.

The small rural village of Loshniv, set in valley near the small city of Terebovlya, was home to about 500 people, including my Aunt. Sitting over a typical mid-day meal of soup and rye bread, I was somewhat surprised and relieved to discover that Aunt Anna now welcomed the opportunity to talk about her epic journey from Poland to Soviet Ukraine in 1945. But, even before launching into a guarded discussion about her journey, she wanted to make a confession, a confession that was perhaps guilt-ridden.

"This home," revealed my Aunt, *"once belonged to a Polish family. It is now our home. The Polish family who once owned this home were forcibly transferred to Poland."*

Only after recognizing and paying tribute to this Polish family was my Aunt prepared to talk about her own trials and tribulations.

"At the time of my re-location," explained Aunt Anna, *"three of my brothers and their families were also transferred from Poland to Ukraine. Can you imagine? In 1939, Poland was attacked by the Nazis in the west and by the Red Army in the east. Poland was divided into two pieces. In the beginning, Gmina Narol was occupied by the Nazis. It was not until 1944 that the Red Army pushed the Nazis out of Narol. Even while the war raged on, this did not stop nationalistic Polish bands from attacking Ukrainians. We had so much to contend with."*

According to Aunt Anna, the transfers of Ukrainians from Poland to Soviet Ukraine were not undertaken at the same time and in the same way in every village. The experiences of those being transferred depended upon the location of the village, the inclination of Polish nationalistic bands to attack the Ukrainians, and the ability of Soviet and Polish authorities to protect Ukrainians identified for transfer to Soviet Ukraine. In listening to my Aunt, I realized that I would have to undertake more research and interview other members of my family in order to understand more fully the experiences of Ukrainians who were forcibly transferred from Poland to Soviet Ukraine after the war.

"So sad," added Aunt Anna with tears welling up in her eyes, *"my whole family was forced to leave the land they had occupied for many generations. They did not want to leave their ancestral homes but the brutality to which the Soviet government resorted in order to remove the Ukrainians from Poland testifies to its eagerness to resolve the minority question."*

Perhaps it was my cousin Vasyl Groszko who best described his experiences during and after World War II. In 1939, at the age of fifteen, he was captured by the German Gestapo in the village of Płazów and forced to work in Austria as an Eastern Worker. The Austrian family for whom he toiled had no children. When the war was over, they begged him to stay behind as an Ostfluchting, a refugee from Eastern Europe. He desperately wanted to do so. However, the Soviet authorities had other plans for him, *"...return to Soviet Ukraine honourably or in a pine box. The choice is yours,"* was the manner in which they defined it.

1999: Vasyl Groszko, Eastern Worker in Austria during World War II.

Much like Aunt Anna's family, Vasyl's family also had to face the horrors of international conflict, the possibility of arrest by the Gestapo and slave labour in Germany, and attacks from nationalistic Polish units. And yet, Vasyl's experiences were in stark contrast to those of my Aunt. Anna Kaszuba-Grokh was arrested in 1940 by the Gestapo and forced to work in Germany as a Zivilarbeiter. However, upon learning that her parents were in poor health and needed her assistance, Anna begged to be returned to Poland. To everyone's surprise, German authorities showed some heart and granted Anna her request. She returned to Poland in 1943.

Even as I digested the heart-wrenching stories of hardship that Aunt Anna had to overcome, I was most anxious to pursue the matter of the composition of my family tree. In particular, I wanted to know if *any* branch of the family was missing. Although Aunt Anna was fully aware of the composition of her immediate family, she seemed less interested in the composition of the extended family. Perhaps the very survival of a family during uncertain political times had a lot to do with this mindset. They had little time to deal with genealogy and the composition of the family during troubled times.

And yet, based upon her comments, I could not dispel the notion that my family tree was not complete. This feeling originated with an earlier visit to Narol, Poland, when a community leader informed me that clan kaszub consisted of two distinct branches, one branch residing in the village of Grochi while another branch lived in the nearby village of Ruda Różaniecka. Unfortunately, neither the local archive in Narol nor the national archives in Warsaw could cast any light upon my search. After all, archives contain information only inserted into the record by individuals. In the event that an archive is destroyed, so is the information contained therein. I concluded that information not available in the archives of a jurisdiction often resides in the hearts and minds of its elder residents.

Of course, it would be relatively easy to confirm this belief if civic or church records were available for my review. In 1782 Austria introduced laws establishing Catholic priests as civil registrars. Then, in 1784, an edict by Emperor Joseph II required Catholic clergy to make civil transcripts of church records. Catholic parish registers were designated as state records and a standardized Latin columnar form was issued. The parish register thus became the official register of births, marriages, and deaths. A duplicate was made for state purposes and separate registers were required for each parish in every diocese. As a result, Greek Catholic and Roman Catholic clergy were responsible for the registration of all vital records.

Unfortunately, all Ukrainian Greek Catholic records in Gmina Narol were destroyed during the war. It is for this reason that I wanted to make another visit to Poland and the village of Ruda Różaniecka. I wanted to meet and interview any senior citizen who would remember the names of those who lived in the village during World War II. I wanted to either prove or disprove the rumour that the kaszub clan consisted of two branches.

"Would you remember," I asked Aunt Anna, *"if clan kaszub consisted of more than one branch in the Narol region? Did one branch of the family live in the village of Grochi and the other in the village of Ruda Różaniecka?"*

"When I was a little girl," confirmed Aunt Anna, *"my grandfather, Ivan, said that he had a bit of a falling out with his brother, Jakub. They went their separate ways. So did my great Aunt, Mariia Kaszuba. She married a Pole, left the Ukrainian Greek Catholic Church, and joined a Roman Catholic Parish. That is all I know."*

With these thoughts bouncing around in my head, I concluded that my family tree was, in fact, missing a branch. My challenge was either to prove or disprove this hypothesis. I realized that intervening world events and the passage of time since World War II would only add to my challenges. At the same time, I accepted that when one door closes, another opens, even though we often look so long and so regretfully upon the closed door that we do not see the one which has opened to us.

Answers to my search for the missing branch in the family would be slow in coming. In the end, I uncovered a well-kept secret. I discovered that two little orphans constituted the missing branch. They were the byproduct of war and victims of ethnic conflict. Without discovering these two little orphans, my family tree would not be complete.

To fully unravel the mystery of how these two infant children became orphans war and ethnic cleansings, my search first took me to Poland and then to Volhynia, a province that today is a part of Ukraine but was an integral part of Poland during the interwar years.

6

A Startling Discovery

Two little toddlers emerge from their torched home

During my first visits to Ukraine and Poland, I discovered that members of my extended family did not readily volunteer information. Their responses to my questions about family had to be considered in the light of the political climate in which they were raised. Members of my East European family grew up in Soviet villages where a misspoken word could be one's ticket to Siberia. Maybe they were remembering the lack of freedom, the poor life, the long queues, and the seven-year wait for a car. Perhaps they were even thinking about the insecurity of today as compared to the security provided under the communist regime, the plice state.

Adding further to Aunt Anna's difficulty in answering my questions was this matter of state control upon the concept of freedom of communication and restrictions to travel within Soviet Ukraine, even for its own residents. The passports which they held during Soviet times were internal passports, limited to travel within the county in which they resided. In the main, it was an identity document used to control and monitor the internal movement and residence of its people. They were also used to record the ethnicity of citizens and to control access to sensitive sites or closed cities. Travel to a foreign country was completely out of question. Even communication with family members residing in another gmina was frowned upon, let alone any communication with a relative living in another country. In the end, I concluded that I would have to search for answers elsewhere.

Fifteen years after my meeting with my Aunt, Anna Grokh, in Loshniv, I found myself in Poland seeking answers to questions of genealogy and my family tree. With this objective in mind, I made a special trip to the small village of Ruda Różaniecka, just two kilometers from the burnt-out village of Grochi, home to the kaszubs in the 18th and 19th centuries. Although Grochi no longer existed, did not necessarily mean that the memories of that village would not live on in the hearts and minds of those old enough to remember the war. In the meantime, I tried to make sense of the life and times of those who lived, worked, and worshipped in the Austrian province of Galicia and in the small village of Płazów.

It could be, I reasoned, *that if a member of the family became estranged from the kaszub clan, he or she would still have taken up residence in the same region.* Perhaps one branch of the clan was set adrift and did not communicate with other members of the family. The question was, *would there be any elderly resident of Ruda Różaniecka who would remember the tragic events of World War II? Would that person remember who survived and who did not? Who was transferred to Soviet Ukraine and who was not?*

As I entered the village of Ruda Różaniecka, I reflected upon the thoughts that my cousin Jaroslaw Kaszuba expressed about family and the important role that religion played in their lives. He impressed upon me that in many respects religion and ethnicity were inexorably intertwined in Poland.

"In Płazów," concluded my cousin, *"the church and state had strong formal ties. Not only that, but religion was the glue that held families together. Religious beliefs held by a family were always passed on from one generation to another."*

Another cousin, Ivan Kaszuba, was also of the opinion that dissension frequently existed between adherents to the Roman Catholic Church and those who attended the Greek Catholic Church. Having regard for this assertion raised an important question, *was it possible that a schism in the family had been caused by religious beliefs or by an inter-faith marriage?*

From my discussions with family members in Ukraine, I concluded that, over time, a family living in the region of Poland bordering on Soviet Ukraine can split into two branches. One branch of the family could have remained as members of one church while, through marriage or for other reasons, another branch of the family would join another church. This raised a very important question in my mind. Within my extended family, *was there any movement from one religious diocese to another? Did any members of the family give up their faith in a Greek Catholic Church in favour of a Roman Catholic Church or the other way around? If so, for what reason was such a change made? What might have been the consequences of any change in religious affiliation?*

Immigrants to Canada from East European countries often spoke of the conflicts that existed between various religious groups. Especially troubling were those conflicts which frequently arose as a result of inter-religious marriages, ethnicity, race, or colour. Frequently, the first signs of trouble in an inter-faith or mixed marriage came about as a result of religious days of obligation falling on different days for each group. This would immediately have an impact upon family customs and family get-togethers. In many cases, the precipitate of such a discord was predictable—a schism in the family and a breakdown of effective communication.

As scarce as were the church and civic records available in Lubaczow and Przymysl for the Roman and Greek Catholic churches, they were quite helpful. For one thing, I discovered that the children of my great-grandfather did not necessarily embrace the same religious beliefs as did their parents and grandparents. Civic records show that my great-grandfather, Jan Kaszuba, had a brother Jakub who married a Polish girl. The members of the Polish family were devout Roman Catholics while most other kaszubs were affiliated with the Greek Catholic Church. However, this was about to change. In order to win the hand of the Polish girl, Jakub had to give up his affiliation with the Greek Catholic Church in favour of the Roman Catholic Church. This seemingly small act caused quite a rift in the household of the kaszubs. Communication between the two brothers came to a virtual halt.

The schism in the kaszub lineage became even more pronounced when Jakub's daughter, Mariia, fell in love and in 1870 married a Polish boy by the name of Mareusz Zaborniak. As can be expected, this marriage had consequences similar to those encountered by Jakub. Communication links between the two branches of clan kaszub were damaged. In fact, it would appear as though the two families rarely, if ever, talked to one another even though they lived in the same gmina. With this realization in mind, I concluded that there could well be a branch of my family that was not yet on my family tree.

In the centre of the small community of Ruda Różaniecka, I stopped to talk to an elderly woman. As it turned out, it was not so much that I was talking, perhaps, to the oldest woman in the village of Ruda Różaniecka, but the realization that she was able to recall events which happened so many years ago. She immediately struck me as having information not available in state archives. Now approaching the second decade of the twenty-first century, World War II had been over for nearly seventy years. I believed that it would be difficult to find anyone in this region who even remembered the war. To most, the war was no more than a vague memory. However, this woman was an exception. Looking around at the small rural village of Ruda Różaniecka, I already knew the questions I was about to ask her.

"Dzien dobry, mowisz, ze masz na imie Karolina Nowak? Że jesteś najstarsza kobieta w tym regionie? Good day to you. I am honoured to meet you, Pani Nowak."

Steadying herself by holding on to the garden gate, she was most happy to have a chat with a visitor from a foreign country.

"Dzien dobry. Yes, I am the oldest woman in this village. And, look at me. I still tend to my garden, my chickens, and my geese."

"How old are you?" I asked the elderly woman. From her quizzical look on her face, I could see that she was not offended by my question.

"Why," she responded with a great deal of pride, *"I will soon reach the century mark!"*

"That is most unusual," was my response. *"With all of the political upheavals and wars, just to survive that period in history is a victory in itself!"*

Looking at Pani Nowak, I could see by virtue of her age that she belonged to that rare group of individuals often referred to in Poland as the *starosta,* a title for an official or unofficial position of leadership that has been used in various contexts throughout most of Slavic history. From the Slavic root *'star...',* meaning *old,* can be translated as *senior* or *elder.* Over the years, it was common for a particular territory to be administered by a *starosta,* frequently referred to as the *starostwo.* In fact, the concept of a *starosta* goes back to the Middle Ages when the *starosta* was the head of one or more Slavic communities. The person designated as the *starosta* was looked upon as being a counsellor to residents and often the master of ceremonies at the traditional Carpatho-Rusyn, Ukrainian, or Polish wedding.

Could it be, I wondered, *that this woman has information about my family not found in any archive? Would she have memories from the war that might help me with my search for my extended family?*

"Do you remember the events before World War II?" I ventured.

I could scarcely believe what I was hearing when I entered into a conversation with this elderly woman. It soon became abundantly clear that she vividly recalled the events of World War II.

"Pamiętam wojnę," was the way that the diminutive but stately-looking Polish woman responded, *"I remember the war as if it happened just yesterday! I remember those terrible times before, during, and after the war. I remember them all!"*

"Did you and your family live in Ruda Różaniecka during this period in history?"

"Yes, yes, my family has lived in this region for as long as I can remember."

"You know, Pani Nowak, we checked every grave marker in the local cemetery. I noticed that there are very few extended families who currently live or have lived in Ruda Różaniecka. I also noticed that there is an absence of Ukrainian names spelled in Cyrillic alphabet on any markers."

"That," thoughtfully responded Pani Nowak, *"is because this cemetery is relatively new. To the best of my knowledge, Ukrainians had never been laid to rest in this cemetery during or after the war."*

"Pani Nowak," I offered hopefully, *"you may be able to help me. Would you remember the names of all villagers who lived here during the war? Would you know the family name Kaszuba?"*

"Yes, I know the family name Kaszuba. I remember them all. But you must know that we lost some of them as casualties of the war. Not only that, but most ethnic Ukrainians were deported to Soviet Ukraine."

"What can you tell me about the Kaszuba family?"

"One Kaszuba family lived in Grochi. Another Kaszuba family lived nearby, right here in Ruda Różaniecka. Adam and Katarzyna Kaszuba lived right over there but their home was burned to the ground in 1944."

"Their home was torched? By whom? Why?"

"Their house was set on fire by a band of Poles. Adam and Katarzyna were murdered by the armed band because they were Ukrainians. They perished but their two infant children survived."

A thousand thoughts reverberated in my head when I heard Pani Nowak declare that two kaszub infants survived the inferno. It suddenly occurred to me that these two little infants could well be the missing branch on my family tree.

"Their two infant children survived? Can you tell me more about them?"

"Yes, little Franek and Sofija escaped from their burning home."

"What happened to those two little infants? Where are they now?"

"They were adopted by Bronislawa and Franciszek Zaborniak."

"Pani Nowak, you remember that those two little orphans were immediately adopted by the Zaborniak family after their parents were murdered? Who told you all of this?"

"No one had to tell me this. I remember all of it. The two infants were adopted by the Franciszek Zaborniak family," explained Pani Nowak. *"I know that Franek's grandmother's maiden name was Mariia Kaszuba. She married Mareusz Zaborniak many years ago. I remember the marriage of their grandson, Franciszek."*

"Where would I look for these two kaszub infants today?"

"They are no longer infants. They would now be senior citizens. Besides, they no longer live Ruda Różaniecka."

"Where do they live?"

"Franek lives in Nowe Sioło. Sofija married a Pole a long time ago and she also lives in Nowe Sioło. The village is about 15 kilometres from here, near the town of Cieszanow."

"Would I be able to find Franek Kaszuba in Nowe Sioło?"

"Pan Stefan, you would not look for a kaszub. They are no longer kaszubs."

"They are no longer kaszubs? Why not? Who are they now?"

"They are Zaborniaks now. Both Franek and Sofija took the family name of their adoptive parents. As far as I can remember, they were always the Zaborniaks."

One would have to go back to 1825, a time when the first member of clan kaszub arrived in the Narol region to understand how, so many years later two orphans would suddenly be taken in by the Zaborniak family.

Mariia Kaszuba married Mareusz Zaborniak in 1871, left the Ukrainian Greek Catholic Church and joined the Polish Roman Church. Their grandson, Franciszek Zaborniak, married Bronislawa in 1931 and by 1940, they would bring into the world three children. The onslaught of World War brought death and destruction to residents of Gmina Narol. Finding themselves to be under Nazi administration was not the only problem or challenge for ethnic Ukrainians. In the face of military conflict and considerable political instability, a new and present danger began to unfold. Ethnic cleansing began to rear its ugly head as Poles attacked Ukrainian families. These attacks would soon have a most deleterious impact upon clan kaszub and the Zaborniak family.

Drawing upon the history of the family, it was during a timeline parallel to that of Franciszek Zaborniak that Adam Kaszuba, the grandson of Ivan Kaszuba and Mariia Zaborniak's nephew, married

Katarzyna in 1937. They would bring into the world Sofija in 1941 and Franek in 1943.

According to Pani Karolina Nowak, Adam and Katarzyna Kaszuba were murdered in 1944, not as a result of the war but as a result of ethnic conflict, leaving behind two infants, Sofija and Franciszek. As fortune would have it, Bronislawa Zaborniak lived next door to the Kaszuba residence. Bronislawa was a direct descendant of clan kaszub. It is for this reason that Franciszek and Bronislawa immediately decided to adopt Sofija and Franciszek.

"Immediately after the war," explained Pani Nowak, *"Sofija and Franek took on a new identity. They became the children of Bronislawa and Franciszek Zaborniak. As orphans, they had no other choice."*

"Do you have any idea, Pani Nowak, who murdered Adam and Katarzyna?"

"There have been all sorts of rumours as to who murdered Adam and Katarzyna. Some believe that the Polish band responsible for the dastardly deed came from Volhynia. A member of the unit told a Polish family living near here that he was from Lutsk but that his family moved from Zamosc to Volhynia after World War I. Who knows for certain?"

"Would you, Pani, know the names of any of the band's members?"

"No, Pan Stepan, I would not know the names of any of the nationalistic bandits. Someone once said that their leader's code name was Kawa. Maybe this family once lived in Zamosc. Whoever is responsible for the crime not only murdered Adam and Katarzyna but also several other residents in Ruda Różaniecka, Grochi, and Płazów."

We sat in silence for the longest time, reflecting on the past and considering what the coming days might bring to each of us. Before leaving the village of Ruda Różaniecka, Pani Nowak approached me with outstretched arms, embraced me warmly, and extended her best wishes in a manner that resonates with me even to this day, *"Szerokiej Drogi, Pan Stepan."*

I could not imagine a more appropriate farewell. In fact, I would find it difficult to find so short an expression with so much meaning, *"...may the roads you travel always be wide."* In turn, my leavetaking was also brief, *"...życząc zdrowia, Pani Karolina."* This common Polish expression also had plenty of meaning, *"May the Good Lord bless you with lots of health and happiness."*

As I set out on the short drive to the village of Nowe Sioło, I had no reason to doubt what Pani Nowak told me. I felt confident that I would soon meet my two long-lost cousins, the missing link on my family tree. But for Pani Nowak, I might never have discovered the existence of the two orphans. At the same time, Pani Nowak raised an important question—who murdered Adam and Katarzyna? Why? I felt duty-bound to set out in search of the perpetrators of the crime.

In order to tell you the heart-wrenching story of how and why Franciszek and Sofija were orphaned, I must take you back to 1939 and the aftermath of the infamous non-aggression pact signed between Nazi Germany and the Soviet Union. From Volhynia to Gmina Narol, the pact unleashed a series of ethnic conflicts—conflicts that took the lives of Adam and Katarzyna Kaszuba, leaving behind two orphans.

PART 4

UKRAINIAN NATIONALISM

7

The Girl Next Door

A romance flourishes despite the war and ethnic differences

Although Volhynia's history goes back hundreds of years, significant migration into the underpopulated region did not occur until the mid-1830s. In 1921, Volhynia was split in two, with the larger western part going to Poland and the smaller eastern part going to the Ukrainian Soviet Socialist Republic. Ethnic conflicts came to Polish Volhynia when its Polish leaders decided to Polonize all ethnic groups, particularly the Ukrainians, even though the Poles constituted only 11% of the population.

During the interwar period, ethnic conflicts between Poles and Ukrainians escalated and began to boil over long before the outbreak of World War II. Following the signing of the Molotov-Ribbentrop Pact in 1939, the Polish part of Volhynia was soon occupied by the Soviet Union, resulting in arrests, deportations, ethnic cleansings, and population transfers.

Deep in thought in the small village of Polonka, Filip Wozniak could not help but reflect upon his own childhood and his life in the town of Zamosc, Poland. He recalled how, after the war in 1920, the Premier of Poland announced that those soldiers who had served on the front would have priority in the government's land-grant program in the newly acquired province of Volhynia. After all, in the opinion of the Premier, the sparsely-populated region, due in part to the postwar Influenza Pandemic which took upwards to 40 million lives worldwide, needed an economic stimulant in the form of new immigrants. Having served in World War I in *Legiony Polskie*, Filip decided to take up the government's offer of free land which was abandoned by the Russian nobility retreating from the region before the arrival of the German forces in 1915.

Firmly under Polish control since the end of World War I, no one living in Volhynia could have imagined that their province would soon find itself on the cusp of another calamity. Yet, if one stops to consider the politics of the day and the process through which Poland was re-created in 1918, the outcome could have been predicted. After all, the majority of the residents were ethnic Ukrainians while nearly all administrative positions were assigned to Poles. This immediately led to many conflicts.

The economy of Volhynia was largely rural and the world-wide depression of 1929 saw hardship in every sector. During the interwar period, the population of Volhynia was only two million, 1.5 million of who were ethnic Ukrainians. This is why the Premier of Poland wanted to give the economy a boost while at the same time increasing the ethnic Polish population. He was of the opinion that this would add stability and strength to the Polish community.

At the same time, Polish leaders wanted to devise a policy towards the minorities that would bring harmony and peaceful coexistence rather than bitterness, confrontation, and strife. They wanted to avoid the pitfalls of an overly aggressive and patriotic Polish government that would be oppressive—persecuting minorities through terror, discrimination, and even murder. However, many ethnic Ukrainians living in Volhynia soon discovered that Poland failed to address this question in a satisfactory manner.

As the decade of the 1930s was drawing to a close, these challenges paled in comparison to other emerging problems. The Nazi regime in Germany was openly pursuing expansionist policies and Poland's policy of equilibrium between potential enemies was failing. By 1939, Hitler had shattered the continental balance of power by a concerted campaign of armed diplomatic extortion that brought most of Central Europe into his grasp.

Even though international events began to consume the energies of many political leaders in Eastern Europe, most residents in Volhynia went about their daily tasks, undeterred. As it turned out, 1939 was also the year when Wiktor Wozniak would turn 17. His father always had something pleasant to say on the occasion of his son's birthday. This day was no exception.

"You know what, my son," was the way his father started his birthday greeting, *"there are lots of good people in Polonka. One of them would like to wish you a Happy Birthday!"*

Blushing, Wiktor suspected that his father was making reference to Tanja Konenko, the pretty teenage girl who lived on a nearby farm. It was obvious that his father must have spoken to her. Otherwise, why would he tease him with the birthday greeting which obviously came from Tanja? Like so many young Poles, Wiktor was also fully aware that in just one more year he would be 18 years of age, the point of departure from boyhood to manhood. Recently, he had attended a friend's 18th birthday party. During the celebration and to the singing of *sto lat*, the Polish equivalent of Happy Birthday, Wiktor delivered one of the 18 whacks to the buttocks of his friend, who, after each belt, would jump up and down with pain, all the while yelling *Kurwa, Kurwa (whore)*.

Confident and self-assured, Wiktor had a question for his father. *"I will soon be completing my secondary education. What do think, Father, about my attending a university in Lwow? Would you allow me to live in a student residence?"*

"Are you out of your mind? You should first think about completing your secondary education. There is plenty of time to think about entry into a university."

It was not so much that Wiktor wanted to attend a university but rather his wish to seek some independence from his parents. Oh, sure, his parents did acknowledge that he was very mature for his age and that he increasingly took responsibility for his actions. What Wiktor did not know at the time was that world events would soon change everything. Wiktor's lack of experience would soon place him on an emotional roller coaster. After all, what 17-year-old would have the background and experience to deal with difficult and complex political situations?

The autumn days in the small rural town of Polonka were always very special. World War I was over for twenty years and much of the Ukrainian animosity towards the Poles had diminished. It was a time when villagers would reap the rewards of their toil, a time to take in the harvest. Located just a short distance from the small but thriving city of Lutsk, Polonka was home to nearly two thousand Poles, Ukrainians, Jews, and Russians. Much like the City of Lutsk, the town had survived military conflicts, fires, and health scourges which periodically wiped out many of its residents.

Doing the morning chores, Wiktor reflected upon his last two years and how he spent his carefree days. At times, he would walk to the village store on a cold and frosty winter's day, fur cap over his ears and a hooded cape around his neck while all the while pondering how he might spend the 20 kopecks his father gave him to buy something sweet, a *sukerka* as the Poles called it. At night, on his way home, he would recite passages from the works of Jan Potocki, a Polish nationalist who wrote about Polish movement against foreign occupation. He could recite many of Potocki's passages by heart, perhaps as a remedy against his fear of rustling sounds and shadows in the dark.

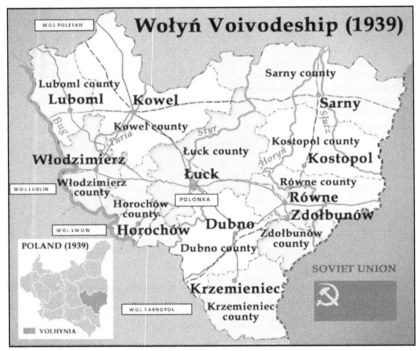

Map of Volhynia showing the location of the village of Polonka and the Voivodeship of Lublin, the destination for members of Brygada Salon.

During the summer months, he would spend his free afternoons in the meadow playing football or boating on the River Styr. He visualized himself sitting on his father's knee in the beautiful local Roman Catholic Church and recall how the family would get together for the Sunday meal of chicken and perogies. He remembered driving to the large marketplace in Lutsk with his parents where in the summertime women would sell hot corn-on-the-cob from huge tin tubs and where venders would sell wood, grain, fruit, poultry, fish, eggs, straw, fir branches, and willow twigs. At times like this, his heart was full of fond memories.

The youthful Wiktor Wozniak's neighbours were other Poles, Russians, Ukrainians, and Jews. To him, it seemed as though the majority of the population belonged to the middle class—small and not-so-small farmers and merchants. In the bustling city of Lutsk there were all kinds of shops and businesses well stocked with commodities, cereals, timber, fruit, foodstuffs, haberdasheries, dry goods, ironware, paint, and tar. There were manual workers, unskilled employees, and journeymen of various trades such as tailors, cobblers, joiners, carpenters, bricklayers, house painters, blacksmiths, furriers, and finishers. Still others were employed in small industries such as tanneries, grain mills, saw mills, and soap-boiling works.

In the transportation business, there were forwarding agents to distribute merchandise to businessmen who had arrived at the depot, and cabbies to drive passengers from the town to the railway station or from the railway depot into the city. There were draymen with their wooden carts and under-nourished horses making a scant living by delivering to a local resident a bag of grain, a casket of herring, a bag of salt, a package with merchandise, some planks, and maybe even a few dozen bricks.

"Wiktor," yelled his father, "stop your day dreaming. Get those cows milked. It's nearly seven o'clock. You'll miss your marshrutka to gymnasia and your history examination!"

"Yes, father. I was simply thinking about my history examination. I was daydreaming about the province of Volhynia and how it became a part of Poland after the war."

"Yes, of course, my son. There is no shortage of tensions between the Poles and Ukrainians in this region. There have been times when I wanted to kill a few of those stupid Ukrainians myself."

"That's a terrible thing to say, father. Maybe there were times when the local Ukrainians wanted to murder a few Poles."

"Of course, our neighbour is a Ukrainian. Maybe you have been spending too much time with their daughter. Maybe your thinking is becoming a bit fuzzy."

Wiktor was well used to this kind of teasing. It was not so much that his father forbade him to fall in love with any girl other than one of Polish heritage but rather the thought that it was normal for a teenager to fantasize about love and romance. The only thing that Wiktor could say to his father was that the tensions between the Ukrainians and Poles reflected their long history over the years.

"Besides," added Wiktor, *"we have friends in the Ukrainian, Russian, and Jewish communities. You have long said that we are all human beings and should learn to get along."*

"Well," concluded Filip, *"we may all be human beings but our people are a little more advanced, don't you think so, my son? Don't you believe that we are a bit more human than those others?"*

Filip Wozniak was well aware of the Polish-Ukrainian tensions which dated back several hundred years with territorial, religious, and social conflicts. While relations were not always harmonious, most Poles and Ukrainians interacted with each other on every civic, economic, and political level as far back as Filip could remember. There was one other mitigating factor that brought the two families closer together; Filip was ever mindful of the fact that the Konenko family, although ethnic Ukrainians, also came from the Zamosc region of Poland to the province of Volhynia in 1923, not directly as military colonists but from among those who had served in the military as civilians and were then seeking land ownership in Volhynia.

With the rise of nationalism in the 19th century, the ethnicity of citizens became an issue, and the conflicts erupted anew after the First World War. Both Poles and Ukrainians claimed the territories of Volhynia and Eastern Galicia during the interwar period, resulting in political conflicts and paramilitary actions by the *Organization of Ukrainian Nationalists (OUN)*. Collective punishment meted out by the ruling Poles to thousands of mostly innocent peasants exacerbated animosity between the Polish state and the Ukrainian population, a topic that Filip did not hesitate to discuss with his son.

"You know what, my son," Filip Wozniak would point out, *"for a very long time, this region was a part of the Polish-Lithuanian Commonwealth. You were not born in this province but in Zamosc. Our family came here after the war as Polish military colonists, the osadniki."*

"So, Father, what happened to the Polish-Lithuanian Commonwealth?"

"Well, in 1795, Poland was partitioned. Lutsk, and the surrounding area, was annexed by the Russian Empire. It was a century ago that Russia increased their efforts to remove Polish influence. Rumours are that the Soviets want to do so once again."

"Is this how," asked Wiktor, *"Russian became a dominant language in official circles even though the population, in private circles, chooses to speak Ukrainian, Polish, or Yiddish?"*

"Yes, my son. This region of Poland does have a very complex history."

During the First World War, the region was seized by Austria-Hungary, subsequently becoming an important military centre. In 1916, Russian forces re-captured the region only to lose it to German forces in 1917. In 1918, the Germans retreated and left the region to military forces loyal to Symon Petliura, leader of the Ukrainian People's Republic. During the Polish-Bolshevik war of 1919, Lutsk was once again taken over by Polish forces. Following the victory of Polish forces over the Red Army in 1920, the region gained twenty years of independence for Poland. Lutsk was designated by the newly-reborn nation of Poland as the capital of the Wołyń Voivodeship. Wiktor was less than one year of age when his father accepted the invitation from the Polish government and moved the family from Zamosc to the Voivodeship of Wołyń.

En route to school and the history examination, Wiktor recalled how his history teacher described the current political situation, *"When the Austro-Hungarian government collapsed following World War I, Poles and Ukrainians struggled for control over the City of Lwow. Although the city was populated mostly by Poles, it was surrounded by a Ukrainian majority in the villages and countryside."*

Wiktor was thankful that his father encouraged him to study the proud history of Poland. He suspected that the history examination would deal with the Polish-Lithuanian Commonwealth, the partitions of Poland, and the annexation of Galicia by the Austrian Empire. *No matter,* thought Wiktor, *I am prepared for any questions about the history of Poland, the Polish-Ukrainian War, or about Symon Petliura's attempt to expand Ukrainian claims westward.*

After a century of partitions, Polish statehood was established by the Treaty of Versailles in 1919, exactly five years after the assassination of Archduke Franz Ferdinand and the outbreak of World War I. However, the borders between Poland and Soviet Russia had not been clearly defined. As a result, the Polish-Soviet war of 1920 broke out, with the Soviets claiming both Ukraine and Belarus, which they viewed as a part of the Russian Empire.

It would not be until 1921 and the Treaty of Riga that Volhynia and Eastern Galicia would join the Second Polish Republic with the proviso that Poland would recognize the eastern part of Galicia's ethnographic condition and grant the Ukrainians autonomous status. At the same time, the Ukrainian Soviet Socialist Republic would become an integral part of the Union of Social Socialist Republics (*USSR*).

The promise to recognize the Ukrainians' autonomous status was never fulfilled by the Polish government. In the following years, the historical discourse between Polish and Ukrainian researchers has often been based on historical stereotypes stemming from ethnic conflicts during the First World War and the interwar period, making it difficult to draw an objective account of bilateral Polish-Ukrainian relations during World War II.

Before entering the examination room in the local gymnasia, Wiktor was immediately cheered when he spotted Tanja Konenko.

"Dzien dobry, Tanja. Good Morning. Do you have an examination today?"

"Cześć. Good day, Wiktor. Yes, I am here to write my mathematics examination. You look nervous. It's that history examination that has upset you isn't it?"

Upon hearing the warm words of encouragement coming from Tanja, Wiktor impulsively grasped her hand.

"Thank you, Tanja. Let me escort you to your examination room."

Their warm relationship was testimony to the fact that Volhynia was home to one of Eastern Europe's most ambitious policies of toleration. At least this was the expressed hope of the architects of those who awarded the province of Volhynia to Poland after World War I. This was why, at first, the Poles supported Ukrainian culture, religious autonomy, and Ukrainization of the Orthodox Church. In effect, this came about as a result of the leadership of Józef Piłsudski and his support and understanding of the politics between the two ethnic groups. However, all of this goodwill began to unravel after Piłsudski's death in 1935.

Civic unrest in the Galician countryside resulted in Polish police exacting a policy of collective responsibility on local Ukrainians in an effort to pacify the region. Ukrainian community centres and libraries were demolished, and property and produce confiscated. Protesters were beaten and Ukrainian parliamentarians were placed under house arrest preventing them from participating in elections. Their constituents were terrorized into voting for Polish candidates. The ongoing policies of the Polish state led to the deepening of ethnic cleavages in the area.

Little wonder that Tanja was worried about her blossoming relationship with Wiktor. At the same time, Tanja was aware that Wiktor's mother, Marta Wozniak, took great pride in the fact that her son had developed a close friendship with her.

To make matters worse, the Organization of Ukrainian Nationalists (*OUN*) stationed in Vienna began to conduct terrorist campaigns in

Poland, including the assassination of prominent Polish politicians. To counteract these activities, the Polish government in Volhynia initiated a campaign to force Orthodox believers to switch to Roman Catholicism. More than 190 Orthodox churches were destroyed and another 150 converted to Roman Catholic cathedrals. The remaining Orthodox churches were forced to use the Polish language in their sermons. In 1939, the last Orthodox Church in Lutsk was forced, by a decree of the Polish Government, to convert to a Roman Catholic cathedral.

The expressed mission of OUN was in stark contrast to the earlier position taken by the Ukrainian National Democratic Alliance (*UNDO*). Founded in 1925, UNDO, the largest *legitimate* Ukrainian political party, was opposed to the terrorism and violence of OUN and declared its loyalty to the Polish state. Unfortunately, after the Soviets annexed Eastern Poland, Dr. Dmytro Levitsky, UNDO's former leader, and many of his colleagues, was arrested, deported to Moscow, and never heard from again. UNDO, along with all other legal Ukrainian political parties, was forced by the Soviet authorities to disband. As a consequence, OUN, already well entrenched, was left as the sole functioning, independent, political organization in western Ukraine.

With an earlier influx of nearly twenty thousand Polish military settlers who came to Volhynia from the western regions of Poland, serious problems began to develop. This led to the Ukrainian peasants' refusal of bringing food into the towns. Ukrainian workers went on strike. In turn, the Polish government crushed the strike, killing 42 Ukrainian workers.

Violence on the part of the OUN resulted in harsh policies being implemented by the government of Poland. The outcome was predictable—a further deterioration of relations between the two ethnic groups. This led to a suppression of the Ukrainian language, culture, and religion. The antagonism continued to escalate. For these reasons, the escalation was quite obvious to Ukrainians. Fully 68 percent of the population was Ukrainian, while practically all government and administrative positions, including the police were assigned to Poles.

The Ukrainian population was outraged by the Polish government policies. A young Ukrainian nationalist was heard to say, *"We will decorate our pillars with you and our trees with your wives."*

Wiktor, an outstanding young Pole was about to find out just how these events would unfold. Despite his love for Tanja, there would be little peace for him or for anyone living in the Voivodeship of Volhynia for that matter.

8

Romance And Tragedy

Two young lovers tiptoe through a series of political landmines

"**T**anja," declared Wiktor Wozniak, picking her up at her home for the short walk to the community centre in Polonka, "*you are the most beautiful girl in the world.*"

"*Wiktor,*" responded Tanja, overcome with the significance of the moment, "*you are the most handsome man in all of Volhynia.*"

On April 23, 1939, Wiktor Wozniak and Tanja Konenko took part in a very popular Polish custom. Held annually for those students about to graduate from *Liceum*, the Polish high school, it was a time to relax and have some fun before writing the *matura* examinations. Considered as secondary school exit exams, their importance for entrance to any university could not be overstated. By tradition, Tanja wore red garters thought to bring good luck. Wiktor, in response, wore red underwear. The celebration was in anticipation of final examinations which would occur exactly 100 days from the date of their celebration of *studniowka*, a word which literally translates to *one hundred days ahead.*

Joined by parents, and friends, they were not alone at these celebrations. Their teachers, in providing the necessary chaperoning required of the party, seemed as anxious to celebrate the academic school year as did the students. The evening started with a dinner followed by the first dance, a polonaise in honour of Frederic Chopin, Poland's most famous composer. There was no shortage of toasts, solidified with a swig of wine, in honour of their teachers and parents. When the celebrations were over, it was time for Wiktor to walk Tanja back to her home.

"Tanja," stammered Wiktor as they arrived at the Konenko residence, *"I love you because you are my life. I don't want to lose you! Do you love me?"*

"Oh, Wiktor, your love is my sunshine. I love my life because it gives you to me. I love you. I know that these are troubled times but don't worry, you will never lose me."

"You and I, Tanja, it's as though we have been taught to kiss in heaven and sent down to earth together to see if we know what we were taught!"

Despite the expressions of love and the memories of a special evening, imagine what the celebrants might have felt had they been aware of a secret international pact. On April 23, 1939, one of the most dastardly events in history of the world took place. This would be the day upon which Germany's Foreign Minister, Joachim von Ribbentrop and the Soviet Union's Foreign Minister Vyacheslav Molotov would sign the infamous Molotov-Ribbentrop Pact.

Even as the dark clouds of international conflict began to gather at the end of the school year, Wiktor successfully completed his matura examinations. As a teenager, he had a goal in mind and that was to continue his education in a university, perhaps in the City of Lwow, and then seek a career in one of the professions. His plans for entry into a post-secondary institution, however, were about to take a sudden turn for the worse.

Wiktor was well aware of the opportunities in the food industry, an industry very important to the Oblast of Volhynia. With major branches in grist milling, sugar refining, liquor distilling, brewing, fruit and vegetable canning, meat packing, and milk processing, gave him a wide range of choices. He also knew that these industries were secondary to the lumber, woodworking, furniture, wood-chemical, and pulp and paper industries. There were other choices for a university graduate, including machine building, automobile development, metalworking, road-building, and farm machinery industries. The future looked bright.

Unfortunately, if Wiktor were to enrol in any of these programs, he would have to attend a university in Lwow. Other than the State Teachers Institute which was about to open its doors for post-secondary education in the fall of 1940, Lutsk did not have an accredited university. So, for Wiktor, there was no other choice. According to oblast administrators, instruction in the Teachers Institute would be provided by a staff of fifty professors working within the departments of physics, mathematics, and geography, and a separate department to deal with the historical development of the Ukrainian and Russian languages. Even at that, the functioning of the university would soon be interrupted by war.

Before the outbreak of the war, the future of post-secondary education was somewhat dampened by events which had taken place two years earlier. Up until that moment, the whole region was under the control of the national government in Warsaw. That was the way it had been since the end of World War I. Suddenly, in 1939, the Russian Red Army moved through the oblast and established Soviet control. Although there was no public disclosure why the Soviets occupied the region, rumours persisted that there was a secret agreement between Germany and Russia. The presence of Soviet soldiers in the region struck an ominous chord. All of a sudden the future did not look so bright for Wiktor Wozniak.

As the youthful Wiktor Wozniak considered his circumstances, the world was not unfolding in the manner he had hoped. His plans for a post-secondary education now dashed, he thought long and hard as to how he could best escape the wrath of the Soviets who were bent on deporting important Poles to Siberia or by simply eliminating them. But that was not the only problem he was facing. There was suddenly the matter of Ukrainians seeking retribution on any and all Poles living in the region.

When Ukrainians saw that the Soviet Army was coming in the direction of Lutsk, many began to take revenge on the Poles. Ukrainians stood by the roadside waiting for the arrival of the Soviets. Polish women and children cried and prayed, begging God to save them. Some Ukrainian families went so far as to attack their Polish neighbours, stealing their cows, horses, pigs, and chickens. Other Polish families fared much worse. The Soviets took away their hay and slaughtered their pigs, cows, and horses for food. Whatever the Soviets could not devour, they took to the railway station and shipped to Russia.

The Soviet Army invaded the City of Lutsk, buying up everything they could from merchants, all the while trying to convince the local population that they were on the side of the Poles. The Soviet Army depleted the stores to the extent that the local population had to line up for hours just to try to buy a loaf of bread.

Early on one Sunday morning, several Ukrainian families on their way to church in Polonka witnessed an NKVD squad knocking on the door of a Polish family, waking them at gunpoint and then interviewing them in their front yard. The family was then ordered to pack up while an official wrote down the name of each member, what they were taking with them, and what they were leaving behind. Minutes later a horse-drawn cart pulled up and took the family to the railway station. Everyone knew what their fate would be.

Marta Wozniak was particularly alarmed at learning of these events, expressing her concern to her husband, Filip.

"Those murdering Soviet dogs cannot be trusted," concluded Marta. *"First, it was our neighbour being shipped off to Siberia; are we next?"*

"Shush, Marta. Be careful what you say. The walls have ears. I don't like Siberia."

"Since the Soviets entered our land, we now feel the lack of everything," continued an undeterred Marta, *"the Soviets buy everything for roubles. The grocery stores are now empty. To buy bread you have to get up at night for the line."*

"Yes, yes, damn those thieving Russian bastards. Synowie suk. Sugar and fat are very hard to get and you pay enormous amounts. Instead of fat, we should be selling rat poison to the Moskali. That would take care of all of them!"

Between 1939 and 1941 the Soviets, without warning, arrested and deported to Siberia a number of officials and educators from the Lutsk region. At first, they arrested all the higher administrators, the police, and village and hamlet heads. In February, they deported military colonists and foresters and their households to the depths of Russia. Before deporting them, the Soviets took their horses, cows, and grain, abolished Polish offices, and put Bolsheviks and Jews in their place. The people were depressed and any minute they expected worse to come. Many Poles disappeared as if into thin air. Word filtered back to the region that many of those arrested perished in the Katyn Forest massacre. All of this spelled nothing but trouble for the Konenko and Wozniak families; trouble because they had been identified as military colonists.

The Katyn Forest massacre was prompted by a proposal from NKVD Chief, Beria, who wanted to execute all captive members of the Polish Officer Corps. Approved by Josef Stalin in 1940, the Soviet political police force had put into place a plan to eliminate all those Poles who had participated in politics, not to mention politically active clergy and former employees of the judicial system. Suddenly, the prisons were filled to brimming with the Polish intellectual elite. Carried out by the NKVD in April and May of 1940, the number of victims in the Katyn Forest massacre was estimated to be 22 thousand.

Even while Wiktor Wozniak was actively examining all of his options for a university education, he could not help but hear about these terrible rumours. There were constant rumours about the Red Army moving into the region. Under the escort of Soviet soldiers, machine guns on wheels moved along the roads. Heavy tanks with their guns directed towards the local people rumbled down the streets. From time to time a shot could be heard, likely a Polish officer who couldn't stand those sights and didn't want to submit to captivity. All public signs were changed to Russian and the civilian population was assigned Soviet officers as tenants. Shortages of bread, sugar, soap, meat, and other products were beginning to be felt.

With the arrival of the Red Army, local Poles had to stand in line to buy foodstuffs, many times as early as two in the morning. Food was dispensed in grams, and shortages of wood and coal forced the local people to take trips to the nearby grove for fuel, a trip from which many never returned. In schools, Russian and Ukrainian languages were introduced along with Russian history. Not only were religion and Latin abolished but the Soviets started to persecute religious institutions by imposing enormous taxes on churches and church property.

The NKVD conducted numerous arrests and deportations to faraway Siberia. More and more families began to experience the early morning rap on their door. Two Soviet officers with drawn bayonets would conduct a search of the house to make sure that no weapons were evident while a third officer stood at the door to make sure that no one escaped.

In the province of Volhynia, Soviet agents had a most devious plan. The Soviets wanted to provoke conflict between Poles and Ukrainians in order to bring about revolution and justify the extension of the Ukrainian Soviet Socialist Republic into Volhynia. By contrast, in the province of Lublin, Poland, the Nazis wanted to expand their living space needed for growth and survival by utilizing pre-existing tensions to let the colonized kill themselves off. In the end, the attrition of war wore down both sides to such an extent that ethnic cleansing could not be prevented. That left the Poles and Ukrainians to rely on their respective underground military organizations as the only source of authority.

Wiktor, determined to enrol in the University of Lwow, received more bad news. Once the Soviet Union took control of Lwow in 1939, the university took on a new name. In October of 1940, it became the Ivan Franko National University. Now under Soviet control, a growing number of Polish professors, assistant professors, associate professors, and administrative assistants were fired. This was accompanied by the liquidation of all departments having any connection whatsoever with free-market economics, capitalism, or the West. In addition, all faculty members who dealt with Polish geography, literature, or history were removed.

By 1940, the university brought in a new faculty specializing in Marxism, Leninism, political economics, Ukrainian and Soviet literature, history, and geography. With the liquidation of the Department of Theology, the structure of the university and the curriculum were adjusted to the Soviet educational system.

With a heavy heart, Wiktor accepted reality and enrolled in the Lutsk State Teachers Institute with the hope of specializing in the sciences and, upon graduation, launching a career as a secondary school teacher.

As fortune would have it, September, 1940, was also the month that Tanja Konenko was about to register at the Lutsk State Teachers Institute. During its first year of operation the institute enrolled 135 students under the tutorship of fifty professors. The politics of the day seemed not to deter 17-year-old Tanja. To her pleasant surprise, Wiktor rushed out of nowhere to give her an enthusiastic hug.

"Tanja, my little sweetheart, I'm so glad to see you. Are you enrolling in the pedagogical program?"

"Yes, I hope to get accepted by the institute. I'm glad to see you, Wiktor. Are you not worried about being seen in public? About being conscripted into the Red Army?"

"I'm more worried about my education. I want to prepare for the future. I feel in my heart that it will be a future with you!"

"On, Wiktor, if I were to live a thousand years, I would belong to you for all of them. If we were to live a thousand lives, I would want to make you mine in each one."

Despite the ethnic tensions and religious differences, Wiktor and Tanja continued to develop a close and loving relationship. Not surprisingly, their relationship began to move away from one of two young people being from the same village to one of mutual respect. Wiktor looked upon himself as providing Tanja with the necessary support and protection during troubled times. The fact that Tanja, a most attractive Ukrainian teenager who attended the Greek Catholic Church while Wiktor, as a Pole, attended the Roman Catholic Church, seemed to make little difference.

*1941: Tanja Konenko in a traditional Ukrainian dress
and Wiktor Wozniak in a Polish costume.*

It was on Saturday, September 21, 1940, that Wiktor left the State Teachers Institute by bus for the family home in Polonka. When he arrived at the family home, he found his mother, Marta, delirious and in tears.

"Good Lord, what is the matter, Mother? Why are you crying?"

"It's those damn Russians again. They are stupid, Godless NKVD synowie suk, sons of bitches. They are no more than a bunch of bloodthirsty criminals. Kurwa."

"What happened?"

"They arrested your Father and took him away. They said he was being deported to Siberia because he exhibited capitalistic tendencies."

"They arrested Father and took him away because we are wealthy? What about my little brother Donek? Is he at home?"

"No, Donek is not at home. My poor Donek is gone, too. God help us all!"

Wiktor was speechless. He didn't know what to say or how to console his mother. All he could do was sit next to his mother, embracing her while tears flowed down his cheeks. Earlier in the week he had heard that the Soviet NKVD started to eliminate the predominantly Polish middle and upper classes. He never suspected for a moment that his family fit the criteria of belonging to the middle class. Why, then, was his father deported? Had he expressed any anti-Bolshevik sentiment? Did the NKVD fear that his father would turn on the Soviets? What would now become of his younger sisters, Monika and Agata? What would become of his brother Donek? Wiktor had so many questions to which there appeared to be no answers.

It took Marta Wozniak the longest time to calm down. Sitting down with her three children, all she could do was think about what happened to her family and what was happening to so many of her Polish neighbours.

"You know, my dear children, maybe we are the lucky ones. There are Polish families in our midst where every member of the family is being deported to Siberia."

Wiktor, deep in thought, said nothing. Neither did his two younger sisters, Monika and Agata. The gravity of the situation was hard to bear.

"Mother," was Wiktor's first question, *"what about Ukrainian families? Are they being deported? Have you heard anything about the Konenko family?"*

"No, I have heard nothing about them. But why should they be deported? Are they not on the side of those murdering criminal communists? Are they not opposed to the Poles living in Volhynia? They are probably singing the praises of God that it is the Poles being deported."

Thinking about his friendship with Tanja, Wiktor elected not to respond to the questions raised by his mother. Worried, he immediately went to the Konenko residence. When he was tearfully invited to come in by Pani Konenko, he immediately sensed that something was dreadfully wrong.

"Why are you crying, Pani Konenko? What happened?"

"What happened, Wiktor? What happened," declared a hysterical Pani Konenko, *"the world has come to an end. Jan is gone. So is Janko."*

"Are you saying, Pani Konenko, that the Moskali arrested your husband and your son? Are you serious?"

"Yes, they are gone. Those communist bastards said that Jan spoke out about those communist murdering criminals, syny sukni. That, they said, was a crime against their country."

"Where is Tanja? Is she safe?"

"Yes, she will be fine. She is hiding out for a couple of days. I don't know where. She would not tell me for fear that the Moskali would find out."

Shocked beyond belief, Wiktor could do little else but return home. His meeting with Tanja would have to wait.

As events would soon unfold, the attacks on Poles living in the Oblast of Volhynia did not come solely from Ukrainian residents. The Soviets looked upon the Poles as enemies of the state. At the same time, several other important events took place. The Lutsk State Teachers Institute shut its doors to student enrolments, thereby leaving Tanja and Wiktor in a lurch. Of course, Filip and Donek Wozniak were nowhere to be found after their arrest. Neither were Jan and Janko Konenko. Marta Wozniak could do little else but hope and pray that she would hear from them once they arrived in Siberia. For whatever reason, it was now obvious that the NKVD had no interest in deporting Marta or hunting down Monika and Agata who were not at home at the time of the arrests. For the strangest of reasons, the NKVD seemed to have no interest in the female members of the family. No one could explain why only two members of the Wozniak and Konenko families were deported while other families were not so lucky.

Events continued to unfold quickly. Those Poles deported from Volhynia to Siberia were soon replaced by Ukrainians and Jews. However, that is not to say that everything went well for all Ukrainians living in Volhynia. The Soviet Union put a damper on the Ukrainian independence movement by abolishing all local Ukrainian political parties. As a result of these Soviet repressions, nearly thirty thousand Ukrainians escaped to the German-occupied areas of the previous Poland. Many of those left behind were deported or eliminated, thereby leaving the Organization of Ukrainian Nationalists to operate underground as the only party with a significant organizational presence.

In the City of Lutsk, the Soviets took houses and various businesses away from the citizens for the benefit of the state. Militiamen visited homes and forced occupants to attend political gatherings. Those Poles who didn't go to the meetings could expect to be arrested. These meetings were preparations for elections. Before the voting itself, the Soviets made lists of citizens who were entitled to vote in a rigged election. A militiaman would lead the people into the hall, give them a voting card and tell them to place a check mark next to the name of a candidate listed on the card, and to then throw the card into a large urn. You couldn't do anything else because there were guards all around and militiamen with bayonets at the ready. Every person feared arrest and deportation to Siberia. The importance of these rigged elections could not be overestimated. It was Stalin's way of approving the Soviet takeover of all of Eastern Poland.

The political situation for the Konenko and Wozniak families would turn from bad to worse. No sooner had the Soviets eliminated one threat than the families had another one on their hands. After only one year of Soviet military occupation of Volhynia, the Nazis shocked Stalin by declaring war on the Soviet Union. On June 22, 1941, Operation Barbarossa, Nazi Germany's code for the invasion of the Soviet Union, began its assault with four million soldiers along a 2,900-kilometer front. Within weeks, Western Ukraine was captured by the Nazis. Two weeks later, the Red Army retreated, leaving the area under the control of the Nazis. In short order, the whole of the Lutsk region lay in ruins.

Believing that the Nazis would eventually help Ukraine gain its independence, several OUN units carried out acts of sabotage. Prior to their retreat, Soviet authorities were unwilling to evacuate prisoners. They chose to kill all inmates, whether or not they had committed a major or minor crime and whether or not they were being held for political reasons. This resulted in the death of nearly 40,000 individuals in Western Ukraine. To further complicate the political landscape, the Germans, with the support of Ukrainian nationalists, rounded up and executed Poles, Jews, and those deemed to be communist sympathizers or Soviet activists.

After the Nazis occupied Poland, Polish nationalists in the province of Lublin began a campaign of terror against Ukrainians, torching their villages and murdering the inhabitants. At the same time, the Germans renamed this region as *Generalgouvernement Polen* and began to forcibly deport the inhabitants of many Polish and Ukrainian villages in Zamosc and Tomaszow-Lubelski to labour camps with the aim of resettling the region with Germans. It was their plan to exterminate most of the Poles and reduce the remaining population to the level of serfs. This led to an upsurge in the Polish underground activity and further German reprisals. It was also a time when Soviet partisans appeared in the Lublin Voivodeship for the first time.

After occupying the Oblast of Volhynia and renaming the region as *Reichskommissariat Ukraine*, the Germans closed the Polish higher education program and placed bans on the teaching of subjects such as history, geography, and Polish literature in lower level institutions. As a result, underground education became a common practice. At first, covert teaching only took place at the primary school level. Since the violation of prohibitions on higher education carried very serious legal consequences, no one attempted to conduct university-level courses, even on a secret basis.

Despite numerous obstacles, the underground Commission for Public Enlightenment was founded in Warsaw as an initiative of the Service for the Victory of Poland. Some teaching organizations took up the task of providing underground education and began functioning as early as October, 1939. By the end of 1940, this initiative oversaw a wide range of smaller organizations and the administration of educational and cultural projects in occupied territories. This new development gave some hope to young people, including Wiktor Wozniak.

Unable to attend a recognized public post-secondary institution, Wiktor, along with a group of other students, elected to continue their post-secondary programs in church buildings and in the home of Professor Oleg Osadnik.

During this period in history, there were a number of individual executions and other acts of persecution against the intellectual elite. Though the Nazis made every effort to conceal the atrocities, word spread fast throughout the academic community abroad, shaking public opinion regarding the nature of the occupation. In 1942, the Germans allowed some post-secondary schools to function; however, none was located in Lutsk.

While all of this was happening, Wiktor Wozniak discovered that the Nazis were recruiting workers to go to Germany. Not only did he have to avoid service in the German military but now he was forced to make certain that he was not rounded up by the Nazis for slave labour in Germany.

In this regard, an important announcement was posted in conspicuous places, *"On January 28, the first special train will leave for Germany with hot meals in Kyiv and Przemysl."*

The announcement proved to be truthful when the first train full of willing and unwilling Ostarbeiters departed for Germany on January 22, 1942. The advertising campaign continued and on March 3, 1942, when a Kyiv newspaper ad contained an important invitation, *"Germany calls you! Go to beautiful Germany! One hundred thousand Ukrainians are already working in free Germany. What about you?"*

Word got back from Germany, however, of the terrible working conditions encountered by Ukrainians. As a result, the campaign failed to attract a sufficient number of volunteers. This led the Gestapo to initiate a policy of forced recruitment. Wiktor, worried by these developments, kept a low profile even as he attended secretive underground classes.

In the spring of 1942, Wiktor got the surprise of his young life. As he was entering Professor Osadnik's evening science class being held in the Polish church, Tanja Konenko was just leaving Osadnik's history class which was scheduled one hour earlier.

"Good evening, Tanja! I am so glad to see you! I didn't know that you were attending Professor Osadnik's evening classes."

"Oh, Wiktor, I am glad to see you! Yes, I knew that you were attending Professor Osadnik's classes. My mother told me that you would be here."

No sooner had Wiktor raised the question about Tanja's attendance than all the students from the two classes were confronted by a Gestapo brigade. Speaking in Polish, the Commander of the brigade informed the students that the Nazis were recruiting workers for Germany. Wiktor could see that the brigade was well armed and that a truck was stationed nearby. Just as the students were being rounded up in the twilight of a late afternoon, Wiktor grabbed Tanja's arm and whispered, *"Quick, Tanja, let's make a dash for safety through the cemetery next to the church."*

As Wiktor and Tanja scurried into the graveyard, the Gestapo brigade leader fired a warning shot into the air, yelling, *"Zatrzymać! Stopp oder ich werde schießen. Stop or I will shoot!"*

But for Wiktor and Tanja, there was no turning back. They knew full well what awaited them if they stopped. They did not stop running until they reached the outskirts of Lutsk. Since Tanja and Wiktor arrived for their evening classes by different means, they spent several hours making sure that the families who transported them from Polonka to Lutsk were safe. More bad luck followed. Earlier, Wiktor had arrived in Lutsk with three other students from Polonka. Unfortunately, Wiktor's two friends did not escape the claws of the Gestapo. Although they were able to find the driver of the Lada who brought them to Lutsk, there was no sign of the two boys. A similar fate awaited Tanja's friend, who also went missing.

At daybreak the next morning, Tanja, Wiktor, and the two Lada operators quietly returned to the church where the evening classes had been conducted the previous evening. Everything was quiet and no one was in sight. When they found Professor Osadnik, he tearfully informed them that the Nazis had rounded up twelve of his students. It was virtually certain that all were now on their way to work in Germany as Ostarbeiters.

Just like that, the educational program for Wiktor Wozniak and Tanja Konenko came to a screeching halt. They would not return to

Professor Osadnik's evening classes. In fact, Professor Osadnik, with a heavy heart, terminated his program. As events unfolded, he would not be able to resuscitate the program, even after all of the hostilities ended.

The situation, however, was quite different in other Ukrainian cities, including Lwow. That year, nearly two thousand Ukrainian students were awarded degrees. Many of the graduates had started their post-secondary education after the start of the war and most were enrolled in the humanities and social sciences, followed by mathematics, and the natural sciences. Yet, despite what happened to Professor Osadnik's evening class, the void in Lutsk was soon filled by other enterprising teachers.

Safely back in the village of Polonka, Wiktor had some important questions for Tanja, *"I didn't know that you wanted to be a teacher. Is that why you started to attend Osadnik's evening classes?"*

"Yes, Viet, I have always wanted to be an elementary school teacher."

"Oh, Tanja, I love it when you call me Viet!"

"Yes, it is my shortened version for Wiktor. It is my little secret. You are the vietyr, the wind in my sails."

"Didn't you know that it would be dangerous to attend any kind of a class during these troubled times?"

"Yes, I knew that there would be many risks. But I also knew that you would be in this class. I knew that you would help me in case of trouble."

"You knew that I would be here? My mother told your mother and your mother told you?"

Squeezing his hand gently, Wiktor could see that she did not have to answer his question. It suddenly dawned on him that Tanja really cared for him in a special way. *Tanja was truly head over heels in love with him.*

In 1939, the Germans had issued a decree which introduced a mandatory work system for all residents aged 18 to 60 in the region of Western Poland controlled by the Nazis. Not able to recruit a sufficient number of labourers by December, the Nazis lowered the age of recruitment from 18 to 14 years of age. By 1942, following the Nazi attack on the Soviet Union, the Volhynian region was under the control of the Germans. No young person was safe from the Gestapo and the likelihood of labour in Germany. Wiktor Wozniak continued to keep a low profile for fear of conscription into the German Wehrmacht or work in Germany as a slave.

More bad luck, however, continued to follow the Wozniak family. Monika Wozniak, alone at home with her mother and younger sister Agata, thought that they were relatively safe and no harm would come to the family. She was wrong, very wrong. Without warning, a Gestapo squad burst into their home. Fourteen-year-old Monika was rounded up by the Gestapo and given two choices, instant death or acquiescence to the wishes of the Nazis for work in Germany as a Zivilarbeiter. Despite the objections and screams from her mother and younger sister, Monika was forcefully removed from her home. She was immediately sent on her way to East Germany to provide domestic help to Adolf Hitler's regime.

A Russian-language Nazi poster reading, "I live with a German family and feel just fine. Come to Germany to help with household chores."

In the meantime, the Ukrainian Insurgent Army believed that it had to move fast while the Germans still controlled the area. They wanted to pre-empt future Polish efforts at re-establishing Poland's prewar borders. The OUN leadership decided that an ethnic cleansing of Poles living in the area was required, through terror and murder, if necessary. In addition to the attacks on Polish citizens by the OUN, Soviet partisans began to operate in the region by raiding local settlements. In retaliation, the Germans began to pacify entire villages for the real or alleged support of Soviet partisans.

In response to the increase in German terror, Ukrainian self-defense groups began to form. The situation also gave rise to the extremist Bandera faction of OUN-B whose ideology stressed a pure national state and language, the glorification of violence and armed struggle, as well as totalitarianism in which the nation would be ruled by one person and one political party. The first OUN-B military groups in 1942 adopted a goal of subduing the other independent groups and in the spring of 1943, the OUN-B partisans started to call themselves the Ukrainian Insurgent Army (UPA).

It was also a year when approximately five thousand Ukrainian occupational police defected with their weapons and joined the UPA. With the addition of these well-trained police, OUN-B forces destroyed or absorbed other Ukrainian groups in Volhynia. The OUN-B then undertook to liquidate *foreign elements* with posters and leaflets urging Ukrainians to murder Poles. Once its dominance over Nazi forces was secured in the Volhynian countryside, UPA began large-scale operations against the Polish population.

Much of this, however, suddenly changed for the Volhynian Poles in 1943 when the Soviet Union gained control of the German Army. This made it possible for Ukrainians to seek revenge on the Poles. Some called it a form of ethnic cleansing through terror and murder. Polish members of the local administration who were murdered were soon replaced by Ukrainians and Jews.

Perhaps it was the decisive Soviet tank battle victory at Kursk in 1943 which acted as a stimulus for Ukrainians to escalate their attacks on Poles. Listening to the rumours about these attacks, Marta Wozniak became convinced that the OUN was responsible for the most egregious of attacks, many of them bordering on ethnic cleansing. She took pains to impress upon Wiktor of the impending dangers.

"Son" cautioned Wiktor's mother, *"our parish priest warned us about the Commander of the Ukrainian Army. The priest said that the army did not hesitate to murder Poles."*

"Yes, mother, I am being very careful to stay away from the Nazis and the Ukrainian nationalists."

"The Ukrainian Insurgent Army wants to liquidate all Poles in Volhynia. You can see that the Nazis are now in full retreat. This is why the Ukrainians are free to roam from village to village, killing our boys. They are burning Polish villages."

No one in the Oblast of Volhynia made any attempt to hide the truth. Perhaps that, in the first place, was the intent of the Ukrainian nationalists. By mid-summer of 1943, hundreds of Polish villages were burned to the ground and thousands of ethnic Poles were deported or killed. Rumour had it that Roman Catholic priests were axed or crucified and churches were burned with parishioners trapped inside. Isolated farms were attacked by gangs of Ukrainians carrying pitchforks and kitchen knives.

The Soviet and Nazi invasions of prewar Eastern Poland, the UPA massacres, and postwar Soviet expulsions of Poles all contributed to the virtual elimination of a Polish presence in Volhynia. Those Poles who remained behind either left Volhynia or planned to leave the oblast, mostly for the neighbouring province of Lublin. As a result of ethnic conflicts from 1942-1945, nearly 70,000 Poles lost their lives in the Oblast of Volhynia.

From 1939 to 1943, the Polish population in Volhynia dropped to just eight percent. Their numbers decreased to the extent that it was only the German Army that could protect them from further annihilation. In the winter of 1943, the UPA launched a series of assaults on the Poles, killing hundreds of unarmed men, women, and children. The only Poles to survive were those who were hidden by sympathetic Ukrainian families.

These attacks worried Wiktor Wozniak to the extent that he decided to discuss the matter with his mother.

"Mother," observed Wiktor, *"I know that the Ukrainians in Polonka are decent and honourable people, but out in the countryside, every day there are rumours about Ukrainians attacking towns and villages. Dozens of villages have been burned to the ground."*

"Yes, my son, the war has been going on for nearly four years and this July has been the worst. There are rumours about massacres, ethnic cleansings, deportations of our people to Siberia, and now these frightening notices."

"Notices, mother? What kind of notices?"

"Notices have been placed in our village by the Ukrainian Army. These notices warn all Poles to leave Volhynia in 48 hours."

"Where do they want the Poles to go?"

"The Ukrainians want all Poles to leave Volhynia within 48 hours and go beyond the Bug or the San River. They want all Poles to go west to Poland."

"And if they don't leave? What will happen?"

"The Ukrainian nationalists will kill all of us. Be careful, my son."

Poles who did not abide by the directive were attacked, not only by the UPA forces but also by local Ukrainian peasants who took part in the massacres by forming their own self-defence units. Despite the killings, many Ukrainians risked and many lost their lives trying to shelter or warn the Poles.

Tanja, fearing that the Wozniak family was now in grave danger of elimination by militant Ukrainian forces, decided to help keep Wiktor out of harm's way. To accomplish this, she approached her uncle, Andriy Konenko, who lived in a sparsely-populated region of the oblast. After introducing Wiktor to her uncle, Tanja had a request.

"Uncle Andriy," Tanja pleaded, *"these are troubled times in Volhynia. The Ukrainians are trying to kill all the Poles in our region. I need your help."*

"Yes, my dear niece. I already know what you are about to ask of me."

"Please, Uncle, can you harbour Wiktor until the troubles are over?"

To Tanja's surprise, her uncle was more than willing to harbour Wiktor until the political situation in Volhynia normalized. Not only that, but Andriy Konenko thought that he might be able to put Wiktor to work on his modest farming operation. After all, the Germans would need all of the garden and grain supplies they could muster to feed their troops. Tearfully, Tanja and Wiktor had a few brief moments together before Tanja left for Polonka.

Somehow, the UPA must have found out about Tanja's role in finding safe haven for Wiktor. When she arrived at her home, she found a brigade of German soldiers watching as her family's home was fully engulfed in flames. Hysterical and in tears, Tanja questioned the German soldiers as to what happened. Unable to communicate adequately in German, she had to turn to an elderly neighbour who, haltingly and in tears, relayed the bad news.

"It's that damn Ukrainian Insurgent Army. One of their bandits came looking for you. They said that you were harbouring the Wozniak family," explained the neighbour.

"What did they want to know?" enquired Tanja.

"They wanted to kill any Ukrainian harbouring a Pole. They wanted to kill you."

Apparently as retribution and while Tanja was at her uncle's farm, a brigade of the UPA soldiers attacked the Konenko family home in Polonka, murdering Tanja's mother and her younger sister Juli. Having done their murderous deed, they torched the Konenko home and barn before disappearing into the forest.

The same fate met the Wozniak family. Marta Wozniak and her only remaining daughter, Agata, were murdered by a UPA brigade and their home set ablaze.

Even while the German Army was retreating in advance of the Red Army, a Gestapo brigade sought more recruits for work in Germany.

Learning of the tragedy unfolding before them, they saw an opportunity to gain more recruits for their Ostarbeiter Plan. After some discussion, the Gestapo brigade arrested the distraught Tanja and escorted her to the local command centre. Tanja was about to join Monika Wozniak in Germany as a Zivilarbeiter.

The massacres prompted Poles to organize their own self-defence units. This decision helped to decrease the number of Poles being killed in the province of Volhynia. As a result, the killing of Poles moved to Eastern Galicia where the majority of the population was Ukrainian but where the Polish presence was strong. Unlike Volhynia, Poles in this region were given the option of fleeing or being killed. Here, the UPA Commander reminded Ukrainians, *"Once more I remind you, first call upon Poles to abandon their land and only later liquidate them, not the other way around."*

With the Soviet successes against the Germans, a UPA Commander stated, *"In view of the success of the Soviet forces, it is necessary to speed up the liquidation of the Poles. They must be totally wiped out and their villages burned to the ground. Remember, only the Polish population must be destroyed."*

While the Nazis actively encouraged the conflict, for most of the time they attempted to avoid direct involvement. However, there were reports of Nazis supplying weapons to both Ukrainians and Poles. Special Nazi units were formed from collaborationist Ukrainians and later from Polish auxiliary police to be deployed in pacification actions.

Unfortunately, those Ukrainians who believed that the UPA had their best interests at heart were wrong. Compounded by casualties inflicted by Soviet partisans and German policemen, Ukrainians who did not embrace the UPA's form of nationalism were frequently murdered along with the Poles.

As the autumn days of 1943 began to recede and the days of a new year were about to descend upon the Oblast of Volhynia, the terrifying impact of armed conflict and ethnic tensions began to unfold.

Most anti-Polish actions came to a stop and terror was used only against those who co-operated with the NKVD. However, for Wiktor Wozniak the long and treacherous road into the future was only beginning. There would be no shortage of missteps and challenges.

9

The Destruction Of
Polish Villages

"We must cleanse this land of every living Pole before war's end..."

Wiktor Wozniak was thankful just to be alive. He realized that without the help of Tanja and her uncle his situation might have ended very differently. The very thought of service in the Red Army or forced labour in Germany or Siberia sent shivers through his body. He recalled how others expressed their fear of being arrested by the NKVD and the shock of being loaded onto cattle cars for transport to Russia's cold and barren wasteland, the tundra as they called it. It was not only the secluded location of the Konenko farm that provided some protection but also the fact that Konenko had a most reliable guard dog.

"Just look at my dog, Wiktor, you say that Boris looks docile to you? Docile, my ass," opined Andriy Konenko, *"he is worth two sentries! Boris can sense danger and loves to strike fear in the heart of any intruder."*

Looking at the German shepherd, Wiktor had to agree that Pan Konenko did not need a sentry post or an armed guard for his farm. Boris was not your ordinary farm dog but a huge and ferocious-looking German shepherd. Just one look at the size of the dog's teeth coupled with his deep growl was sufficient proof that an intruder would not want to get into any kind of confrontation with the dog.

"Are you certain, Pan Konenko, that Boris has a natural instinct to protect your home and family?"

"Boris has a sense of smell far superior to yours. Not only that, but he hears sounds that you would never hear."

"What about people, would he attack me?"

"Boris never forgets a person he has met. When he picks up the scent of a stranger, he gives me a low growl. He will attack any unwelcome guest if I give him my secret wistle. Boris is loyal, courageous, and loves to attack and bite the shit out of any suspicious-looking stranger. He provides the stranger with an unforgettable experience of terror."

"I noticed that Boris is not securely tied down."

"He doesn't have to be tied down. I trained Boris to always stay within the perimeter of my front yard."

Assigned to a secret hiding place in a vegetable root cellar adjacent to the barn, Wiktor knew that he would be safe. After all, who would even think that a farmer would have a root cellar with a hidden entry to it from inside a barn? Wiktor had to agree that entry into the root cellar through a camoflaged door not readily discernible to the naked eye was pure genius.

"Thank you, Pan Konenko. Not much light in the root cellar but then I won't have to spend all of my time in hiding, will I?"

"Don't get too comfortable," cautioned Konenko, *"the Nazis and Soviets have binoculars and are able to spot their prey from long distances. Stay out of sight, especially during daylight hours. Stay put until any danger passes. Learn to listen to Boris. If he barks, be very careful."*

In this way, Wiktor escaped detection by both the Gestapo and the UPA. On three different occasions, an armed brigade appeared at Konenko's farm in search of Poles. In each case, Boris announced their arrival by barking long before they entered the front yard. On one occasion Konenko had to convince the UPA that all members of his family were of Ukrainian heritage. In another case, a Gestapo squad entered his property looking to recruit additional foreign workers. Konenko had great difficulty controlling Boris during these intrusions.

As a result of such ever-present dangers emanating from various sources, Wiktor could do little to assist Konenko with his farming operation. When he did, he liked to dress as an old woman, thinking that this might offer him some protection, at least from the UPA. Despite the dangers, Wiktor did his best to help Konenko take in the harvest.

"Over our long history," explained Konenko over a late evening meal of potato pancakes, *"Poland and Ukraine have long been subject to conflict and changes of power."*

"This is why, Pan Konenko," acknowledged Wiktor, *"I am so thankful that you and your niece are willing to help me. The Poles are under attack by Ukrainians, Germans, and Russians. Only God knows where all of this will end."*

"I shall protect you from harm. I do this for you because I know that Tanja truly loves you. I have nothing against the Poles. Our fight is with those Nazi krauts and the Soviet suka dogs, not with our Ukrainian neighbours."

"Yes, Pan Konenko, these are difficult times for all Poles. First, it was the Soviet invasion and the annexation of this region. Now it is those damned Nazis who are occupying our land."

"I must tell you this Wiktor, it is not the Nazis but the Ukrainian Nationalists who worry me the most. Militant and ruthless, they are the ones who are distrustful of Polish territorial ambitions and want to create an independent Ukrainian nation."

"Yes, Pan Konenko, I understand why Ukrainian nationalists want their own homeland. In another time and in another place, wouldn't you support Ukrainian nationalists and their ambitions? Wouldn't you agree that Ukrainians want to exact retribution for the Polonization of this region which occurred after World War I?"

"Of course I am in support of the ambitions of Ukrainian nationalists but I am not in favour of armed conflict between anyone. I believe that our differences can be settled diplomatically in Kyiv and Warsaw."

As events unfolded, it mattered little how Wiktor and Pan Konenko felt about the conflict unfolding before them. As early as 1939, citizens of Volhynia were fully aware of the Soviet Union's policy of the cleansing of borders through the forced resettlement of Polish people from the 22-kilometer border zone of Soviet Ukraine because they were suspected of being disloyal to the Soviet Union. At the same time, neither Wiktor Wozniak nor Andriy Konenko was fully aware of the secret protocol between Hitler and Stalin. Konenko, however, was painfully aware that the Soviet NKVD had already started to eliminate the predominantly Polish middle and upper classes, including social activists and military leaders.

Even more alarming was the rumour that Stalin identified Polish military colonists as the first group to be earmarked for deportation to the Gulag. How the Soviets managed to get their hands on the list of soldiers who served in a Polish Legion Brigade during World War I was a mystery in itself. Unfortunately for the Konenko and Wozniak families, they had been identified by the NKVD as military colonists. Now living in Volhynia placed them on Stalin's hit list, eligible for arrest and deportation to a labour camp in Siberia.

Not only did the Soviets begin the deportation of Poles to Siberia but they also deported thousands of Polish political prisoners of war to the eastern region of Ukraine, a location where, in April and May of 1940, most were executed by the NKVD operatives. These deportations and murders deprived the Poles of their community leaders. In addition, tens of thousands of Poles fled from the Soviet-occupied zone to areas controlled by the Germans, concluding that their chances of survival were far greater in a region under Nazi control as opposed to a region controlled by Stalin.

When the extremist arm OUN realized that the Soviet Union had eliminated many of the Polish elite in Volhynia, they felt confident that they could attack Poles with some degree of immunity. In the opinion of OUN, the situation made it much easier for them to operate underground as the only political party with a significant organizational presence among Volhynian Ukrainians. With this in mind, the OUN immediately put into place a purposeful policy of removing, by violence and terror-inspiring means, all Poles living in Volhynia.

"What about all of these violent attacks on Polish farmers by Ukrainians," pursued a curious Wiktor, *"are they occurring all over Volhynia? What about you and your neighbours?"*

"It is a crazy world that we live in. The stupid war has changed everything. We are now in the middle of a war but we are not fighting the Nazis or the Bolsheviks. We are at war with our Polish neighbours. As for me, I feel quite safe right here."

Residents of Galicia and Volhynia had to admit that they were living at a time when World War II raged on while at the same time the Ukrainian and Polish communities were intent upon destroying each other. If these events were not enough, partisans and self-defense formations, representing the interests of the Ukrainians, Poles, or the Soviet Union began to spring up in their midst, adding to the horrors of armed conflict. Ethnic cleansings, according to Konenko, were wide-spread and had the characteristics of a civil war in a geographic region first occupied by Poland, then by the Soviet Union, and more recently by Germany.

"It is my view," explained Konenko thoughtfully, *"that the occupation of this region by the Poles after the First World War resulted in many problems. It might have been better for Poland to help Ukrainians gain independence, don't you think, Wiktor?"*

"Yes, Pan Konenko, my father often said that the Ukrainians objected to their treatment as second class citizens by the Polish elite."

"We must also remember, Wiktor, in this region the Ukrainians outnumbered the Poles by a ratio of three to one. The Ukrainians formed the majority in Volhynia and felt that Polish occupation was thrust upon them."

"I know this to be true," responded Wiktor, *"my father had the greatest respect for Ukrainians and their territorial ambitions. However, he also said that Polish leaders supported the occupation of Western Ukrainian lands, a decision necessary for state security."*

The thoughtful opinions of Pan Konenko and the youthful Wiktor Wozniak seemed not to matter. Poland was no longer a major player in Volhynia. Neither was Ukraine. Although Volhynia was occupied by the Nazis in 1941, the political landscape was about to change. Volhynia would soon be under the control of the Soviet Union once again.

Throughout this period of history, Volynians could not escape massive state-organized political and ethnic violence carried out by both super powers. The brutality introduced a divided Poland to its first exposure to massive ethnic cleansings. In the process, an unprecedented terror swept through the recently conquered areas. Tens of thousands of Poles were killed and hundreds of thousands were deported by both occupational regimes. Nazi occupation was one thing; however, Soviet occupation spawned even more hatred among the Ukrainian population, radicalizing it.

The OUN had but one solution for Poles living in the province of Volhynia, however, not all factions of the OUN supported the total ethnic cleansing of Poles to accomplish this goal. As a result, OUN had split into two factions in 1940, the moderate OUN-M faction under the leadership of Andriy Melnyk and the radical OUN-B faction under the leadership of Stepan Bandera. The radical OUN group came to believe that it had to move fast while the Germans still controlled the area in order to preempt future Polish efforts at re-establishing Poland's prewar borders.

Stepan Bandera, the controversial leader of the OUN, seen as a hero in Western Ukraine but as a Nazi collaborator in Eastern Ukraine.

Even as World War II raged on, Stepan Bandera, the son of a Greek Catholic priest, sought a tactical relationship with the Nazis in an effort to defend Ukrainian nationalistic ideas. In search of funds to subsidize his campaign, Bandera had led members of his OUN unit in robbing banks, post offices, police stations and private households. The extremist faction of OUN, under his leadership, did not shy away from killing Poles in Volhynia in an effort to attain their goals. Supported by other Ukrainian political and military groups, OUN gained sufficient strength and popularity, creating the conditions necessary for massacres to occur.

For OUN, their program of ethnic cleansing began in earnest in March of 1943. Ukrainians abandoned their roles in the German police, took their weapons with them, and began their attacks on Poles. Numbering in excess of 20,000, the OUN set out to resettle all Poles west of the Curzon Line, thereby preventing any future possibility of claims toward the territory. In the process, not only were Poles killed but so were thousands of Ukrainians who sided with Roman Catholicism or with any partisan group opposed to their point of view.

Ukrainians could not forget the harsh policies implemented by Poland during the interwar period. With this in mind, they felt justified in seeking retribution by attacking the Poles. At the same time, violent attacks on Polish villages undertaken by the OUN contributed to a further deterioration of relations between the two ethnic groups. The rumours that the Poles were attacking Ukrainians in the province of Lublin did not help the situation in Volhynia.

One year earlier while under the occupation of the Nazis, the Volhynian region became a part of *Reichskommissariat Ukraine.* In a similar move, Galicia became a part of *Generalgouvernment,* thus becoming a part of Greater Germany. New social and political divisions were established in a short period of time. In Galicia, Ukrainians were elevated to positions of authority whereas in Volhynia, Poles retained authority within the German administration.

The Soviet counteroffensive that followed the battle of Stalingrad in January of 1943, led to a westward push by Soviet forces as they recaptured Ukraine proper, leading Ukrainian leaders to reason that a pre-emptive elimination of Poles from Ukraine would be the most they could gain in a short period of time. The Soviets celebrated victories in the Tank Battle of Kursk, the Battle of the Dnieper, and the Battle for Ukraine. Due to the successes of the Soviet Army, Ukrainians felt that it was necessary to speed up the liquidation of Poles. Ukrainian insurgents believed that the war would soon end.

In the neighbouring province of Galicia, Polish families were notified of OUN's actions by way of an ultimatum.

"Because the Polish government and Polish people are collaborating with the Bolsheviks and are bent on destroying the Ukrainian people on their own land, all Poles are hereby called upon to move to native Polish soil."

This dictum would soon have considerable impact upon Wiktor Wozniak and his Polish friends. In August of 1943, the OUN placed notices in every Polish village in Volhynia, *"In 48 hours leave beyond the Bug River or the San River, otherwise Death."*

"Your challenge, Wiktor, is to avoid conscription into the Red Army or arrest by the Gestapo for slave labour in Germany," concluded Konenko. *"If that is not enough, you must also avoid capture by a Soviet or Ukrainian partisan group."*

"What about you, Pan Konenko? Will you be safe?"

"Thank you, Wiktor, for your concern. I am too old for military service. As for the partisans, they are not interested in old farmers. They want to recruit young people. The Ukrainian Insurgent Army will not bother me. They will be after you."

Despite many successes throughout Volhynia, the OUN was not able to completely control the situation. In addition to Soviet partisans, many independent Ukrainian self-defence groups started to form up in response to the growth of German terror. By consolidating their power and control, the UPA set out to subdue all independent groups. Well trained and well armed, the UPA was able to achieve dominance over other Ukrainian groups who were active in Volhynia at the time.

The UPA undertook steps to liquidate all foreign elements with posters and leaflets, urging Ukrainians to murder Poles. Starting in March, approximately 7,000 men, women, and children were murdered in the first days of operation. Village after village was razed to the ground. By mid-1943, after a wave of killings of Polish civilians, the Poles tried to negotiate, without success, a cessation to the killings. In the process, the negotiators were captured and murdered.

After gaining control over the Volhynian countryside from the Germans, the UPA began large-scale operations against the Polish population. The peak of the massacres took place in the summer of 1943 when UPA ordered the liquidation of the entire male population between 16 and 60 years of age. However, and despite this order, UPA forces experienced limited success. Perhaps the bloodiest day of attacks on Poles came on July 11, 1943, when the Ukrainians simultaneously attacked 167 towns and villages. The UPA continued the ethnic cleansing, particularly in rural areas, until most Poles had been deported or killed. These actions were conducted by many units, well coordinated and thoroughly planned.

Interestingly, Ukrainian attackers limited their actions to villages and settlements. They did not strike towns or cities.

One UPA leader's report presented some interesting conclusions, *"I have liquidated all Poles, starting with the youngest ones. Afterwards, all buildings were burned and all goods were confiscated."*

Another account of the atrocities committed by UPA units painted a most horrific picture. Curiously, the language and images used in the report could not be confirmed. Many believed that much of the message was pure propaganda put into place to encourage more attacks on Polish villages. The intent of the message was quite obvious.

"Our units torched villages. They axed and crucified Roman Catholic priests and burned their churches. Several of the churches were full of parishioners. Isolated farms were attacked by gangs carrying pitchforks and kitchen knives. The throats of many Poles were cut. Pregnant women were not spared and infants were cut in two. Polish men were ambushed in the field and led away. The perpetrators could not determine the province's future but at least they could determine that it would be a future without Poles."

Another UPA directive to Ukrainians living in the region was clear.

"Liquidate all Polish traces. Destroy all walls in the Catholic Churches and other Polish prayer houses. Destroy orchards and trees in the courtyards so that there will be no trace that women ever lived there. Pay attention to the fact that when something remains that is Polish then the Poles will have pretensions to our land."

Deprived of their elitist leaders when so many were deported to Siberia, the Poles were soon dispersed around the countryside, with neither a local partisan army nor state authority to protect them.

By the fall of 1943, UPA forces, under Bandera's leadership, established control over substantial portions of Volhynia. They set up military training schools, hospitals, and a school system involving tens of thousands of personnel while at the same time fighting against the Germans and later against the Soviets.

UPA Insurgents in the Rivne region of Volhynia during World War II.

During this period of the war, Soviet partisan groups were also operating in the area. Composed of Soviet POWs, they initially specialized in raiding local settlements. These attacks disturbed the UPA and the local Polish self-defence units. As a result, the Nazis began pacifying entire village in retaliation for real or alleged support for the

Soviet partisans. In several cases, the Nazis murdered Polish villagers or supervised such actions.

By September of 1943, as the Soviet Battle of the Dnieper was in full swing, Konenko and Wiktor had taken in the garden and the grain from the fields. Fearing that he might be discovered, Wiktor was forced to make a very important decision.

"Pan Konenko, I cannot thank you enough for keeping me safe. But, it is now time for me to think about my future. Soon, I will have to leave the safety and sanctuary of your home and seek safe haven in Poland."

"What are you saying, Wiktor? Do you know the dangers that exist in this region from the Soviet partisans, Ukrainian butchers, and Nazis? Are you sure that you want to leave the safety of this farm?"

"Yes, Pan Konenko, my mind is made up. First, however, I want to take some time to meet with my friend in Zaborol. I need your support to find him. The village is not far from here. Once I meet with him, I shall return to your home."

"I can see that your mind is made up. After you meet your friend in Zaborol, I want you to return. I know that Tanja would want you to return."

While harbouring Wiktor, Konenko was well aware that local Ukrainian squads were intent upon ridding the region of all Poles. The Nazis did not help the situation when they turned a blind eye to the atrocities. Caught on the horns of a dilemma, Wiktor was forced to protect himself from roving Ukrainian bandits, UPA forces, the Wehrmacht, and the Red Army.

The distance that Wiktor had to traverse from Konenko's farm to Zaborol was less than fifteen kilometres, a distance that one could cover in three hours under normal circumstances. However, the circumstances were anything but normal. Following the Omelyanivka River, the first sign of trouble occurred when out of nowhere, three heavily armed partisans jumped him.

"Stop, you son of a bitch, hands up," was the command.

Thinking quickly, with hands held high in the air, Wiktor realized that the command was spoken in Polish. *Perhaps,* he thought, *they will not shoot me without first finding out more about me.*

"What is your name, suka, you son-of-a-bitch? Where do you live?"

"My name is Wozniak," replied Wiktor in Polish.

"What the hell are you doing wandering around the countryside? You are one stupid bastard. You must have some sort of death wish."

"I am on my way to see a friend in Zaborol."

"You dumb shithead. Suka, you know that you are not safe. Come with us. We will provide safe haven in the Przebraze settlement. It is located near here"

"How will I be safe in Przebraze? I have never heard of it."

"Przebraze is a self-defence centre for Poles who want to protect themselves from those murdering Ukrainians. Our Polish sentries are armed with weapons taken from the Nazis. In addition, Armija Krajowa helps us by providing supplies, weapons, and money."

"Thank you for reaching out to help me. God only knows, these are dangerous times for all of us. How many Poles are you able to protect?"

"At the moment, we are protecting thousands of Poles in the fortified Przebraze settlement. They are safe from the units of marauding Ukrainian Insurgent Army and those murderous Nazis."

The massacres of Poles prompted Polish leaders to organize self-defence organizations. Sometimes the self-defence organizations obtained arms from the Germans. At other times, the Germans confiscated the arms from self-defence units and arrested their leaders. Many of the smaller organizations were destroyed by the UPA. Only the largest self-defence organizations that were able to obtain help from the Armija Krajowa or from the Soviet partisans were able to survive. In some cases, Polish self-defence organizations had the protection of Poland's Armija Krajowa and were able to take part in revenge massacres of Ukrainian civilians.

According to the Polish officer, the Przebraze paramilitary unit consisted of several hundred men charged with defending a vast area, including all surrounding settlements. Polish families occupied several houses within the compound while others had to live in temporary mud huts. A field hospital was organized for the sick and wounded. Skirmishes with Ukrainians were frequent and beds were usually full. This was why Polish units from Przebraze scouted the area, encouraging all Poles to leave their homes and move to the fortified settlement.

Unfortunately, not all agreed to move to the fortified settlement. In many cases, their reluctance turned out to be fatal. UPA units tried to destroy Przebraze, burning neighbouring villages and murdering its inhabitants. Throughout the summer of 1943 the war for grain persisted. In the fall of 1943, the local Polish Home Army units, assisted by Soviet partisan forces were able to push back the UPA forces. It would not be until February of 1944 that Volhynia would be liberated by the Red Army. The Poles were thankful that the Soviet regime considered the UPA to be their enemy, finally stopping the UPA attacks.

It took a considerable amount of persuasion to convince the Polish partisan unit to release him from captivity. In order to be released, Wiktor promised that he would find his way back to the fortified settlement after a meeting with his friend at Zaborol. Now being more aware than ever of the dangers of travel, Wiktor decided to wait until nightfall before completing his journey. Only then, he concluded, would he have a chance to avoid further trouble. Arriving safely at Zaborol the next day, Wiktor was able to find his friend, hiding out in the family barn.

"Good Lord, Wiktor Wozniak," was the reaction from Igor Kawa, *"What are you doing in Zaborol?"*

"Shush, Igor, not so loud. I barely escaped from Polonka with my hide. It's those murdering Ukrainian Nationalists. My father and brother have been deported. Our family home has been burned to the ground. I want to talk with you."

"That is most tragic. Just like my family. There is nobody left. That is why I am hiding out in this smelly old barn. I am the only surviving member of my family."

"You are? What happened to your father and mother?"

"Those pigs, the Soviet suka bastards, they deported my parents and my two brothers to Siberia. God only knows what will happen to them. I may never see them again."

"And you? How did you survive?"

"I got word from my closest friend's younger brother who warned me. We hid out with a Ukrainian family to escape persecution. I wish that my best friend was still living. I miss him very much."

"You miss your best friend? Tell me more about your friend. What happened to him?"

"It all happened near Polonka. When the war began in September, the Soviets attacked the Lutsk region. That was when all the trouble began. They dismantled the factories in Lutsk and transported everything to Russia. Thousands of citizens, political and business leaders were deported to Kazakhstan. Those who resisted were arrested and murdered by the NKVD."

"So, what happened to your friend?"

"When the Nazis attacked the Soviet Union, the retreating Red Army executed political prisoners. They murdered countless Jews and non-Jews."

"Did the Germans kill your best friend?"

"No, that's not what happened. Out of curiosity, we watched as the Germans rounded up all the Jews in this region. They placed all the Jews in a ghetto in Polonka."

"You saw this happen?"

"Yes, that was stupid of us. I wish that I had not seen those thousands of Jews being murdered in the Jewish labour camp. I heard that thousands of people were executed at point-blank range by the Nazis."

"You witnessed this terrible slaughter? Were the Nazis murdering the Jews?"

"Yes, I witnessed all of that. I still have nightmares about the murders. I escaped from the area but my best friend, Pawel Barczak, lost his life."

"Do you mean to tell me that they killed him too?"

"Yes, and I blame myself for allowing my friend to get closer to those criminals from Germany. He was shot by a Nazi sniper."

Now a refugee in a land that was home to his family since 1923, Wiktor tried to assimilate what he had seen and heard. The rumours, he suddenly realized, were now reality. He was witness to some of the atrocities as Ukrainian partisans burned homes, shot, or forced back inside those who tried to flee, and used sickles and pitchforks to kill those they captured outside. In some cases, beheaded, crucified, dismembered, or disemboweled bodies were displayed in order to encourage remaining Poles to flee.

Rumours about whole villages being wiped out, men beaten to death, women raped and mutilated, babies bayoneted, actions that one might see in a medieval rebellion, began to circulate. The methods used in most of the attacks were the same. At first, local Poles were assured that nothing would happen to them. Then, at dawn, a village was surrounded by armed members of the UPA. Behind them were peasants with axes, hammers, knives, and saws. Sometimes, Poles were herded into one spot to make it easier to exterminate them.

After a massacre, all goods were looted, including clothes, grain, and furniture. The final part of an attack was setting fire to the village. All vestiges of Polish existence were eradicated and even abandoned Polish settlements were burned to the ground. According to reports, those who did not speak Polish but were considered to be Poles by the perpetrators were also murdered.

Even though it may be an exaggeration to say that the massacres had general support of Ukrainians, it has been suggested that without wide support from local Ukrainians these atrocities could not have taken place. In many cases, Ukrainian peasants, in support of the UPA also created their own self-defence units and took part in the massacres.

Ukrainians in ethnically mixed settlements were offered material incentives to join in the slaughter of their neighbours, or warned by the

UPA's security service to flee by night, while all remaining inhabitants were murdered at dawn. Many Ukrainians risked and in some cases lost their lives trying to warn or shelter Poles. Such activities were treated by the UPA as collaboration with the enemy and severely punished. In the case of Polish-Ukrainian families, one common UPA instruction was to kill one's Polish spouse and children born of that marriage. Those who refused to carry out such orders were often murdered together with their entire family.

While the Nazis actively encouraged the conflict, most of the time they avoided direct involvement. However, there were reports of Germans supplying weapons to both Ukrainians and Poles. The Germans were actively prodding both sides of the conflict against each other, stating that, *"We have to do everything possible so that a Pole meeting a Ukrainian would be willing to kill him and conversely, a Ukrainian would be willing to kill a Pole."*

During that summer of 1943, Polish partisan forces killed many defenceless Ukrainian villagers, even though these villagers had nothing to do with the killing of Poles. In these retaliatory measures, hundreds of Ukrainians perished. Additionally, a Home Army Infantry Division was formed with the objective of fighting the UPA and bringing some order to the conflict. Despite this initiative, however, the Commander of Armija Krajowa was critical of his troops for burning neighbouring Ukrainian villages, killing any Ukrainian that crossed their path, and robbing Ukrainians of their material possessions without cause.

By late 1943, most Poles living in Volhynia had either been killed or fled the conflict to the neighbouring province of Galicia. In East Galicia, unlike cases in Volhynia where Polish villages were usually destroyed and their inhabitants murdered without warning, Poles were given the choice of fleeing or being killed. The UPA commander once again warned his troops against the wanton killing of Polish citizens, *"I remind you, first call upon Poles to abandon their land and only later liquidate them, not the other way around."*

In the province of Galicia, the Poles developed better self-defence units, resulting in a significantly lower death rate. However, the methods used by Ukrainian nationalists followed a procedure similar to that used in Volhynia. Polish residents were rounded up in a village, slaughtered, their homes looted, and then burned to the ground.

In the final analysis, the ethnic conflict between the Poles and Ukrainians resulted in as many deaths as from the armed conflict between the Nazis and the Soviets. Wiktor, in particular, tried to make sense of the atrocities being committed by both groups. In his mind, he could not understand how a man of God, a parish priest in a small Ukrainian village was able to proclaim from the pulpit, *"Mother, you are suckling an enemy. Strangle it."*

During the campaign to remove all Poles from Volhynia, a UPA commander stated, *"In view of the success of the Soviet forces, it is necessary to speed up the liquidation of the Poles. They must be totally wiped out, their villages burned. Remember, only the Polish population must be destroyed."*

By the end of the summer and under the slogan, *"Poles behind the San,"* mass acts of terror aimed at Poles were taking place in Eastern Galicia with the purpose of forcing Poles to settle on the western bank of the San River. With tears welling up in his eyes, Wiktor Wozniak, now a refugee on the run, considered the poster prominently displayed in the village square, *"In 48 hours leave beyond the Bug River, otherwise death."*

Turning to Igor Kawa, Wiktor had made up his mind, *"Those ruthless bastards. Kurwa, the time has come, my dear friend, to heed those warnings. We must get our asses out of Volhynia just as quickly as we can. We must go to Poland."*

"Synowie suk, sons of bitches, that's all I can say about those UPA units. Be very careful when you return to Konenko's farm. Hurry back."

"Yes, I shall be back in three days. At that time, we shall plan our escape from Volhynia to Poland. I hate the very thought of this decision and the impact it will have upon our lives and those of our family who remain behind."

It was time for Wiktor to make a most agonizing but necessary decision. His love for Tanja must now be put on hold. His family decimated and his father and brother somewhere in Siberia, Poland now beckoned, even if that territory was still under German control.

PART 5

POLISH NATIONALISM

10

Seeking Refuge In Poland

"Soon, very soon, Poland will once again be an independent country..."

Even as Wiktor Wozniak set out to leave Zaborol, he was once again confronted by that ever-present warning, *"In 48 hours leave beyond the Bug River or San River, otherwise Death!"*

To Wiktor, it was no longer a question of the seriousness of the UPA threat. The actions of the UPA spoke volumes, none of them being good for Polish citizens. Now convinced that his life would be danger if confronted by the UPA, Wiktor was forced to take immediate action. From the amount of death and destruction inflicted upon Poles, he could do little else but treat the warning as having real meaning. He also knew why the UPA selected the Bug River as the boundary between Poland and Ukraine.

Historically, the Bug River had real significance. It is a left tributary of the Narew River flowing from the Oblast of Lviv in the west of Ukraine, northwards into the Volhynian Oblast before passing along the Ukraine-Polish border into Poland. Traditionally, the Bug River was considered to be the ethnographic border between the Catholic Polish peoples and the Orthodox believers; between the Poles and Ukrainians; the dividing line between the German Wehrmacht and the Russian Red Army forces following the 1939 invasion of Poland.

Realizing that the territory between Zaborol and Konenko's farm might be inundated with Ukrainian nationalistic bands or the Gestapo,

Wiktor decided to return along the Omelyanivka River in the dead of night. In this way he felt certain that he could avoid running into any UPA or Gestapo units or Polish security officers from the Przebraze settlement. Only this time, thanks to Igor Kawa, Wiktor carried a Luger P08 semi automatic handgun tucked neatly under the belt of his trousers.

Arriving safely at Konenko's farm in rural Polonka, Wiktor Wozniak felt as though he was a member of the family when Pani Konenko gave him a warm hug.

"I am so glad to see you again. I was very worried that you might have run into trouble. This region is full of those Ukrainian butchers and Nazi thugs. Did you get to see your friend in Zaborol?"

"Yes, thank you, Pani Konenko. I am glad that Boris recognized me when I entered your front yard. I had visions of being mauled to death by your dog."

"Yes, yes, Boris has a most keen sense of smell. Tell us about your friend in Zaborol. What are your plans for the future?"

"While in Zaborol, I did get to meet with my friend Igor Kawa. I was shocked to see that the UPA had posted notices commanding all Poles to immediately leave this region in favour of Poland. They must have taken the idea of posting notices in public places from the Russian Tsars. They looked very official to me."

"Very true, Wiktor, the Russian Tsars used ukases to post their proclamations."

"Do you think, Pani Konenko, that these ukases have the force of law?"

"Those crazy Ukrainian bandits," objected Pani Konenko, *"have no right to post such proclamations. Only the government in power has the right to post them. And, sure as hell, the government in power is not the UPA."*

"I would not argue with a UPA soldier while staring into the barrel of a Kalashnikov rifle. Pani Konenko, I must take their warnings seriously."

"I understand, Wiktor. Now that you are back safely, you can stay as long as you want."

The heat of summer coupled with the destruction of war made it look as though all of the Oblast of Volhynia was on fire. As early as the mid-summer of 1943, the Soviet Union was in full control of Eastern Ukraine while the Nazis still controlled the western region of Poland. Peering into the eyes of Wiktor, Andriy Konenko concluded that, like it or not, he would have to share some shocking news with him, not about war but rather about his family.

"I have some terrible news for you, Wiktor. My neighbour just returned from Polonka. He informed me that your family home in Polonka was set ablaze and your mother and sister were butchered by the UPA."

In hearing the shocking news, Wiktor fell to his knees in silent prayer. No one said anything for the longest time. When Wiktor stood up, Konenko could see that although shocked and saddened by the news, Wiktor was also mad as hell.

"Those goddamn murdering criminal pigs. Why would they kill innocent people?"

"The whole world has gone crazy. Who can you trust today?"

"What about the Konenko family? Have you received any word about them?"

"A similar fate met their family. The Gestapo showed up at my brother's home in Polonka just as the UPA set the house and barn on fire. Maria and Juli perished in the fire."

"Have you any news about Tanja?"

"Tanja was not at home when the UPA appeared. But once again the news is not good. The very next day, Tanja was arrested by the Gestapo. I was told that Tanja is being taken to Germany by Hitler's henchmen. I suppose that she will be working in Germany as a slave labourer. There is very little that we can do about these tragedies."

"Those damn Nazi bastards. This means that my sister Monika and now Tanja have been taken to Germany. I have lost both of them. I may never see them again."

Wiktor could not find the words to describe how he felt about the devastating news. Recognizing the gravity of the situation, Konenko didn't know how to console Wiktor. After all, it was Tanja who worked so hard to save Wiktor's life and now Wiktor was not able to save Tanja from slavery in Germany. Embracing Pani Konenko, Wiktor declared his intentions.

"I will go to Polonka during the night. I want to make certain that the victims are all laid to rest according to our beliefs. I know it is risky but I have to do the right thing. I also want to contact Myron Mora, a childhood friend of mine."

In the darkness of night, Wiktor set out for Polonka. Just as he was wending his way through the neighbour's farm, a dog began to bark. Lying motionless in the wheat field, cradling the Luger, Wiktor decided to stay put until any danger passed. He did not have to wait long to get his answer. A volley of shots rang out and then silence. Whoever the intruder, Wiktor was thankful that he was not the victim.

Giving the farm a wide berth, Wiktor slowly continued on his way to Polonka. He wanted to see firsthand as to what happened to his mother and sister. Most of all, he wanted to know what happened to Tanja Konenko.

An eerie silence greeted Wiktor when he arrived in Polonka. The UPA brigade responsible for torching several buildings and murdering a number of villagers were nowhere to be seen. It appeared as though the onslaught on helpless villagers showed no mercy. The Konenko and Wozniak homes were no more than piles of ashes. To approach the smouldering ruins would be folly. All that Wiktor could do was to observe a German Gestapo squad as they, too, looked on as the final embers gave moot testimony to the burnt-out homes. To make sure that he was not arrested by the Gestapo, Wiktor spent the night in the woods near his family's burnt-out home.

At sunrise, sleep-deprived and cold, Wiktor made certain that no member of the Gestapo was in sight before getting together with his neighbours and the local priest. Keeping an eye out for the UPA, Wiktor helped with the burial of his mother and sister. He also helped his neighbours with the burial of Danuta Konenko and her daughter, Juli. While grieving the loss of loved ones, there was shortage of tears. Wiktor was thankful that the Gestapo respected those who grieved by keeping their distance.

Stealthily approaching the Mora residence, Wiktor hoped to be able to meet up with his friend, Myron Mora. At a time like this, he needed a friend—someone to talk with who might share the pain of his loss. At the same time, Wiktor knew that Myron, not wanting to be forcefully recruited into the Wehrmacht or arrested by the Gestapo for slave labour in Germany, would be keeping a very low profile.

Discreetly, Wiktor waited until someone in the family appeared out of doors to do the morning chores before trying to get their attention. While waiting, Wiktor checked to make sure that his Luger semi automatic was safely tucked away in the belt of his midsection. After a couple of low-keyed whistles, he got the attention of Myron Mora's mother.

"Good morning, Pani Mora. Are we free to talk?"

"Yes, but please speak in a low voice. Do not attract the attention of the Gestapo or the neighbours."

"Pani Mora, where is your son Myron?"

"Shush, he is hiding out in the hayloft in the barn. This is not a safe time for any Polish boy. If it is not the murdering Ukrainian bandits, it is the Gestapo butchers."

Quietly and making certain that no one was watching, Wiktor crept into the barn and called out Myron's name.

"Good Lord, Wiktor," excitedly exclaimed Myron, *"I glad to see you! You are very lucky to escape the UPA brigade."*

After a quiet embrace, Wiktor and Myron had a lot to talk about.

"It's God's will that I am still alive," confessed Myron. *"Why the Ukrainian thugs did not kill my mother, I shall never know. Mother must have convinced them that she was an ethnic Ukrainian. Why else would they spare her?"*

"You heard those Ukrainian butchers talking to your mother?"

"Yes, I did. Imagine what would have happened to me in this hayloft if they set the barn on fire? I would be a goner. Maybe I would be in heaven by this time."

Wiktor and Myron talked for the longest time. The decision they were about to make would not be easy. When Pani Mora heard of their plan to set out for Poland, she expressed ardent opposition.

"Pani Mora, you can understand. We have no other option. To remain in Polonka would mean certain death for the two of us."

Following more discussion about what the future held for the boys in Volhynia, Pani Mora reluctantly agreed. Packing some personal belongings and snacks, Wiktor and Myron agreed that it was now time to heed the directive of the UPA. It was time to leave Volhynia for the safety of Poland.

"Please be careful," pleaded a tearful Pani Mora, *"promise to write and tell me that you have arrived safely in Poland. When this war is finally over, we will once again get together as a family, God willing!"*

With much of the village of Polonka in ruins, the hellishness of war unnerved Wiktor. Even his sense of youthful exuberance could not diminish the seriousness of the situation. With the telegraph and telephone lines out of commission, accurate information about what was happening in Poland was hard to come by. Rumour had it that the Zamosc region was under the control of the Nazis who were doing little to stop roving Polish armed bands from killing Ukrainians or from Ukrainians killing Poles. Bidding farewell to Polonka, Wiktor and Myron set out for the village of Zaborol.

Arriving safely in Zaborol, Wiktor Wozniak and Myron Mora joined Igor Kawa. Now a unit of three, they wanted to discuss the current political situation in Volhynia in contrast to what they assumed would be the safety of Poland.

"We can only assume," argued Igor, *"that we will be safer in Poland where the Ukrainians will have to keep an eye out for Polish units. If the rumours are correct, it will be the Ukrainians who will be on the run."*

"My cousin, Szymon Woycik," offered Wiktor, *"lives in the town of Zamosc. Except for this damned war, I would have been able to contact him and seek his help. But thanks to the krauts, the telephone and telegraph systems in Poland have been destroyed."*

"I have a famous uncle who lives in Poland," added Igor, most excitedly, *"an uncle that I would love to contact. I heard that the only telephones in use are the field telephones used by the Nazis and the Red Army."*

"To send a postcard to someone we know in Poland is of no use," agreed Myron. *"No telephones, no telegrams, and no postal service."*

"Even if I could telephone my cousin," clarified Wiktor, *"the conversation would be monitored by the the Nazis or the NKVD. What good would that do? On the other hand, the Soviets would not stand in our way. It is they who want us to get the hell out of Volhynia."*

"Yes," agreed Myron Mora, *"that is the reality. We all understand that the NKVD and those war-mongering Ukrainians want all Poles out of Volhynia and Galicia in 48 hours. Those bastards will kill all of us if we are not out of here in two days."*

"Suka, son of a bitch, those damned Nazis," angrily swore Wiktor as he derisively spat in the direction of Germany, *"maybe all of this is for the better. Since we cannot telephone anyone, no one will be able to monitor our conversations or discover our whereabouts."*

Having considerable knowledge about the situation in the province of Volhynia, Wiktor's unit was anxious to leave the Lutsk region and arrive in their next destination of Radekhiv before that region could fall under UPA control. Believing that Radekhiv was under the control of Armija Krajowa made it easier to select the town as their next destination. However, getting safely from Zaborol to Radekhiv was the real challenge.

"From Radekhiv," Wiktor surmised, *"we can find our way to Rawa Ruska at which point, God willing, we shall safely cross into Poland. Once in Poland, we should be able to get to Zamosc without too many problems."*

Even after being alerted of the general location of several Gestapo brigades did not make their escape from Volhynia to Poland any easier.

Since every avenue of escape to Radekhiv was under the control of either the Nazis or the UPA, the unit decided to spend some time under the protection of a Ukrainian family sympathetic to their plight before exiting Volhynia.

This is how, after some reconnaissance work, the unit decided to spend some time with the Melnyk family sympathetic to the plight of Poles. Much like the Konenko family before them, the Melnyk family held no animosity towards the Poles and wanted to extend a helping hand, especially at a time when Poles were being forced to vacate Volhynia.

"These are dangerous times for us all," explained Adam Melnyk, *"especially for our Polish neighbours. Pani Melnyk and I want to help."*

In exchange for their protection, the three boys promised to help the Melnyks take in their cereal crops. During the very first week of their work on the Melnyk farm, all went well, too well. Early one morning while still asleep in the hayloft of the Melnyk's barn, Wiktor heard the clippetty-clop of several horses stop next to the Melnyk home. Listening intently to a conversation between a member of the UPA and Adam Melnyk, what Wiktor heard spelled nothing but trouble for his unit.

"Melnyk, your name is Melnyk?" enquired a member of the UPA unit.

"Yes, my name is Adam Melnyk. What is it you want?"

"I am the leader of this UPA brigade. Where are those three little Polish bastards? Where are you hiding them?"

The loud conversation got the attention of Wiktor's unit. *Why was Adam yelling at the Ukrainian bandits?* Suddenly, it occurred to Wiktor as to the reason for the yelling. It was Adam Melnyk's way of warning the boys of impending danger.

"Yes," shouted Melnyk, *"my hearing is not the best. Those three boys have been helping me with my farming duties. They have been working on my small farming operation."*

"Where are those little snivelling thieves now? We want to take care of them."

"Do you see that hay meadow to the north?" yelled Melnyk, *"The boys are cow-herding over there. They are looking after my herd of cows."*

Suddenly, the four heavily-armed Ukrainian bandits left the farmyard in the direction of the meadow. Melnyk did not have to tell Wiktor that they must make a dash for the forest to the south. In just a few moments, the three boys were gone, disappearing into the forest. Once clear of the Melnyk farm, Wiktor decided to call a stop. What they witnessed from their hiding place was most disheartening. They heard a volley of rifle shots and then watched as the Melnyk home and barn were set ablaze by the UPA.

Hiding out in the forest and deep in thought, Wiktor, Igor, and Myron shared their deepest thoughts. To the surprise of Wiktor and Myron, it was Igor Kawa who was most adamant about getting even with Ukrainians once they reached Poland. Igor confessed that he lost many of his friends as a result of the war and ethnic cleansings imposed upon the Poles by Ukrainians. He felt justified in harbouring this secret desire for revenge. However, with Tanja on his mind, Wiktor was most reluctant to express any desire to harm Ukrainian families. After all, without the help of the Konenkos and Melnyks, where would he be on this day?

"I must agree with you, Igor," offered Wiktor, *"that not all Ukrainians are of good will, especially the UPA. We must keep in mind that the Melnyks saved our lives."*

Wiktor reserved most of his anger for Germany. *Those damned murdering Nazi dogs,* thought Wiktor, *first they kill the Poles in this area and then they capture and send our young people to Germany. Why would they want to torture my sweetheart by sending her to Germany? What did Tanja ever do to them?*

The more Wiktor thought about the past, the angrier he got. Yet, as the three boys set out in the direction of Radekhiv, Wiktor realized that their very survival might well depend upon the good will of other Ukrainian families.

Wiktor recalled the stories he had heard from his father about the proud history of the thriving town of Radekhiv and the beautiful gardens surrounding a spectacular castle on the river. Although in normal circumstances the distance could be covered in one day, the circumstances in this case were anything but normal. Hungry, thirsty, and wet after having to swim across a swollen brook, the boys sought refuge in what they thought was an isolated farm barn near Radekhiv. Unfortunately, the farmer must have heard his guard dog barking, alerting him that an intruder was in the vicinity. Approaching the direction from whence the barking came, the farmer came upon the boys hiding in a thicket.

"Hands up, you bastards," yelled the farmer, pointing a rifle in their direction, *"or you are dead. What are you doing here? Your explanation had better be a good one."*

"*We are trying to find our way to Poland,*" calmly explained Wiktor. "*We lost all of our families in Volhynia. My father has been deported to Siberia.*"

"*Where are your belongings? You have no personal effects?*"

"*All we have in our small satchels is some food and a few personal things.*"

"*You lying bastards are criminals. All three of you are armed. I should shoot all of you.*"

Realizing that this could suddenly happen, the boys remained silent with their hands raised over their heads. After examining their documents and considering their plight, the farmer instructed them to stay right there. In a few minutes he returned with a loaf of fresh bread and some words of advice.

"*I believe that you boys are leaving Volhynia and want to find your way to Radekhiv before entering Poland. Here is a sketch of the roads you must take. Most Ukrainians along the route know that the Poles are leaving Volhynia. There is a truce in place and you should not encounter too much difficulty.*"

That evening, while quenching their thirst from a brook, the unit was thankful for the bread they received from the farmer. Stealthily, they wound their way into a villager's garden. In the darkness of night, they were able to dig up a few carrots, a head of cabbage, and some kernels of wheat from a freshly threshed field of wheat. Knowing that the area around the town of Radekhiv was once home to many Poles made it easier for the boys to spend a day hiding in the grounds of a castle. In a stack of hay, they made a bed of straw and promptly fell asleep. Unfortunately, when they awoke early the next morning, they were discovered by a group of teenagers who were playing a game of soccer nearby.

"*Who are you?*" asked one of the soccer players in Ukrainian.

"*My name is Wiktor, Wiktor Wozniak,*" responded Wiktor in Ukrainian, "*and these are my friends, Igor Kawa, and Myron Mora.*"

"*The sons-of-a-bitches are not Ukrainians, they are Polish criminals,*" asserted one of the soccer players. Turning to his colleagues, he shouted, "*Let's kill all three of these Polish scum. They are no more than hoodlums.*"

Instantly, Wiktor was attacked by three members of the soccer team. Luckily, none of the soccer players had a weapon. Otherwise, all of them might have been shot by Wiktor's heavily-armed unit. One very physical soccer players jumped Wiktor from behind while a second player started to pummel him. Although Wiktor could feel the blows landing on his head, he knew better than to retaliate. A kick to his groin by one of the players brought Wiktor to his knees. At that point, the father of one of the soccer players suddenly appeared, yelling at the boys, *"Leave them alone. We've had enough killing. Let them go."*

Barely able to get to his feet, his left eye beginning to swell and a terrible pain in his groin, Wiktor groggily got to his feet most unsteadily. Igor, as well, seemed as if he had taken several blows to his head. Slowly and in obvious pain, the three Polish youths made their way into the countryside in the direction of Rawa Ruska. What the soccer players did not realize is that the three Polish boys were well armed. Had their lives been in serious peril, the soccer players might have met an untimely end.

Despite the beauty of the surroundings, their time in the town of Radekhiv was anything but peaceful. Staying away from any area that might cause them further problems, it took the three boys two more days to find their way to Rawa Ruska, the line of demarcation between Soviet Ukraine and Poland. However, unlike the town of Radekhiv, Rawa Ruska had a much larger Polish presence, making it easier for the unit to meet other Poles who were also preparing to leave Volhynia for the safety of Poland. The town square in Rawa Ruska was almost deserted until an obviously curious young Pole approached them.

"My name is Krawczyk, Adam Krawczyk. I overheard you say that it is your plan to leave Volhynia in favour of Poland."

"Yes, that is true. We are from the village of Polonka. We are on our way to Poland. We feel lucky to escape the guerrilla warfare being waged in Volhynia."

"Yes, you boys are lucky to be alive. This region is safe. It is under the control of Armija Krajowa."

From Adam Krawczyk, Wiktor learned that Armija Krajowa, using secret radio transmissions, was in constant communication with the Polish government-in-exile in London. In this way, Polish officials were able to keep abreast of developments in Poland. At the same time and as a part of Poland's underground struggle, young Polish males were carrying out sabotage activities virtually everywhere. In particular, their target was the seaport of Gdansk. According to Adam Krawczyk, over 85,000 children had enrolled in classes in Warsaw to learn how to conduct clandestine sabotage activity. Many became skilled in fabricating false documents in order to provide its members with a change of identity when this became necessary. Since the Gestapo brigades were constantly on the prowl trying to track down the sources of radio and telephone transmissions in Poland, the danger was immense.

Deep in thought, Wiktor turned to Adam Krawczyk, *"Didn't this Armija Krajowa Commander cooperate for a time with the German military in a fight against the Soviet partisans?"*

"You heard about this Commander? Yes, he did cooperate with the Nazis but that was last year. This year it is different. Those goddamn Nazis will soon be gone. It's even worse with those butchering Ukrainians. This is why I plan to join Bataliony Chłopskie, a self-defence unit made up of farmers; a battalion that will report to Armija Krajowa."

"You will be joining Armija Krajowa? Where is this army located? What is their mission?"

"Armija Krajowa is the army for the people of Poland, an army that wants to secure our lands. My friends and I want to be a part of this organization. There is a rumour that Armija Krajowa is preparing to cause a large scale operation behind the German lines to prevent a Soviet takeover of the territory by establishing a local Polish administration."

"I am most impressed with your knowledge. What about Rawa Ruska, what's happening here?"

"Well," explained Adam Krawczyk, *"most of those damned war-mongering, money-grubbing Jews have been gathered up by the Nazis. They have all been shipped to some unknown destination by the Nazis. Soon, this area will be under the control of the Red Army. God only knows what will happen when Stalin's butchers arrive."*

"Yes," explained a friend of Adam, *"the Soviets are a ruthless bunch of murderers. The Ukrainians know that the Red Army wants to recapture this region. This is why they posted their ukase in the centre of town ordering all the Poles to immediately find their way to Poland."*

"I know, I know," nodded Wiktor in agreement. *"I saw this edict myself. This is why we are leaving Volhynia. Not only is Volhynia under attack but so is Galicia."*

"The most dangerous squads," added Adam's friend, *"are those under the command of Bereza. Some of his squads had from eight to ten soldiers. Others had only three or four volunteers."*

"Wiktor," suddenly blurted Adam, *"can I join your group? I want to leave this region. I know the area very well. Your unit will be much safer with me."*

After a brief discussion, Wiktor's unit agreed to invite Adam to join them. Now consisting of four members, Wiktor was satisfied that Adam Krawczyk would be of great help.

"This region," pointed out Adam, *"is famous for training guard dogs. Not only will our concern be with the Ukrainian partisans but also with their vicious dogs."*

At a nearby railway siding, Wiktor observed that one train, with carriages loaded with soldiers, was waiting for other trains to pass. The roads alongside the railroad were lined with people walking or riding in horse-drawn carriages and wagons in the direction of Poland. Everywhere they looked there seemed to be activity on horseback or on trucks, often pulling artillery pieces and military supplies. Soldiers seemed to be moving in one direction while civilians moved in another. On the narrow roads, civilians had to make room for the military vehicles to pass.

Near the border between the two political entities, the locals were aware that Poles would likely get plenty of encouragement to find their way to Poland. Wiktor, Myron, Igor, and now joined by Adam, soon found themselves in the village of Hrebenne, Poland. But what they thought would be a town with a Polish majority turned out to be a town reflecting a Ukrainian majority. Not only that, but it would be the Ukrainians burning Polish villages and not the other way around. To make matters worse, the youths discovered that the UPA partisans from the Lemko region of Ukraine were operating in the region, making it increasingly dangerous for them.

Adam Krawczyk, the newest member of the group, knew the region well. He proudly explained that from an historic perspective, the largest church in the Hrebenne community belonged to the Greek Catholic parish which had a membership in excess of one thousand. True, the church was also used by the Polish Roman Catholic parish but only on certain occasions when a Polish priest would come from Lubaczow for a church service. Most astounding was the discovery that any Pole marrying an ethnic Ukrainian would be encouraged to embrace and become a member of the Ukrainian Greek Catholic Church. Many Ukrainians in the town belonged to the Ukrainian Prosvita organization which helped unite the Ukrainian community. For whatever reason, the Poles did not mind this arrangement and the Russians saw no reason to take over the church in favour of the Russian Orthodox Church.

Hrebenne, and the surrounding wooded countryside, revealed no shortage of burned-out homes. As the youths continued their westward journey to Zamosc, it was difficult to reach any conclusion as to which of the two warring nations was responsible for the damage. Along with the burned-out homes, barns, and storage sheds, there seemed to be the smell of death everywhere—thanks to the Nazis, Russians, Poles, and Ukrainians.

"Adam Krawczyk, earlier you mentioned that you have family in Tomaszów Lubelski. You said that we should set our sights on that town. Why is this your suggestion?" enquired Wiktor.

"Yes, Wiktor, I think that this would be our best plan. I have family in Tomaszów Lubelski. I know that they can help us."

Now in the relative safety of Poland and only 22 kilometres from Tomaszów Lubelski, Wiktor's unit decided to hitch a ride on a military transport truck. Looking at the destruction in and around Tomaszów Lubelski, they did not have to use too much imagination to visualize the battle that must have occurred in the region between the Nazis and the Poles, resulting in the destruction of the Polish forces. Even though the Polish forces included one of the largest armoured units of the time, they were no match for the Germans. Lacking food, antitank ammunition, petrol, and maps, the Polish units were soon reduced to half of their original strength. Poland's military leader, General Piskor, surrendered and some 11,000 Polish soldiers were captured, with only small groups managing to hide out in nearby forests.

Bad luck followed the Polish military when Army Krakow was separated from the main Polish forces and inadvertently marched towards the town of Narol. Surrounded by Germans, one by one the Polish units were destroyed. Several units did manage to reach the area of Rawa Ruska where three thousand Polish soldiers surrendered, ending this phase of the battle between Poland and Germany.

Wiktor's unit eavesdropped on the conversations and rumours being discussed by locals. They learned that Ukrainian partisan groups were not only fighting each other but also the Communist resistance organizations. With so many recent military successes, however, the Red Army was confident that they would soon push the German Army beyond the River Bug, the current border between Poland and Ukraine.

"Our Polish brothers," declared Adam, *"will soon be able to administer this entire region."*

"Are the Poles out of their minds, Adam? Have they taken leave of their senses? What do you think the Poles will administer?"

"Well, for one thing," pointed out Adam, *"what the hell are we going to do with all the damned Ukrainians living in our territory? This is why we are here. The Ukrainians kicked our asses out of Volhynia. Don't you want to return the favour and kick their collective asses out of Poland?"*

"Are the Poles at that stage of retribution already, Adam? Don't you think it's a bit early to think about eliminating the Ukrainians in this region? What about the Germans? Don't they still control this region?"

"Yes, the Nazis still control this region. But, there is a rumour in Zamosc that Komorowski, the commander of the Polish Home Army in Warsaw, wants Poles to begin an armed uprising against those murdering German dogs. Not only that but he wants to fight the Soviets as well, if necessary."

Reaching the relative safety of Tomaszów Lubelski, the unit faced a new possibility when an emotional Igor Kawa bragged about his uncle, Bartek Kawa, a long-time resident of Tomaszów Lubelski. They wanted to know more about Bartek Kawa.

"When I was a young boy, my father loved to tell a good story," proudly explained Igor. *"He often bragged about Uncle Bartek. He said that my uncle attained a high rank in the Polish cavalry. My father was very proud of his brother."*

"Where does your uncle live?" asked Wiktor.

"My father told me that he lives somewhere in Tomaszów Lubelski."

"Why don't you try to contact your uncle? He might be of some help to us."

It did not take Igor Kawa long to contact his uncle. Most everyone in Tomaszów Lubelski seemed to know of Bartek Kawa, referring to him, in respectful tones, as Kapitan Kawa.

"So, my dear nephew, you say that all of the members of your group are from the Lutsk region of Volhynia?"

"Yes, Uncle Bartek. Wiktor Wozniak is from the village of Polonka and Myron Mora is from the city of Lutsk. Adam Krawczyk is from the town of Radekhiv."

"Let me tell you," expounded Kapitan Kawa, *"about what is happening to our Polish brothers in Eastern Galicia and Volhynia. Those warmongering Allied leaders, Franklin Roosevelt, Winston Churchill, and Josef Stalin, held conferences in 1943 in Tehran and Yalta."*

"Uncle Bartek, how do you know about these conferences?"

"That's not important, Igor. What is important is that those monkeys decided that all Poles living in the region east of the Curzon Line annexed by the Soviet Union in 1939 should be transferred to Poland. That's why those Ukrainian butchers burned so many Polish villages in Volhynia. They also torched Polish homes in Galicia. Ukrainians want our Polish brothers to suffer as much as they say they suffered under Polish rule."

"So, Uncle Bartek, how many Poles in Volhynia and Lwow are impacted by the actions of Ukrainians?"

"Who knows? Maybe one million souls are suffering. Even as we speak the Poles are being removed from the Polish lands annexed by the Soviet Union. Maybe one day we will know how many of our people have been killed by that tyrant Stalin."

"Yes, Uncle Bartek, I heard that those murdering Bolsheviks have been shipping our brothers to Siberia for years."

"It is all so sad," responded Bartek Kawa, "can you imagine? The Kresy regions are now a part of Soviet Ukraine! Will Poland ever regain this territory?"

"Listen up, you lads," cautioned Bartek Kawa, "what I am about to say should never, ever be repeated. These are troubled times for our Polish brothers. I want you lads to get together and form up a brigade."

"Uncle Bartek, I knew that you would come up with a good idea. What would be the purpose of this brigade?"

"Soon, very soon, Poland will once again be an independent country. Before that happens, there is a lot of work to be done. Armija Krajowa, Poland's Home Army, supports the formation of underground units to operate as guerrilla or partisan organizations."

"So, Uncle Bartek, you have a plan for us?"

"Yes, I do have a plan for you boys. Here is the plan."

Kapitan Kawa did have a plan for the Polish teenagers, a plan that would soon spell nothing but trouble for ethnic Ukrainians living in the border region, especially for those living in Gmina Narol.

11

We Shall Serve Our Fatherland

"I swear to the Polish land and to the Polish nation..."

Kapitan Kawa was not your ordinary decorated war hero. Over the years, especially since the end of the First World War, Bartek Kawa had gone through extensive character development, becoming a vivid, real, jovial, and cunning hero. Living in Tomaszów Lubelski during the inter-war period, it seemed as though he had led a meaningless life of a lesser Polish noble. A lesser life, it seemed, until this moment of opportunity. He no longer had to survive by exploiting the good faith of others, becoming drawn into the company of hero-like personas, and slowly changing to become worthy of their trust and friendship. Suddenly, the time had come for Kapitan Kawa to spring into action.

Kawa was no stranger to being treated as a hero. He liked to embellish each of his exploits, always ending up as the hero. By 1943, he had become a widely-known person in the Tomaszów Lubelski region, treated with respect by powerful magnates. He liked to offer counsel to anyone who would listen, even at times when not asked for advice. Although hard of hearing, he loved to drink and tell stories, always glorifying his own exploits while at the same time poking fun at everyone and everything around him. He was of the opinion that as a sixty-year-old veteran of world conflict he had earned the right to brag about himself and to talk about his vision for the future of Poland.

This is how, as a result of world events and his service in the Polish Cavalry, Kapitan Kawa became known as a cunning tactician and this is why the young members of Wiktor's unit took an immediate liking to him.

Following the German attack on Poland, every branch of the Polish armed forces produced heroes and myth. Polish cavalrymen were employed to cover retreats, gather intelligence and, when possible, capture key terrain to support infantry counterattacks. As a senior member of the Polish Cavalry, Kawa participated in the Krasnobrod military campaign near the town of Zamosc. Unfortunately, this campaign put the troopers directly into many of the initial skirmishes with the Nazis, some successful, more not.

"During that first campaign," bragged Kawa, *"there were dead horses and dead Polish soldiers everywhere. I was seriously wounded and barely survived the skirmish."*

Kawa's bragging about the use of mounted Polish troops who took part in several battles during the month-long Battle of Poland was no more than a metaphor for stupid futility. The problem with Kawa's take on these battles where Polish cavalrymen charged German tanks with lances in a much different war was no more than a myth fostered by propagandists. Yet, what really happened is a story of bravery and professionalism displayed by the Polish Cavalry in the face of overwhelming odds.

Long before World War II broke out, the future looked anything but rosy for the *Old Country*. Old beliefs were solidified and new fears replaced old hurts. As hostilities between Germany and the Soviet Union escalated, another world war was about to break out. Many were of the opinion that the flash point between Poles and Ukrainians would likely come from either the Zakarpattian or the Volhynian regions. The spectre of Polish nationalism and Poland's determination to control these regions was a strong motivating force for Ukrainian Insurgent Army units. It was obvious to most that Poland was prepared to use military force, if necessary, in order to achieve her vision of a New Poland.

From the perspective of history, both Poland and Ukraine had a legitimate argument as to the rightful rule of Eastern Galicia and Volhynia. For Poles, Eastern Galicia and Volhynia were legitimate parts of a Polish state. They were included in Poland by international treaty after the First World War and had been governed legally by the Polish state for thirty years. On the other hand, Eastern Galicia and Volhynia were territories subject to a legitimate Ukrainian claim. This claim was based upon the simple ethnographic fact that Ukrainians outnumbered Poles in these lands by a ratio of two to one during the interwar period.

This disagreement about the idea of legitimate rule powerfully influenced the conclusions that the residents of these two regions reached. The two diametrically opposed points of view led to intended and sometimes unintended conflicts. Both groups questioned the reasonableness of the aspirations of minorities and the justice of the policies of the state.

Although there were a number of significant international military events that took place before World War II ended, no other event had a greater impact upon my family than what transpired in Eastern Poland. World War II was winding down and it was very clear to most every Pole that the Nazis were facing defeat. Believing this to be true, the Poles living in the Chelm Voivodeship of Eastern Poland were confronted with another challenge—it was now time to settle old scores. Small Polish vigilante groups began to form. Each had a vision of a free and independent Poland.

"Yes, my Polish brethren," explained Kapitan Kawa, *"the time is right to form a brigade, a brigade to help Armija Krajowa remove all Ukrainians from our land. This will be our way of settling a score for what they did to our people in Volhynia. The methods used by the Ukrainian bandits consisted of rounding up and killing all Polish residents in a village. If that was not bad enough, they then looted the village and burnt it to the ground. A witness to these crimes heard terrible cries and the roar of cattle being burnt alive. It is now our turn to return the favour."*

Fancying himself as a great orator, Kapitan Kawa noted, with a mischievous grin, that he had the undivided attention of the members of Wiktor's unit.

"A brigade," explained Kawa, *"is a subdivision of the army. Our brigade will be a small armoured cavalry unit on a special mission. I shall give our unit a special name, Brygada Salon. The home base of Brigade Saloon will be Tomaszów Lubelski."*

It did not hurt Kapitan Kawa's cause to personally know Kazimierz Tumidajski, the Commander of the Polish Home Army of the Lublin District. In organizing Brygada Salon, Kawa assured the unit that it would function under his guidance and that of the Polish Home Army, subordinate to the Polish Commander-in-Chief of the Polish Government-in-exile in London.

"One important request," commanded Kawa, *"from this moment forward you are soldiers of my unit. You shall refer to me as Kapitan Kawa. Familiarity is dangerous and not acceptable in the military. This is now a military unit embracing the principles of discipline and rank. Each of you will display honesty, integrity, and loyalty to each other. That is an order."*

Armija Krajowa was well aware that nationalistic Polish units were springing up everywhere. With this knowledge, they knew that it would be nearly impossible to maintain an inventory of all the units. This was why Brygada Salon would soon be able to operate as an independent unit without the obligation of having to report to the Polish Home Army.

Gathered round their brigade leader in a secret country hideaway near the town of Tomaszów Lubelski, Kapitan Kawa once again addressed Brygada Salon with a great deal of authority. Tall, with a handlebar moustache, he looked every bit the veteran of an earlier war.

"Your work," stressed Kapitan Kawa, *"will be in the Powiat of Lubaczow. It is there that the beautiful Polish countryside is littered with too many of those war-mongering Ukrainians. The war is quickly coming to an end. Soon, we will not have to contend with the Nazis. However, the Ukrainian underground soldiers will continue to operate. Bad luck for them. Not only will they have to contend with Armija Krajowa but also with our unit, Brygada Salon."*

Kapitan Kawa was no stranger to the manner in which a military unit operated. This was why he did not hesitate to repeat instructions so that mistakes could be minimized. In the process, he was also well aware that certain questions would be raised, questions that he anticipated and was more than willing and ready to answer.

"Armija Krajowa does not want any unit to operate in its home base. This is why Brygada Salon will not operate in Gmina Tomaszów Lubelski. We need troops from outside this region, a nationalistic unit that will not hesitate to burn Ukrainian homes and kill a few of them, if necessary. This is why we are creating Brygada Salon with members from other regions."

Kapitan Kawa was aware that there was no policy to govern the composition of a Polish nationalistic unit. If necessary or expedient, other members could be added to the brigade at any time. After all, what young Pole would not hold a war veteran in high regard and serve the national will of the people, especially in light of the atrocities committed by the Nazis and Ukrainian nationalistic groups in the province of Volhynia.

Although it may have been true that the Red Army was intent upon eradicating partisan groups and nationalistic units, this did not mean that they were having any success. In addition, the Soviet Union's attempt to transfer Ukrainians from Poland to Soviet Ukraine in a peaceful and orderly manner was meeting with considerable resistance.

"Next week," explained Kapitan Kawa, *"Brygada Salon will begin its operations. I will provide you with a list of Ukrainian villages that you will attack and burn to the ground, if necessary. You must eliminate any Ukrainian who interferes with your work."*

"Won't this mission be dangerous?" enquired Wiktor Wozniak.

"Yes, of course, your mission will be dangerous. Many Ukrainians are well armed and many will be protecting their property. They will be reluctant to leave Poland. You will also have to keep an eye out for units of the Ukrainian Insurgent Army operating south and west of this region. Ukrainian nationalists are of great concern to Armija Krajowa."

"Kapitan, are you referring to Stepan Bandera's cutthroats?"

"Yes, Adam, Bandera is a dangerous criminal, a soldier who is leading the anti-Polish crusade. Bandera and the UPA began a deliberate campaign of murdering Polish civilians in 1943, particularly in Volhynia. In retaliation for burning dozens of Polish villages, the Polish Home Army killed thousands of Ukrainians in Volhynia."

In considering the mission of Brygada Salon, Kapitan Kawa wanted to make sure that the unit was made aware of the pitfalls and the obstacles to success.

"Remember, this region will soon be occupied by the Soviet Red Army and the Soviets will work hard to disband Polish partisans. This is why our operation will be underground. I want each of you to commit to memory all I have to say. Do not carry any incriminating notes. Just carry your identification as a resident of Tomaszów Lubelski. You will travel as one unit, a low-level, quiet, and efficient brigade. All of your work will take place in Gmina Narol."

"Kapitan Kawa," interjected an impatient Wiktor Wozniak, *"there is no shortage of Ukrainians in the town of Lutsk either. Some of them have been murdering our brothers since the outbreak of the war. But there are also many honest Ukrainians who respect all Poles."*

"Never mind your sweet talk about Ukrainians in Lutsk, Wiktor. Forget about your place of birth and those lawless Ukrainians. Your job will be to make sure that the Ukrainians living in the Gmina Narol leave for Soviet Ukraine, one way or another."

Kapitan Kawa knew that his first task was to address and then gain control of the members of Brygada Salon. With this objective in mind he spent a considerable amount of time explaining why the brigade would soon be assigned a special mission. Quietly but in earnest, the brigade discussed the horrors perpetrated upon Poles by Ukrainians, Russians, and Germans in the Oblast of Volhynia. In preparation for their mission, Kapitan Kawa was duty-bound to perform a special ceremony.

Polish partisans (soldiers in Armija Krajowa) taking the oath of allegiance in Volhynia during the winter of 1944—procedures similar to those followed by members of Brygada Salon in Zamosc, Poland.

"I want each of you to take an oath of allegiance to Armija Krajowa and the new nation of Poland. It is true that you are not officially in Poland's Home Army. However, the work that I want you to undertake will be for the honour of our nation. You will represent the hopes and aspirations of our nation. Now stand at attention and remove your caps. Place your right hand over your heart and repeat each phrase after me. When finished with the oath, I want each of you to warmly embrace each other. Repeat after me:

I swear to the Polish land and to the Polish Nation that to the last drop of my blood, to the last breath shall I hate the enemy, the German who destroyed Poland. To the last drop of my blood, to the last breath shall I fight for the liberation of my Fatherland. Only then can I live and die as a rightful and honest soldier of Poland. So help me God!"

After the oath of allegiance, Kapitan Kawa impressed upon the members that their mission would be a very serious one. Each was asked to keep secret the mission and to discuss their duties only with members of the unit.

"In a couple of days we will discuss and define your special duties. Tomorrow is Sunday," continued Kapitan Kawa, *"I want each of you to attend Sunday Mass. We will need the Lord's blessing for the work we are about to undertake."*

After a long pause, Adam Krawczyk put words to an important concern, *"Kapitan Kawa, if we undertake work that will bring harm to another human being, will God forgive us?"*

"Yes, God lives within the soul of every Polish citizen. God will honour the wish of our government. Our government-in-exile in London wants all Ukrainians deported east of the Curzon Line. During this resettlement campaign, all eligible individuals will be required to register with local district commissions. These commissions are set up in several locations. You will concern yourself with only two population transfer locations, Jaroslaw and Lubaczow."

As promised, the day following the oath of allegiance, the members of the brigade did attend Sunday Mass. Once again in their secret location, they were anxious to get on with their duties. To emphasize his expectations of the brigade, Kapitan Kawa took out a map of the Powiat of Lubaczow.

"Most of the peasants living in Gmina Narol," explained Kapitan Kawa, *"are those stupid, stubborn Ukrainians. The villages that you will attack may be home to some Poles but the majority of them will be Ukrainians. The County of Lubaczow contains three towns, Cieszanow, Oleszce, and Narol. Do not undertake any activity in any of these towns. Leave that to the Polish Home Army. Start with the villages of Huta Różaniecka and Ruda Różaniecka. Undertake some reconnaissance work. The starosta in each village will give the Ukrainians two hours to leave the village. Use the means we discussed to remove all traces of Ukrainians."*

Even as Kapitan Kawa fired up the members of Brygada Salon, he was also aware that Polish authorities, with the assistance from the NKVD, had already put out a directive as to who was eligible for resettlement and what property they were able to take with them. The job of Brygada Salon was to expedite the process.

"Your role will be a military one," explained Kawa. *"This notion of registering and helping Ukrainians get the hell out of our country will be the role of the Soviets and our provisional government in London. Armija*

Krajowa has informed me that Ukrainians who are required to register for resettlement are identified by ethnicity and not their country of birth."

"When I lived with my family in Polonka," explained Myron Mora with a great deal of anger in his voice, *"the Russians hated the Poles. Even some of the Ukrainians in our village hated the Poles. I heard that the Russian soldiers changed into the uniforms of bandits and wandered into Polish villages where they encouraged all Poles to immediately leave for Poland."*

"And if they did not immediately leave the Oblast of Volhynia, what happened then," asked Kapitan Kawa, *"were they kind and gentle while kicking Poles out of Volhynia?"*

Wanting to make certain that every member of Brygada Salon was aware of the atrocities and horrific crimes committed by the UPA on the Polish civil population, Kapitan Kawa summarized his argument.

"The policy of UPA in the Subcarpathian Voivodeship was to liquidate all Polish traces. They destroyed the walls of our Catholic Kościoły and Polish prayer houses. They destroyed orchards and trees in the courtyards so that there was no trace that someone lived there. It is now our turn to teach the Ukrainians a lesson or two."

"You don't believe, Kapitan Kawa," interjected Igor Kawa, *"that it was the Germans who burned the Polish villages? Maybe even the Russians?"*

"Sure, the Germans and Russians may have had a hand in the killings. But now, as we look into the future, it is the Ukrainians who want our land. The war is nearly over. The Germans will soon be routed. The Russian Army will leave after the war; however, the Ukrainians will want to remain."

"I know this to be true," thoughtfully added Myron Mora, *"because this happened in Polonka. Our Ukrainian neighbour was heard to say that when something remains that is Polish the Poles will have pretensions to the land. Ukrainians murdered the Poles who did not want to leave Volhynia. The shoe will now be on the other foot."*

"I want to reinforce that this is why the Ukrainians torched our villages," argued Kapitan Kawa. *"They axed or crucified our Roman Catholic priests and burned our churches with all their parishioners inside. Those Ukrainian criminals even attacked isolated Polish farms with pitchforks and knives. They did not hesitate to cut throats and bayonet pregnant women. Worst of all, they killed our young children and ambushed our brothers in the fields. They wanted to make sure that the future of Volynia would be a future without Poles."*

If it was the intent of Kapitan Kawa to prepare the brigade for retribution on Ukrainians in Gmina Narol, his passionate speech exceeded all expectations. On the other hand, what Kawa did not tell his troops was that many Ukrainians living in Poland during the interwar years truly believed that they were being forcefully pacified by the Polish government. They, too, had a bone to pick. In fact, many hoped for the emergence of an independent Ukrainian nation.

Ukrainians were well aware that elements within the Polish government went to extremes to eradicate any element of Ukrainian culture among those Ukrainians living in Galicia. The Ukrainian language was banned, Ukrainian books burned, and libraries closed. Ukrainian national dress elements were forbidden in any remote form. One such rumour was that young people caught speaking Ukrainian amongst themselves were hung for their crime as an example to others. This was supposed to pacify the population, kill the Ukrainian soul, and Polonize the people. While many people complied as a way to survive, at least publicly, this did not breed love between Poles and Ukrainians.

"Kapitan Kawa," ventured Wiktor Wozniak, *"my girlfriend is an ethnic Ukrainian. She often said to me that being Ukrainian was not easy under Polish or Russian rule. Both Poles and Russians wanted to eradicate any element of a Ukrainian ethnicity with equal fervour. Life in Polonka was especially hard when those German butchers controlled the area. I very much support the objective of removing Ukrainians from this region but I am not in favour of killing Ukrainians."*

"Yes, Wiktor, we understand that among us live many Ukrainians of good heart. The goal of our government, however, is to secure our lands by getting rid of all Ukrainians, by making sure that Ukrainians leave Poland."

"Kapitan Kawa, I know that those Poles who did not want to leave Volhynia were threatened with death. Many Poles were shot. Many homes were set ablaze and those caught inside were burned to death. Thank God I left Polonka when I did," added Myron Mora.

"Yes," explained Kapitan Kawa, *"the Polish government has legislation in place to deal with the transfer of Poles from Volhynia to Poland. Fortunately, you boys left Volhynia before this legislation came into effect. Otherwise, you might have been butchered just like your brothers and sisters were butchered and burned to death by those lawless Ukrainians."*

Although Brygada Salon would have preferred to work with a population transfer commission closer to their home base, this was not to be. It was the decision of Kapitan Kawa to stay away from a local commission where preferred treatment might have been extended to Ukrainians and to work with commissions farther to the west. The function of the commissions, staffed with Polish communists and Soviet personnel, was to register, co-ordinate, and facilitate the transfer of individuals and to conduct propaganda work among the target population. The Polish Government was of the opinion that Ukrainians should be told that living conditions in Soviet Ukraine were far better than were those in Poland. In this way, the government of Poland would have some assurance that Ukrainians would want to leave Poland voluntarily and not hide out in the forest until the war was over. The mission of Brygada Salon was to make sure that they left immediately.

"If they don't leave immediately," warned Kapitan Kawa, *"fire a couple of warning shots over their stupid heads. Then burn their homes and barns. If they still don't leave, shoot them, but do not harm the animals."*

Brygada Salon was well aware that many of the residents in the targeted villages were bilingual. This made their mission all the more difficult. Not wanting to harm Poles, the brigade had the added responsibility of finding out in advance of their attack which homes were truly Polish and which homes belonged to Ukrainians. Despite these important considerations, their task was to make sure that the target villages on their list were cleansed of every Ukrainian man, woman, and child.

"Once again," stressed Kapitan Kawa, *"it will be useful for your unit to identify the village starosta in each village. The village elder will then tell the Ukrainians that your unit does not want to kill Ukrainians. However, any Ukrainian remaining in the village after two hours will be shot on the spot and their homes, barns, and farm buildings burned to the ground."*

With these arguments, Brygada Salon became fully convinced that ethnic Ukrainians had been a blight upon their land for too long. The Commander of Home Army assured Kapitan Kawa that provisions had been made for Ukrainians living in Gmina Narol to take their personal belongings to Lubaczow or Jaroslaw, at which point they had three options—exit Poland by train, horse-drawn wagon, or on foot.

"The last thing we want," explained Kapitan Kawa, *"is for the Russian Empire to rise again. I hope that the Ukrainians will not hate Poles so much as to help Russia attain its goals. This is why it is so important that we remove all Ukrainians from our land. By removing the Ukrainians, we will also neutralize the Russians. Remember, the Ukrainians are a very religious*

lot. They gather at their dilapidated little churches for their Holy Days of Obligation."

Kapitan Kawa was aware that most Ukrainian Greek Catholic religious days of obligation were similar to those of the Polish Roman Catholic Church. As a result, the brigade discussed the inherent advantages of confronting Ukrainian parishioners on their special days of religious celebrations. Of particular interest were the Ukrainian celebrations of Easter, the birth of John the Baptist in June, the Annunciation of the Mother of God in July, and especially the Day of Exaltation of the Holy Cross celebrated in September. These, surmised Kawa, would be the days of religious holidays during which Ukrainians would attend their church. Some would come to church to worship while others would come to seek refuge from roving nationalistic units. It was the plan of Brygada Salon to attack the parishioners before they entered the sanctuary of the church or immediately after they left the church.

Although Kapitan Kawa did not spell out precisely what Brygada Salon would do in such situations, his tone and gestures left no question in the minds of the members of the brigade.

"There is one other important matter for Brygada Salon," continued Kapitan Kawa, *"our unit cannot operate without a leader. Igor Kawa, I want you to lead Brygada Salon. Are there any objections to this selection?"*

Noting that there were no objections, Kapitan Kawa continued, *"Under the leadership of Corporal Kawa, your first task will be to take up residence in the town of Narol. You will take your rifles, ammunition, and supplies. For transport, you will have a small army vehicle and sufficient funds for your operation. In addition, I plan to make several military-trained horses available to you."*

"Kapitan Kawa," asked the newly-anointed Corporal Kawa, *"where will we live when we are in Narol?"*

"You will contact Karol Korsyk in Narol. I have alerted him that you are coming to undertake a special mission. The Korsyk family will look after your needs."

In further planning for their duties, the question of the condition of the roads to the small villages was brought up. Although a truck was made available to Kapitan Kawa, he preferred the use of military-trained horses, horses that were regularly reviewed at local fairs and the best breeders rewarded.

"I can tell you this," pointed out a proud Kapitan Kawa in support of using horses, *"the Polish campaign of September 1939 counted fifteen*

significant cavalry actions. My brothers claimed twelve victories, including successful breakout attempts against these murdering Nazis. I am most proud to have served Poland in that campaign!"

The first problem encountered by the Brygada Salon was one of acquiring weapons. Using heavy army equipment was out of question. The unit looked upon itself as being an infantry unit that would require no more than light arms. Mostly, these arms came from arms caches that had been buried by the Polish armies on battlefields after the 1939 invasion of Poland. In the meantime, other brigades were able to acquire arms from the Germans and their allies, or arms manufactured clandestinely by the Home Army itself. Efforts to capture weapons from the Germans proved highly successful. Raids were conducted on trains carrying equipment to the front as well as on guardhouses and gendarmerie posts.

"Keep in mind," advised Kapitan Kawa, *"that Gmina Narol is an urban-rural region in Lubaczow County. Its seat is the town of Narol, which lies approximately 26 kilometres north-east of Lubaczow. The population of the gmina, with numerous Ukrainian villages, is about eight thousand."*

Brygada Salon was aware that Ukrainian partisans were operating out of the densely forested areas of Gmina Narol. Of particular concern was the matter of coming into contact with well-trained Ukrainian partisans from Sanok and the Carpathian Mountains. While undertaking their attacks upon the Ukrainian villages, Brygada Salon would, of necessity, have to keep an eye out for these UPA units. The villages of Huta Różaniecka, Ruda Różaniecka, Lowcza, Płazów, and Grochi were now clearly in the gun sights of the brigade.

"Why have you selected these villages for destruction, Kapitan?" asked Corporal Kawa.

"These villages, Corporal, are the villages that have a high concentration of ethnic Ukrainians. Your work will have to do with making sure that the Ukrainians leave their homes forever. If and when necessary, you have the support of Armija Krajowa to burn their homes, their barns, and their farm buildings."

Just as the members of Brygada Salon were about to disband for the day, Kapitan Kawa stopped them. What he had to say surprised them.

"From now on, you will never, ever, use your Christian names. You will always refer to each other using a fictitious name to protect your identity. My operational name will be Kapitan Kon."

"So, Kapitan, from now on you will be known as a horse?"

"Yes, that is it, a well-trained military horse. You can simply refer to me as Kapitan."

"Have you a brigade name for each of us, Kapitan?"

"Yes, I have prepared operational names for each of you. Wiktor Wozniak, from now on you will be known as Wilk (Wolf), Corporal Igor Kawa as Kula (Bullet), Myron Mora as Puma (Cougar), and Adam Krawczyk as Lew (Lion)."

"This means," noted Corporal Igor Kawa, "that Brygada Salon will now consist of a wolf, a bullet, a cougar, and a lion, all led by a horse!"

"Yes, yes," confirmed Kapitan Kon impatiently, "practice these operational names. Commit them to memory."

That evening, the members of Brygada Salon had great difficulty falling asleep. Each drew upon his past experiences with visions of the tasks that lay ahead. Unfortunately, they were young men who never served in the military. In a way, they were innocent of war. Their mission was particularly troublesome for Wilk. He could not get out of his mind his love for Tanja, realizing all the while that he would not be alive today were it not for her intervention.

Soon, Brygada Salon would set out on a reign of terror, a reign of terror that would impact countless Ukrainians. They would be joined by other Polish nationalistic bands. Many Ukrainian villages would be selected for destruction and many Ukrainians would lose their lives at the hands of this and other nationalistic groups. As for Wilk, his feelings would play themselves out in a shocking way, testimony to the belief that reality is sometimes stranger than fiction.

The work of Brygada Salon would soon be undertaken without regard for human suffering and loss. Countless combatants would perish during World War II. That is to be expected. What was not expected is that even during the war, ethnic conflicts did break out, adding considerably to the mortality rate.

PART 6

UKRAINIANS GET THE BOOT

12

Narol In The Crosshairs

"We must cleanse Gmina Narol of all Ukrainians, by force if necessary…"

K apitan Kon had difficulty suppressing a smile just thinking about a rosy future for his beloved Poland. Somehow, he knew that the message he had in his pocket from Armija Krajowa headquarters would be of great significance. In order to achieve its political objective of relocating Ukrainians living in Eastern Poland to Soviet Ukraine, the Polish government was about to abandon its relatively benign character of the relocation policy in favour of a more aggressive approach.

The very first line of the communiqué did not disappoint, *"Poland's campaign to resettle Ukrainians will now enter a new phase."* Unfortunately, the earlier plan met with significant resistance. Most Ukrainians did not want to abandon their ancestral lands and resettle in Soviet Ukraine. To accelerate the process, Polish and Soviet security forces were about to be deployed. At the same time, Polish authorities began to conduct mass arrests of local Ukrainian elites, usually clergy, and applied a variety of coercive measures to pressure families and individuals to relocate to Soviet Ukraine.

Once again gathered in a secret location at the outskirts of the town of Tomaszów Lubelski, the four members of Brygada Salon, Wiktor Wozniak *(Wilk)*, Igor Kawa *(Kula)*, Myron Mora *(Puma)*, and Adam Krawczyk *(Lew)* were most anxious to hear what the leader of their brigade had to say. The late fall day of 1943 had finally arrived when an action plan would be put into place. That the brigade was rather small in membership did not in any way diminish its enthusiasm or importance. Whatever the plan, it would have dire consequences for several Ukrainian villages and their families living in Gmina Narol. At precisely eight in the morning, Kapitan Kon convened the meeting with a short prayer and, in his ever optimistic way, restated the Oath of Allegiance to the emerging nation of Poland. Before getting down to the business of the day, Kapitan Kon wanted to first brag about his earlier exploits.

"When the war broke out, our cavalry unit had a remarkable victory near Tomaszów Lubelski. The cavalry unit laid waste to a German Schutzstaffel Garrison in a daring, well-executed attack, eliminating over one hundred enemy soldiers. We captured a cache of weapons, liberated partisan prisoners, and headed off a planned roundup of the male population by the Gestapo, losing only three of our own men. Soon," bragged Kapitan Kon. *"Brygada Salon will be using some of those techniques and the weapons we captured from the Krauts!"*

As Brygada Salon set out on its 17-kilometre trip from Tomaszów Lubelski to Narol, they could not help but notice the peculiar colour of the sky. Perhaps it was the Red Army's attack on Nazi positions near Warsaw which resulted in the formation of dense clouds from the explosions of munitions and the entrails of the flight of dozens of military aircraft undertaking hundreds of bombing missions. That the battle lines were far removed from Tomaszów Lubelski did not mean that the atmosphere would not be polluted through these military actions. Somehow, it seemed as all of this was a harbinger of things to come.

In many ways, Brygada Salon could not have picked a better time to set out for Narol. Although the Nazis still controlled the Lublin region of Poland in August of 1943, there was also some good news. The Red Army had just defeated the Nazi forces in the Tank Battle at Kursk as well as at the Battle of Kharkov. Feeling more confident with every victory, the Red Army was about to engage the Nazis in the Battle of Smolensk. These major battles challenged to the extremes the very core of the Nazi military. On this day, it seemed as though the whole of the region was left to the operation of either the roving Polish gangs or the Ukrainian nationalistic units. Kapitan Kon was anxious to present his final instructions to Brygada Salon.

"Your first task will be to take up residence in the town of Narol. Take your rifles, ammunition, and supplies. For transport, you will have a small Russian-made military vehicle, four military-trained horses, and sufficient

funds for your operation. This truck has been used on all war fronts. Once in Narol, you will contact Pan Karol Korsyk. He is a military associate and I have alerted him that your brigade is coming. He will look after your needs."

"The hell you say, Kapitan Kon. Look at that monstrosity. Swinia. What a pig. That ugly Russian workhorse has no front bumper," observed *Lew.*

"This truck," explained Kapitan *Kon "is of basic construction. Sure, the wings are flat and the foot boards are made of wood but the motor runs fine. You will have to watch the brakes. They were removed from the front wheels and the beast has no tail lights. It was greatly appreciated for its remarkably simple and reliable construction. You will need some firepower for your work. I commandeered the use of six Russian-made bolt-action rifles. They have been used successfully as sniper rifles for a very long time."*

"Dammit," complained Wilk, *"bolt-action rifles sound like a piece of końskie gówno, a piece of horse shit to me. Can't we get something more modern? Even my revolver is better. What about Kalashnikov rifles? What about the cache of weapons your cavalry unit confiscated from the German Waffen-SS garrison? Only a dupak would use a Russian bolt-action rifle!"*

"Stop complaining, Wilk. Yes, we did capture a cache of weapons. But Armija Krajowa needs all of those weapons for other very important partisan units. Getting the six rifles was difficult enough. Getting the ammunition for them was even more difficult. We now have the rifles and a sufficient number of rounds of ammunition for your use."

Finally, the brigade was ready for its first assignment. Lew and Puma took care of the horses while Wilk and Kula elected to take charge of the truck. But to everyone's surprise, the truck refused to cooperate. Try as they might, they could not start the old beast. As a result, they abandoned the idea of using a truck in their operations, relying now completely on the military-trained horses. Travelling in a southerly direction from Tomaszów Lubelski, Brygada Salon reached the village of Bełżec where they planned to stay long enough for a road-side rest. According to plan, they would then travel west to the town of Narol. In mid-Bełżec, the brigade made the turn to the west, stopping long enough to talk to a curious group of local Poles. It seemed as though everyone wanted to discuss the conduct of the war. Turning to three young women exiting a small groceteria, Kula wanted to confirm that the brigade was on the right road to Narol.

"Excuse me, panienka, is this the road to Narol?"

"Yes, this is the road to Narol," responded the young woman, *"but be careful. This region is full of Ukrainian bandits and Armija Krajowa brigades."*

Kula could see that the young woman was reluctant to answer his questions. But he persisted. By this time, several more Poles gathered to listen to the conversations. All were curious about the fine-looking military-trained horses. Try as they might, they were not able to pry any information from the brigade as to the purpose of their mission.

"*Panienka,*" continued a most persistent Kula, "*you have a suitcase with you. Where are you going?*"

"*I am going home,*" replied the young woman.

"*Did you say that you were going home? Where is home?*"

"*My family lives near here. They live in the village of Płazów.*"

"*You live in Płazów? Where are you coming from?*"

"*I am coming home from Germany.*"

"*You have been to Germany? What in the world were you doing in Germany?*"

"*I was captured by the Nazi Gestapo in 1940 and forced to work in Germany for three years. I am now on my way home.*"

"*You worked in Germany during the war? How is that possible? I have never heard of anyone being released by the Nazis from slave labour.*"

"*Yes, I was one of the lucky ones. I was released by the Nazis. My family needs me.*"

"*And you say that your name is Anna? Did you say that you were replaced by another slave when the Gestapo released you in Germany?*"

"*Yes, another young girl by the name of Tanja, a very pretty Ukrainian girl.*"

"*Well, good luck to you, Anna.*"

With that, the three young women disappeared into the surrounding neighborhood. As members of Brygada Salon hurriedly ate their lunch, the conversations with the local Poles naturally turned to the government's new policy of forcibly removing all Ukrainians from the region. Lost in thought and with Tanja on his mind, Wilk was suddenly overcome with a twinge of conscience. The thought of harming Ukrainians did not sit too well with him. Resuming their journey to Narol, the unit stopped at a railway crossing at the outskirts of Bełżec. While waiting for a train to pass, the members of Brygada Salon had an opportunity to exchange a few thoughts about what they had earlier heard.

"*You know what, Wilk,*" concluded Kula, "*it is no different here than it was in Lutsk. Those damned skurwielu Nazis have been capturing young people since 1940 for work in Germany.*"

"*Tell me, Kula, you say that you met someone in the group who worked in Germany?*"

"Yes, I did, Wilk. One of the three young women that I talked to worked in Germany for three years. Her name was Anna."

"What did she have to say about her work in Germany?"

"She had very little to say about her work in Germany except to that she was coming back home to the village of Płazów. The Nazis released her from her work as an Ostarbeiter."

"Was she a Polish or a Ukrainian woman?"

"Who knows? She spoke most fluently in Polish. She said that when she left Germany she was replaced by another slave labourer, a pretty Ukrainian girl from Lutsk by the name of Tanja. If her recall of events is true, this Anna related a most interesting story."

Upon hearing the name of the girl to be Tanja, Wilk nearly fainted. Kula had all he could do to calm him down.

"She was replaced by a Ukrainian girl named Tanja from Lutsk? What else did she say about Tanja?"

"She had nothing else to say about Tanja. Why should she say anything else?"

Wilk wished that he could have asked Anna a few questions himself. However, that was not to be. The shock of hearing Tanja's name left him confused and speechless. As they were finishing their lunch, Brygada Salon was approached by a couple of local seniors, showing considerable curiosity. In hushed tones and while pointing in the easterly direction with a cane, the brigade received some startling news from an elder by the name of Konopski, news that Bełżec was the site of a German extermination camp for Jews. Although uncertain as to the exact dates of its operation, Konopski thought that the camp operated from 1942 to 1943.

"I know that this information is not a rumour," explained Konopski. *"I witnessed many trains pulling into Bełżec fully loaded with Jews crying out in pain for water. Thousands upon thousands of Jews were murdered in the extermination camp. At the same time, the Germans warned the locals to stay away from the camp. It was under constant guard by the Nazis who said that anyone caught near the camp would be shot."*

"Why is there so little evidence of this tragic event?" questioned Wilk.

"No matter how much time those sons-of-bitches tried to cover up their dastardly deeds, they were not able to hide all of the evidence from observant villagers," added Konopski's friend. *"One day the world will learn about what happened to the Jews in this region."*

It was in October, 1941, that Heinrich Himmler gave the German Waffen-SS an order to start Germanizing all those living in Gmina Zamosc. In order to accomplish this, he planned to exterminate all the

Jews living in eastern Poland. The site near Bełżec was chosen for this purpose for several reasons. Located on the border between the Lublin District and the German Distrikt Galizien, the extermination camp, according to the SS, would be able to process the Jews from both regions. The ease of transportation was secured by the railroad junction located near Rawa Ruska and by the highways between Lublin and Lemberg. According to Konopski's friend, the extermination camp operated by using Polish villagers, Ukrainian guards, and Jewish slave workers.

"Good Lord," asked a curious and shocked Puma, *"do you mean to tell us that the Jews were gassed to death? Kurwa!"*

"Yes, they were all murdered. The carbon monoxide gas from the exhaust fumes of a large diesel engine, contained in an enclosed space, was very poisonous. The poisonous gas quickly killed the Jews."

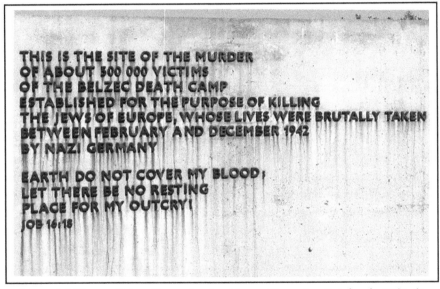

Memorial Plaque, Belzec Extermination Camp, Operation Reinhard, 1942-43.

The members of Brygada Salon could not get what they had heard out of their minds. What made the news even more startling was Konopski's statement that the German soldiers serving the Waffen-SS Squadron under Himmler pledged loyalty to Adolf Hitler and to him alone. In serving the Nazi protection squadron they also took a secondary oath—*obedience unto death!* This explained, according to Konopski, a veteran of World War I himself, why the Waffen-SS was so feared by everyone.

By late afternoon Brygada Salon reached the town of Narol, nestled deep within a Polish state forest. Upon meeting Pan Korsyk, a well-known resident of the town home to nearly two thousand residents, the first order of business was to inform the brigade about the community. To the surprise of the brigade, Pan Korsyk was most intent about extending a warning and some advice to Brygada Salon.

"Be aware," stated Korsyk, *"that the castle at the outskirts of Narol housed a small German Wehrmacht detachment. The Nazis recently lost control this region to the Red Army. It looks like this region will soon be under the complete control of the Soviets. We are located in the midst of a major state forest making it a most dangerous region for armed conflict. Stay away from the castle and always keep an eye out for Ukrainian partisans and Polish nationalistic units."*

"What about our accommodation and meals, Pan Korsyk?"

"You will be on your own for meals. You can purchase your daily needs at the local rynek; the food market. Kapitan Kon asked me to tell you about the various Ukrainian settlements and villages in Gmina Narol. All of these villages are accessible by military horses. Your first mission will be to identify all Ukrainian families living in the village of Płazów. You will frighten the shit out of them so that they will want to get the hell out of Poland. By using military-trained horses, you will not have to worry about the condition of the roads to the villages of Płazów, Huta Różaniecka, Ruda Różaniecka, and Łówcza."

That night, the members of Brygada Salon retreated into slumberland. Each accepted that their murderous mission was justified by events that took place the previous year in the Oblast of Volhynia. It was there that the Poles paid a very high price for their prewar policies towards Ukrainians. The Poles, on the other hand, were of a different mind. They felt that their administrative policies were fully justified. Unfortunately, it was now the turn of Ukrainians living in Gmina Narol to experience the wrath of nationalistic Poles.

The next morning, the Korsyks served coffee and freshly-baked bread to members of Brygada Salon. *"I see,"* observed Pan Korsyk, *"that your brigade consists of only four members. Would you be interested in having another soldier from Armija Krajowa, presently stationed in Narol, join you?"*

Realizing that their brigade might well be able to use a military-trained soldier, Kula invited Starszy Strzelec (*Lance Corporal Rifles*)

Michal Komarski to join them with the proviso that Pan Korsyk would provide an additional military-trained horse.

"I know this region well," explained Corporal Michal Komarski, *"I can be of great help in planning Brygada's attack on local villages and settlements."*

"Good. Very good," commented Kula. *"You will first have to take the oath of allegiance to our Fatherland."*

Once the oath was administered, Kapitan Kula decided to provide Corporal Komarski with a pseudonym.

"Michal, your code name while serving in this brigade will be Karabin (Rifle). From now on you shall refer to each of us by our code names only. In turn, we shall call you only by your code name. Now that you have taken the Oath of Allegiance, please embrace each member of our group."

"Thank you, Corporal Kula. I feel honoured to be a part of this special brigade."

"Corporal Karabin, you know the general plan of our operation. Where do you suggest that we start with the cleansing process?"

"I would suggest that we start in the village of Płazów. The village is near Narol. This would be a good place to start because I know a person in Płazów who would be of great help to Brygada Salon."

"You are recommending a contact in Płazów? Who is this contact, Karabin?" asked Corporal Kula.

"He is a nationalist, a medical doctor by the name of Voljanchuk. For whatever reason, he has come to hate Ukrainians. It is true that his father was a Ukrainian and his mother a Pole. However, he is now very hostile to the Ukrainian people and does not have any mercy for them."

"Can we trust this Voljanchuk? After all, he is an ethnic Ukrainian, is he not? Shouldn't he have taken the language and the ethnicity of his father?"

"You need not worry about Voljanchuk. Brygada Salon can trust him."

When the members of Brygada Salon met Voljanchuk, they could immediately see the importance of having someone join them who knew something about the local villages.

"Płazów," explained Doctor Voljanchuk, *"is a village in Gmina Narol in the administrative district of Lubaczow. This picturesque village has been a part of Poland for a very long time. It is located in the so-called Zakersonskiy Land, the territory of Ukrainian lands which were given to Poland after World War I. It lies in the intersection of four directions, Horynets, Ruda Różaniecka, Lubaczow, and Tomaszów Lubelski."*

"*Doctor Voljanchuk, do you believe,*" asked Kula, "*that the Poles will support our mission? Is it important for our brigade to get rid of those Ukrainians once and for all?*"

"*Yes, we want to make all villages completely and totally Polish. The village of Płazów once had the status of a town. A long time ago it was destroyed by the Turks and Tatars. Unfortunately, the village has become inhabited by too many Ukrainians. Poles also live here, but too few of them. The River Plazivka served as a border between the Ukrainians and Poles.*"

"*When they lived apart from each other, did they live in peace? Did Polish and Ukrainian children attend the same school?*" asked a curious Wilk.

"*Yes, they did live apart from each other at one time and, yes, all the children of the village attended the same school. Płazów has a Ukrainian Catholic Church, a Roman Catholic Church, and a synagogue, as the Hebrews also live here. Well, the Hebrews once lived here. They are now gone.*"

"*Doctor, what do you mean that the Jews once lived here? What happened to them?*"

"*Well, they did live here until last year. The Germans gathered all of them and sent them to Bełżec. Rumour has it that they were exterminated. That has solved one problem for us.*"

"*Why was their synagogue destroyed? Why were the Jews murdered in Bełżec?*"

"*Who knows? You will have to ask the Nazis, ci mordercy, those murderers.*"

"*Doctor, is there anything else we should know about the history of Płazów?*"

"*People who lived in prewar Płazów lived peacefully. There were many mixed marriages. The villagers celebrated their religious holidays together. When the Ukrainian Bishop from Przemysl came to consecrate the Ukrainian Greek Catholic Church to God, the Hebrews first met him as their synagogue was the first place on his way to Płazów. The Bishop then came to the Polish community and blessed them. Their church was then consecrated according to the Greek Catholic Ceremony. Peace and understanding reigned among the people.*"

"*And, so, what has changed today?*"

"*Sure, before the war we had small problems. The Polish government did not hire Jews. That's why they went into commerce where they could be independent. The Jews created a market on Monday and Tuesday where they sold all kinds of goods. The Jews bought from the farmer, took the stuff to*" *the market, and sold it at a profit. If someone was sick or in trouble the Jews collected money for him. The villagers looked after one another."*

"Now the Nazis are killing the Jews. Why?"

"World War II has changed everything. In Eastern Poland, those damn Russians killed or deported all the Polish community leaders. The Ukrainians are no different. They burned Polish villages and killed Poles without regard for gender or age."

"Is it true Doctor Voljanchuk that Stalin wants all Ukrainians in Płazów to register and leave? Is it your understanding that many do not want to leave? Should we burn the houses of those who do not want to leave and kill only those who show any resistance?"

From Doctor Voljanchuk, Brygada Salon learned that war brought disagreement and hate to Płazów. Right after the German attack on the Soviet Union the troubles began. Young working people were sent to work in Germany. The Poles opposed losing their young people to work in Germany. In some cases, the Nazis were helped by the Ukrainians who wanted their lands back. In 1942, it was the Poles who helped the Gestapo round up young Ukrainian girls. Many Poles were opposed to this policy and hid out in the nearby forest. Those who ran away and were caught by the Nazis were sent off to concentration camps in Germany as punishment.

Numerous tragic things also happened in the nearby villages of Ruda Różaniecka and Huta Różaniecka. The Nazis refused to allow the Poles to bury their dead in the cemetery in Płazów. They had to bury them in the nearby forest. After such acts by the German administration, friction between Ukrainians and Poles escalated.

"Is this the reason," asked Corporal Kula, *"that you, Doctor Voljanchuk, want to get even with the Ukrainians? That you want to do this even though the Ukrainians living in Płazów defended the Polish families before the Nazis? Even though they pleaded with the Germans, telling them that the local Poles did not take up arms against them?"*

"Of course," confirmed Doctor Voljanchuk, *"the Poles are very thankful for the assistance received from many Ukrainians. However, much of this good will was lost because of nationalistic Ukrainians who formed underground organizations."*

"Are these nationalistic bandits operating in this region?" asked Corporal Kula.

"Yes, they are. Headed by Ivan Maczaj, the underground organization set out to fight the Poles and to rid this land of all Poles. In 1943, Płazów

was occupied by the soldiers of OUN. Those bandits, with the help of a local Ukrainian by the name of Stepan Mykhailovych and his unit, agreed to do this."

"Did those Ukrainian murderers succeed in their mission?" asked Kula.

"No, OUN did not succeed, thanks to the Germans who occupied this region in 1941. In turn, those bloody Nazis are being pushed out of eastern Poland all the way to Warsaw. This is why the OUN bandits had no real opportunity to succeed."

"Well," concluded Kula, *"the Polish Nation's turn has come to rid this territory of all Ukrainians. It is time to burn their homes and villages, if we have to."*

"By the way, Doctor Voljanchuk," ventured Wilk, *"we met a young woman in Bełżec by the name of Anna. She said that she was coming back from Germany after having served as a slave for three years. Have you heard of her? Do you know who she might be?"*

"Hell, man, there are many girls by the name of Anna. Dozens with that name ended up in Germany. These girls are still probably working in Germany," responded Doctor Voljanchuk.

"These girls are still in Germany?"

"Who knows? Many of them were kidnapped by the Gestapo after the Nazis occupied this region in 1939. They are all probably slaving away in Germany. Maybe this Anna that you talk about is no longer living."

Deep in thought, Wilk didn't know what to make of his chances of ever meeting Anna. In the end, he had to admit that it was not so much about Kula meeting Anna but the nonchalant manner in which Anna had mentioned Tanja. Wilk kicked himself for being distracted during the moment when Kula entered into a brief conversation with Anna in Bełżec.

All too soon, the answers would come to Wilk. And yes, they would shock him to the very core and bring into question the very purpose of Brygada Salon's mission.

13

Torching Ukrainian Villages

"Quick, let's make a dash for the protection of the forest!"

Robert Burns, a well-known Scottish poet once penned the famous words, *"The best laid plans of men and mice often go awry. No matter how carefully a project is planned, something may still go wrong with it."* The words of Robert Burns could be applied to this story.

It was their first evening in Narol and the soldiers of Brygada Salon were looking forward to a good night's sleep, a good night's sleep, that is, until an important message was delivered to them by Karol Korsyk. Opening the sealed envelope, Corporal Kula immediately noted that the message was signed by Kapitan Kon. He knew that the letter would contain important information.

"Corporal Kula, Brygada Salon is hereby ordered to immediately return to your home base. Emerging events call for a change in your first assignment. You will leave behind your weapons and horses in the care of Pan Korsyk. Once again, this is an order, Signed, Kapitan Kon."

Early the next morning, the members of Brygada Salon left their rifles and ammunition in the care of Pan Korsyk and immediately returned to Tomaszów Lubelski. Kapitan Kon did not mince his words.

"Our plans to hasten the departure of those stubborn Ukrainians this fall will have to wait until the spring of next year. Those murdering Nazis are planning to colonize the Zamosc region with German settlers. We must help Armija Krajowa put a stop to those bastards."

"Kapitan Kon," enquired Corporal Kula, *"is it your decision to have Brygada Salon act as a Polish partisan unit during the winter months and attack those German settlers?"*

"Yes, Corporal Kula, Brygada Salon will attack railway lines and any and all German communications lines. You will place explosive devices on rail tracks. You will assassinate a few German settlers. We want to discourage the Nazi murderers from taking over our land. While on this mission, all of your needs will be provided by Armija Krajowa."

"How many settlers is Hitler planning to bring to this region?"

"The rumour is that the Germans plan to bring at least 60,000 ethnic Germans to this region by the end of 1943. They want to remove our brothers and sisters and replace them with their own ilk. Your job will be to help Armija Krajowa put a stop to this invasion."

Local people resisted the action with great determination. They escaped into forests and organised self-defence units, helped people who were expelled, and bribed kidnapped children out of German hands. This is why Brygada Salon, with support of Armija Krajowa, got involved in trying to stop the German settlement. Polish partisan units assaulted German colonists and forces in the Zamosc region from December, 1943, until the autumn of 1944. The resistance forces numbered several thousand citizens and forest firefighters. After several battles between the partisans and the German units, the Germans had to halt the action. In the end, very few German settlers were successfully brought to the area.

During the same period of time, the Soviet Union organized *Operation Concerto,* a major operation composed of thousands of partisans put into action in November against railroad communications with the intention of disrupting German reinforcements and supplies for the Battle of the Dnieper. During the tenure of the campaign, the partisans, which included the actions of Brygada Salon, claimed the destruction of thousands of rails, hundreds of trains and bridges, and several Axis garrisons. According to the Soviets, over 300,000 partisans took part in the operation, killing over 53,000 German soldiers in the process.

Throughout this campaign, Kapitan Kon followed the conduct of the war. By March of 1944, he felt certain that the Nazis would soon be defeated. He listened to rumours about the Red Army's plan to launch a major attack on the Nazis with the object of destroying the German Army Group Centre. *"This operation,"* according to Armija Krajowa, *"would be followed by another offensive with the object of destroying German Army South."*

With each Soviet victory, Kapitan Kon wanted to jump up and down with joy. He felt good about the work of Brygada Salon. In his mind, it was time to re-set the clock and reinstate Brygada Salon's original mission. Early in the spring of 1944, Kapitan Kon once again called a meeting of the members of Brygada Salon. *"Soldiers,"* he declared, *"the time has come to once again set out on our mission."*

Upon returning to Narol, Karol Korsyk alerted Brygada Salon that their brigade was not the only Polish nationalistic paramilitary unit operating in the region with the sole purpose of ridding the landscape of all Ukrainians. On the other hand, no one seemed to know what unit was operating and where, not even Armija Krajowa. Communication between and among the units was minimal, leading to a total absence of any coordination, other than some feeble attempts on the part of Armija Krajowa.

As early as March, 1944, Polish partisans massacred 1,500 Ukrainians in the Chelm region of Poland alone. Seventy percent of those who were killed were women and children. In the campaign, approximately 150 villages, home to 15,000 Ukrainians, faced the so-called *retaliatory measures.* Ethnic cleansings of Ukrainians that started as early as 1942 were now in full swing. In many cases the attacks on Ukrainians occurred even when no direct orders from the Polish government-in-exile were given. These so-called *indiscriminate retaliatory measures* undertaken by Poles resulted in Ukrainian civilians being killed on sight. Retaliation also took place by proxy in several regions. For instance, upon hearing news of killings in Volhynia, Poles in Galicia would take up arms against local Ukrainians.

To pick up where they left off some four months earlier, Brygada Salon wanted an audience with Doctor Voljanchuk. By all measures, he proved to be a reliable source of information about the conduct of the war, not only in the County of Lubaczow but also in all of Poland. Being mindful of his importance, Corporal Kula listened intently to what Doctor Voljanchuk had to say about the Ukrainian-Polish conflict and the upcoming role of Brygada Salon in its mission of cleansing all Ukrainians from the settlements and villages within Gmina Narol, starting with the village of Płazów.

"Corporal Kula," pointed out Doctor Voljanchuk, *"you asked me about the attitude of Poles towards Ukrainians. As early as 1943, Polish partisans*

and nationalists warned Ukrainians that for every Polish village burned, two Ukrainian villages would be razed and for every Pole killed, two Ukrainians would be killed in their place."

"That is one crazy policy, Doctor," observed Kula, *"who in his right mind would be able to determine precisely how many villages were torched by the UPA in Volhynia or how many Poles were killed by Ukrainians?"*

"Crazy as it may sound, Corporal, this is an order issued by Colonel Babinski in the Oblast of Volhynia. He said that only children should be spared. I believe that his policy came from Adolf Hitler who stated that for every German soldier killed by the enemy, 100 villagers would be shot. I do believe that the Nazis adopted and carried out this policy."

Exacerbated by the presence of the forces of UPA, the situation in all regions across the Polish border was far more complex. The Soviet and Polish governments were in agreement that the UPA insurgents needed to be eliminated in order to facilitate the forced transfer of ethnic Ukrainians to Soviet Ukraine. Unfortunately, the transfer of Ukrainians from Polish lands to Soviet Ukraine failed to discriminate between the militant insurgents and peaceful villagers who were attacked and assaulted without reason. Ukrainian transferees faced an arduous journey to their assigned homes on the Soviet Ukraine side of the border.

Although an agreement was in place to resettle Poles living in Volhynia to Poland and Ukrainians living in Poland to Soviet Ukraine, the provisions under that agreement were not necessarily carried out. Certainly, they were not followed in Gmina Narol. In fact, even before an agreement between the Soviet Union and the Polish Committee of National Liberation was signed, numerous bands of Polish nationalists took it upon themselves to advance the removal of Ukrainians. In the process, many Ukrainians were killed and many homes were torched.

In essence, the expressed mission of Brygada Salon was tantamount to ethnic cleansing. After the retreat of the Germans and supported by the organs of Polish authority, Brygada Salon was now intent upon carrying out the genocide of entire communities. Such would soon be the fate of the villages of Płazów, Ruda Różaniecka, and Huta Różaniecka, home to a number of members of my extended family for several generations.

Once satisfied that Gmina Narol was clear of all Germans, Poles took command of community life in the villages. They began encroaching on the rights of Ukrainians who decided to stay behind with the hope of weathering the storm. Polish vigilantes began to harass Ukrainians for any manifestations of nationalist sentiment, which might include keeping portraits of Hetman Bohdan Khmelnytsky or pictures of the Ukrainian national bard, Taras Shevchenko. These attacks spread from Polish villages to isolated Ukrainian settlements.

This is how Brygada Salon was able to take on the mantle of Polish vigilantes. Their assigned task, as defined by Kapitan Kon, was to ensure that every ethnic Ukrainian left Gmina Narol, willingly or at the point of a rifle. With the help of Doctor Voljanchuk, Brygada Salon identified all the homes of Ukrainians living in Płazów. It would soon be their goal to remove them from the village. However, the initial attacks on Płazów were not undertaken by Brygada Salon but rather by other loose-knit Polish scoundrals and thieves who were more interested in personal financial gain and not independence for Poland. They stole cattle, horses, sheep, and goats from Ukrainian villagers. They took away most everything they saw.

Even before Brygada Salon arrived in Płazów, the continued persecution of Ukrainians caused many to leave their native villages and seek refuge in other places. A number of Ukrainians living in the villages of Ruda Różaniecka, Huta Różaniecka, and Płazów had already escaped into the nearby forest when attacked by marauding Polish bands. It would have been most dangerous for members of any nationalistic group to venture into the pine forest in search of the escapees.

To escape certain death, many Ukrainians took refuge in the local Greek Catholic Church in Płazów, even though they were aware that the Polish nationalistic bands liked to attack Ukrainians during religious holidays. It was a time when many Ukrainians would gather in one place to conduct religious celebrations. Those who sought the safety of the church would not leave until safe to do so and only in the darkness of night. Once leaving Płazów, many found safe haven in Łówcza, Nowe Sioło, or Gorajec.

*The Ukrainian Greek Catholic Church of Nativity of Most Holy
Mother of God, Gorajec, Poland, one of the successor churches to the
acceptance of Christianity by Grand Prince Vladimir of Kyiv, 988.*

For Ukrainian Greek Catholics living in Gmina Narol, there was no
shortage of Holy Days of Obligation upon which parishioners felt obliged
to attend church services. In accordance with the Julian calendar, they
celebrated the birth of Christ on January 7, following which nearly every
second week constituted a Most Holy Day of Obligation, a Solemn Day
of Obligation, or a Simple Holy Day of Obligation. Brygada Salon was
well aware of this and made their plans accordingly.

Most parishioners were of the opinion that trouble would not come
to their church in Płazów, especially not on the day of the celebration of
Holy Saturday. It would be the week before the celebration of Easter, the
Holy and Great Week. Through Him, the parishioners believed, that they
could receive gifts of the Holy Spirit for their benefit. However, this was
not to be. In spite of the warnings and obvious dangers, religious holidays
did bring Ukrainian believers together. Unfortunately, this provided
Polish partisans with more opportunities for ethnic cleansings.

During the celebration of the Holy Spirit of God, a member of the
Polish community burst into the Greek Catholic Church in Płazów, even
though it was most unusual for anyone to interrupt the word of God.
Shouting excitedly, it was Michal Sikora who interrupted the religious
ceremony. He had a very important message.

"People," loudly shouted Sikora, *"I give you two hours to leave Płazów. At the meeting of Voljanchuk's bandits, it was decided that they would kill all the Ukrainians this night. You can go only in the direction of the village of Łówcza. Since Poles live there, the land and village will not be under attack by Polish bandits. You will be safe there."*

Truly, it would be at that very moment that the Greek Catholic Church in Płazów would cease to function. The Catholic priest stopped the Liturgy and left the church. He would not return. The beautiful Iconostases in the church portraying a wall of icons and religious paintings would no longer serve the parish. That day, all the people who were in the church rushed home to tell their loved ones about such impending trouble. They also told their neighbours and all those living in the village about the ultimatum. Many fussed over the news. *What to do?*

Some people took their most precious belongings, their children, and any cattle not already confiscated by the bandits, and left their village by horse-drawn carts. In their minds, they felt that the forest would provide some protection. Others who did not have horses, ran away through the forest in the direction of Łówcza. Some did not believe, however, that something bad would happen. They elected to stay behind but at last most decided to go. But so much time had been wasted. Marauding Polish bandits were spotted in nearby Ukrainian villages. First eye-witness reports began to filter in about Ukrainians being attacked, not only in their homes but in the forests as well. The bandits showed no mercy, destroying and pillaging everything in their path.

Earlier, an informant from the settlement of Grochi had contacted Doctor Voljanchuk and confirmed that the small village of Grochi contained 28 homes, 25 belonging to Ukrainian families and only three belonging to Poles. This made Grochi a prime target for attack. Five members of Brygada Salon entered the settlement on their horses. As luck would have it, many Ukrainians had already fled. Three of the houses belonged to clan kaszub, one of which was the pride and joy of the patriarch of the clan, Andrij Kaszuba, while two newly-built homes nearby belonged of his sons, Mikhailo and Dmetro.

During those moments, the level of apprehension reached a crescendo for the residents of the village of Grochi. Perhaps under normal circumstances, all members of clan kaszub might have gotten together to discuss and plan their exit from the village before registering for transfer to Soviet Ukraine. However, the circumstances were anything but normal. When the village was attacked, it was impossible for family members to organize their escape.

Andriy Kaszuba, my grandfather, had been warned earlier about the impending attack. Gathering up his wife, Maria, he immediately left the village by a horse-drawn cart. He knew that his children and their families, younger and far more energetic, would be more capable of looking after themselves. In accordance with whispered agreements, all those who survived the attacks were to meet in the Greek Catholic Church in Płazów.

While driving their cart in the direction of Ruda Różaniecka, Andriy and Maria Kaszuba suddenly came upon Brygada Salon. Mounted on five horses and heavily armed, Andriy Kaszuba knew that trouble awaited them.

"Stop right there," shouted Corporal Kula, *"this is Brygada Salon. Declare yourself. Where the hell are you going?"*

Being perfectly fluent in Polish, Andriy Kaszuba introduced himself and his wife, adding, *"We are on our way to Płazów. There is much trouble in this area."*

"This is not the direction to Płazów, you stupid deceitful dumbbell. Sukinsynu, you are lying about your intention. You look like a murdering Ukrainian thief to me, you son-of-a-bitch."

"I know that this is not the direction to Płazów," responded Kaszuba, *"but the shortest road to Płazów is not safe."*

Suddenly, Wilk realized what the elderly couple had said about their family name. It was as if he had slowly emerged from a fog.

"Your family name is Kaszuba?" asked Wilk.

"Yes, that is what it is."

"Do you know Anna Kaszuba? Are you related to her?"

Andriy Kaszuba didn't know what to say. It occurred to him that this member of Brygada Salon knew something that he did not know. Otherwise, why would he ask such an important question and so directly? No matter, to answer in the positive or negative might well lead to the same result. He could now see that his very life might well be in jeopardy.

"Yes," replied Andriy Kaszuba, *"Anna is my daughter. She is hiding out somewhere in the forest. We have not seen her for some time."*

For whatever reason, Wilk decided not to force the issue. Perhaps he feared that some calamity might befall the couple, thereby destroying any possibility of his getting any information about Anna's time in Germany. Even more important, Wilk suddenly realized that the senior kaszubs might also be his conduit to information about his sweetheart, Tanja Konenko, and his sister, Monika, both forcibly working in Germany.

Corporal Kula looked at Andriy and Maria Kaszuba for the longest time. For whatever reason, perhaps because of Wilk's initial questions of the kaszubs and Andriy's fluency in the Polish language, Kula waved the elderly couple on, wishing them a safe journey. Surprised by this sudden turn in events, Wilk was the first to speak.

"Thank you, Kula. I only hope that they survive. It is my wish to find Anna Kaszuba. I feel that she will have some important information for me."

Mounted on their military horses, Brygada Salon continued in the direction of Grochi. Unbeknownst to them, the very first home they came upon belonged Andriy and Maria Kaszuba, the senior couple they had just met. Left behind in the home but planning to leave shortly, the youthful Anna Kaszuba wanted to spend a few more moments with Damian Klymus, the next-door neighbour and a member of her extended family. Klymus, nearly blind and hard of hearing, had no place else to go to seek safety. Despite any danger from Polish bandits, he wanted to stay right there in the village of Grochi. Suddenly, all hell broke loose. Shouting and shooting into the air, Brygada Salon, astride their horses, burst onto the scene. Frightened out of his wits, Damian Klymus immediately turned to Anna, shouting, *"Quick, Hanka, jump out the window and run for your life!"*

Instantly, Anna Kaszuba jumped out the open window and raced into the nearby forest. Moments later, Damian Klymus, sitting in his chair, was shot by a member of Brygada Salon. A neighbour's teenage boy, also visiting at the time, tried to escape through the window. He, too, was shot in the back.

"Dammit, Lew, why did you shoot them? Can't you see that the old man was crippled? You also shot the defenceless little boy, damn you."

"How was I to know that the old fart was crippled, Wilk. We have our orders."

As the brigade watched Anna scrambling out the open window and disappearing into the forest, Wilk suddenly realized the last words uttered by Klymus were, *"Anna, run for your life."* Immediately, Wilk realized that Anna was the woman Brygada Salon met in Bełżec.

"Don't shoot her," shouted Wilk, *"I want to talk to her."*

Wilk yelled at the young woman to stop, but to no avail. In a moment, Anna disappeared into the pine forest. Wilk knew better than to try to follow her. Yet, he also knew that he had to talk to her. In his mind, he was certain that this was the young woman Brygada Salon met in Bełżec—the woman who recently returned from Germany and had mentioned Tanja Konenko's name.

Mikhailo, Andriy Kaszuba's son, lived a short distance from his father's home. Earlier and in a separate manoeuvre, Mikhailo began herding the family's cows to safety with the hopes that no harm would come to him or his cows. Meanwhile, he ordered his wife Ewa, along with their children, thirteen-year old Marika, eight-year old Oksana, six-year old Misha, and two-year old Ivanka to escape into the forest in the direction of Płazów and the Greek Catholic Church. Mikhailo did not get very far with the family's cows. On foot and not able to escape, he was attacked by members of Brygada Salon.

"*You suka,*" shouted Corporal Kula, pointing a rifle at Mikhailo's head, "*where are you taking those cows?*"

"*There is trouble in our village. I am taking the cows to safety. These cows belong to my mother,*" answered Mikhailo, in Polish.

"*Screw your cows, you lying son-of-a-bitch. We don't believe that you are Polish. First, we shall teach you a lesson. Then, we want you to get the hell out of our country.*"

Mikhailo took a severe beating. Sore all over and his cows now gone, he could hardly get to his feet as he staggered in the direction of Płazów. He was thankful that he was able to answer the brigade in Polish. Perhaps this was what saved his life.

Dmetro, Mikhailo's younger brother, also lived nearby in his new home. When warned about the imminent attack, he immediately took off into the forest with his wife Maria, their two children, and the family's sheep. However, a heavily-armed nationalistic Pole by the name of Tadyk stopped him. Pointing a Kalashnikov rifle at his head, he was about to shoot the unarmed Dmetro.

"*Where the hell are you going with those sheep?*"

"*I am taking them to market in Narol. Mój brat tam mieszka. My brother lives there.*"

"*Your brother lives in Narol? Who gives a shit where your brother lives. You are a lying son of a bitch. You stole those sheep.*"

Suddenly, two of Tadyk's comrades jumped out of the forest. The three bandits beat Dmetro severely and stole his sheep. Barely able to move with sore ribs and a groin injury, Dmetro staggered off into the forest and in the direction of Płazów. For whatever reason, the brigade did not harm Maria or their two children, five-year old Dima, or an infant son, Ivan, born just a few days earlier.

Now scattered in the pine forest, the kaszubs knew that if they could safely get to the Ukrainian Catholic Church in Płazów, the sacred place of worship would provide them with some measure of safety, so long as they remained inside the confines of the church. Once there, they knew that they could neither leave the church during daylight hours nor as a group. They would have to wait until darkness before escaping Płazów.

Undeterred in their mission, Brygada Salon looted the homes, beating, and killing several villagers. Any surviving peasants hurriedly fled into the surrounding forest. They wanted to escape the savage butchery and the murderous attacks. Women in the village came out of their homes screaming and sobbing bitterly. All the men in the village scattered into the nearby forest while others attempted to hide in the attics and cellars but to no avail. Members of Brygada Salon were looking everywhere so that not a single place was left without being searched. Whenever they captured a man who had not left the village but was trying to escape, he was instantly killed. Where they could not find a man, they beat the women and children.

Attacking the home of the Romaniuks, Brygada Salon ordered Maria Romaniuk to climb the ladder to the attic in search of her husband, Ivan Romaniuk. The order was accompanied by severe rifle-butt blows. When Maria started to climb, the ladder suddenly broke under her. Lying on the floor with a broken arm, she was beaten unconscious by the brigade who then set the house on fire. Both Maria and Iwan Romaniuk perished in the fire.

In all, several Ukrainians living in the settlement of Grochi were shot and every house and barn in the settlement torched, including those buildings belonging to Michal Kruczko, the Polish informant. Not only that but the homes and barns of two other Polish families residing in Grochi were also torched. Having done their dastardly deeds and with several homes in Grochi now on fire, Brygada Salon decided to return to Płazów.

The attack on the village of Płazów took place on Holy Saturday, the day before Easter. According to the 1944 Julian calendar, Easter Sunday fell on April 16. Holy Saturday, as a result, fell on April 15. That was the sad day upon which the villages of Grochi and Płazów were attacked. The actions of Brygada Salon were not spontaneous or carried out in the heat of the moment. Only a small number of crimes committed by Polish vigilantes were spontaneous. Most attacks on Ukrainian villages were thoughtfully planned and brutally carried out, as was this one.

At the entrance to the village of Płazów, there was a religious shrine, a figure of Jesus Christ's Crucifixion. For whatever reason, two cow herders, Iwan Horoszko and Andriy Palichuk must have thought that the religious shrine would provide some protection from Polish bands. They believed in the adoring, inconceivable, and unfathomable mystery of God's mercy. They felt that no harm would come to them in the immediate vicinity of the image of Jesus. Unfortunately, they were terribly wrong. Lew and Karabin shot both of them, leaving their mutilated bodies next to the Crucifixion of Jesus.

Brygada Salon continued to the centre of Płazów. An elderly woman screamed at the bandits, only to be shot on the spot. Not one member of the brigade had asked the woman her identity or ethnicity. More problems precipitated when Katarzyna Klymus refused to give up her cow. She was tortured and then shot. Hubert Horoszko, who happened to appear on the scene, was shot without being given an opportunity to speak or even identify himself.

In a moment, the brigade turned to the home of the Mazurkos. Corporal Kula rapped on the door with the butt of his rifle. Reluctantly, a frightened Maria Mazurko came to the door.

"Who lives in this house?" shouted Corporal Kula.

"Moja rodzina tu mieszka, our family lives here," said Maria, *"but my husband is in the Polish kościół, the Roman Catholic Church in Cieszanow. He is the organist in the church."*

"Who else is with you? Who is the old woman in the chair?"

"Ona jest naszym sąsiadem. That is Tetyana Groszko, our neighbour."

"Czy ona jest polska kobieta? Is the woman Polish or Ukrainian?"

For whatever reason, Tetyana Groszko rose from her chair declaring, *"No, I am not Polish. I am a proud Ukrainian woman."*

"But," objected Maria Mazurko, *"what about me, what about the Polish members of your family?"*

The brigade bandits did not wait for any explanations. They dragged Tetyana Groszko, my grandmother, out of the chair into the yard, broke both legs and arms and then threw the unconscious Tetyana into the well. Another woman, in coming to her defence, was first shot and then also thrown into the well. Distraught beyond belief, Maria Mazurko attacked Corporal Kula with her bare hands. Kula defended himself as best he could. Had Maria not told the brigade that her husband was an organist in the Roman Catholic Church, she, too, might have been shot.

"You bunch of murdering low-down stupid beasts! Why did you murder Tetyana Groszko? She did no one any harm."

Even in the midst of critical situations, it was not unusual for members of Brygada Salon to pause long enough to raise questions of potential victims about their ethnicity. For whatever reason and despite the tragedy before her, Maria wanted to know what kind of people would exhibit such cruelty.

"Our mission, woman, is to remove all Ukrainians from Polish lands," responded Corporal Kula. *"Our soldiers are from Lutsk. We are here to defend the rights of all Poles."*

"It's so pathetic, killing innocent people. I am sure that Pani Groszko's family in Lutsk would not condone what you have done."

"You say that the dead woman's family name is Groszko? That she has family living in Lutsk?"

For the longest time, Wilk stared at Maria Mazurko without saying a word. Finally, he did have a question.

"What is the name of Pani Groszko's family in Lutsk?"

"I believe that the name of her family is Konenko."

Shocked beyond belief, Wilk realized that Tetyana Groszko, the woman that the brigade had just murdered, was an Aunt of his sweetheart, Tanja Konenko. The realization left him without words for the longest time. Falling to his knees and raising his hands heavenward, Wilk could do little else but ask for the Lord's forgiveness.

"Lord Jesus, my God, what have we done? We have just killed Tanja's Great Aunt. Forgive me and my troops, Dear Lord."

As Brygada Salon surveyed the scene in Płazów, they took notice of the Ukrainians seeking refuge in the Greek Catholic Church. Even after they realized that their troop may have erred in murdering several innocent people, they were not deterred from continuing their attacks on the residents of Płazów. However, only God knows why they refused to enter the sanctity of the Ukrainian Catholic Church. For, just one week earlier, a Polish unit from Rzeszow did enter the church, divided the victims; pregnant women and children less than four years of age were left inside while several Ukrainian adults were taken to the Moskali cemetery where they were shot and dumped in a pit. The parish priest was included among the victims.

Operating on horseback and in the process of exiting Płazów, the members of Brygada Salon continued to shoot anyone in the village to whom they spoke and who was not fluent in Polish. The shooting continued until late afternoon. By this time the local Ukrainian Greek Catholic Church was crowded with Ukrainians seeking refuge. Having done their cruel and dirty deed in Płazów, the armed brigade decided to head in the direction of Ruda Różaniecka, some three kilometers to the west.

Meanwhile, local Poles from families of mixed marriages organized the burial of those who perished. Unfortunately, the dead could not be laid to rest in the cemetery in Płazów. It was common knowledge that a mass burial of Russian soldiers who lost their lives in World War I had taken place in the forest between Ruda Różaniecka and Płazów. Over the years, the mass burial place came to be known as *Moskali,* a derogatory word meaning *Russian Soldiers.* All those who were murdered in Płazów, whether of Ukrainian or Polish heritage, were laid to rest in this graveyard.

En route to Ruda Różaniecka, Corporal Kula suddenly brought Brygada Salon to a halt.

"I have heard that the UPA is operating in this region. We must keep an eye out for those criminals. It will soon be dark. They like to murder their victims in the dead of night. The commander of their troop will be seeking revenge for what we did in Grochi and Płazów."

Considering what Corporal Kula had to say, it was Puma who was the first to speak.

"Why don't we return to Narol and *get a good night's sleep before attacking Ruda Różaniecka tomorrow morning?"* asked an exhausted Puma.

Corporal Kula did not need any further encouragement to call it a day, especially in light of the belief that the Insurgent Ukrainian Army may be operating in the immediate vicinity. The brigade's attack on the village of Ruda Różaniecka would have to wait until the next day.

The following day, the people of Płazów got togather to discuss what had happened. Under a warm and sunny day, survivors realized that Brygada Salon had not spared anyone. In the bloody orgy, they even killed the village's postman, Pan Kostritsky, an ethnic Pole. In this particular case, his wife, Nadia, was lucky. The bandits did not know that the postman's wife was an ethnic Ukrainian. Perhaps the outcome would have been very different had Brygada Salon set out in search of her. Not only that, but Nadia Kostritsky was the sister of Ivan Machaj, the head of

UPA's underground organization in the region. This oversight would soon prove to be fatal to the very existence of Brygada Salon.

A fate similar to that of Pan Kostritsky also befell Victor Borsovych, the local intellect. Viktoria Groszko was spared but her twenty-year-old son, Vlada, was shot. So were her two neighbours, Kusina Ju, and Iwan Groszko. Thirty-seven year old Natalya Kordupel, the servant of the Polish priest, was also shot. She was guilty only because she was an ethnic Ukrainian. Strangely, it was her master, the Roman Catholic Parish Priest, who decided that she must be killed.

That evening, many people worked hard to pull Tetyana Groszko and Maria Klymus out of the water well. No one in the village got any sleep. Ukrainians who sought refuge in the Ukrainian Catholic Church were helped out of the community by local Poles who lived in the village, knew them, and looked upon them as trusted neighbours. Most Ukrainians elected to escape through the forest in the direction of **Łówcza** with the hopes of finding safe haven in that village before continuing on to Gorajec, a small community protected by a Ukrainian military unit and assisted by members of the UPA. They also heard that when in Gorajec, the Soviet authorities would help them find their way to Soviet Ukraine. But, what kind of safety could that be? Almost every night, not one but several bands of Poles would wander around the countryside, robbing and killing Ukrainians.

Early the next day, Brygada Salon rode their horses, without interruption, through Płazów en route to Ruda Różaniecka. It seemed as though the village of Płazów was devoid of any life. With the help of Kruczko and Voljanchuk, they had already decided who to look for in Ruda Różaniecka. Being a small village, there weren't that many Ukrainians who called it home. Michal Kruczko, the brigade's informant from Grochi, told them that all surviving Ukrainians living in the nearby settlement of Grochi, with most of their homes burned to the ground, left in a hurry. Those who had not left were shot dead the previous day. Now it was the turn of Ukrainians living in Ruda Różaniecka.

Upon entering Ruda Różaniecka, Kula had the name of one particular Ukrainian nationalistic family in his mind that he wanted to remove. Earlier, it was Doctor Voljanchuk who informed Brygada Salon as to the ethnicity of families living in the village. Approaching a home at the outskirts of the village, Kula rapped on the door of the home with his rifle. Almost instantly, a woman appeared at the door.

"Who lives here? What is the name of your family?"

"The Zaborniak family lives here."

"Your name is Zaborniak? Is your family completely and totally Polish? You swear that you are not of mixed marriage?"

"Yes, that is true. My family is Polish. Moja rodzina jest polska."

"Where does the Adam Kaszuba family live? Which house?"

Not wanting to implicate them, Bronislawa Zaborniak was most evasive.

"I do not know of the family. They do not live here."

"That is not the truth. You must tell us or we will shoot you and your four children."

Reluctantly and against her best judgement, Bronislawa Zaborniak pointed in a northerly direction saying, *"They live somewhere over there."*

Leaving Lew to guard the Zaborniaks, the other members of Brygada Salon headed in the direction of the Kaszuba residence. It would be at that very moment that Ivan Maczaj, the local leader of the OUN-B had sent a patrol unit to the Ruda Różaniecka region. It was the mission of the patrol unit to determine whether or not any Polish paramilitary units might be operating in the region. He wanted to know if ethnic Ukrainians needed the assistance of the UPA. Suddenly, a rifle shot rang out, followed by screams emanating from the Zaborniak residence. A member of UPA's patrol unit, hiding out in the nearby forest, must have concluded that a Ukrainian family was being confronted by a nationalistic Polish unit. Instantly, Lew fell to the ground, shot through the head by a UPA sniper. Returning quickly to the Zaborniak home, Corporal Kula found a very upset Bronislawa Zaborniak standing over Lew.

"You bitch," yelled Kula, *"who shot my soldier? Did you shoot Lew, you suka?"*

"God only knows who shot him," replied a shocked Bronislawa. *"It wasn't me. I do not have a weapon."*

"God damn it, where did the shot come from?"

Once again fearing for her own safety, Bronislawa pointed in the general direction of the Kaszuba residence, *"The shot came from that direction."*

Had Bronislawa known for certain the source of the assassin's bullet, the outcome for Adam and Katarzyna Kaszuba might have been very different. On the other hand, and even though Bronislawa incorrectly identified the exact direction of the source of the bullet, the outcome for the kaszubs might have been the same. *Here is why.*

Strangely, right from the start, the marriage of Adam Kaszuba and Katarzyna Waszny in 1938 was inundated with interesting incidents, foisted upon them not of their own volition but rather as a result of world politics. From 1939 to 1941 and in accordance with an agreement between Nazi Germany and the Soviet Union, all of western Poland, including Gmina Narol, would come under the control of Nazi Germany. When in 1941 Nazi Germany attacked the Soviet Union under the name of Operation Barbarossa, Katarzyna had some startling news for her husband, Adam.

"My dear Adam," announced Katarzyna, *"I have some news. It may be good news or the news may not be so good. After all, we do live during troubled times."*

"Not good news? How can it be any worse," responded Adam, *"than the attack on Eastern Poland by those damn Nazis?"*

"I know, I know. This is not a good time to make this announcement, but I am pregnant."

Adam didn't know what to say. After some thought, he said nothing. In the end, world events and the outbreak of World War II did not deter the young couple from starting a family. In 1941, Katarzyna and Adam welcomed the birth of their daughter, Sofija.

As the Nazi blitzkrieg marched through the region, mostly by-passing Gmina Narol, just staying alive was a full-time challenge for the next two years. War would rage on and on and there would be little good news for Adam and Katarzyna between 1941 and 1943. However, as fate would have it, the hostilities in the Narol region diminished in 1943. Perhaps this is the reason why Katarzyna had more news for Adam in 1943.

"Don't tell me," was Adam's reaction, *"that you are pregnant again?"*

Just about the time that the autumn season brought myriad colours to the region, Sofija was about to have a brother, Franek, born in 1943. It was also a time when the Red Army would once again take control of Eastern Ukraine. That, unfortunately, was the least of their problems. They were about to face the wrath of Brygada Salon. Soon, their lives would be in mortal danger, not as a result of the war but because of a nationalistic Polish unit.

Under duress, Bronislawa did reveal the location of the Kaszuba residence as being the likely source of the assassin's bullet. She did not know that the bullet came from the rifle of a UPS band member, who, by this time was long gone. Immediately, Brygada Salon surrounded the Kaszuba residence, being careful to stay out of gun range. In possession of sniper rifles, they began shooting out the windows of the residence while at the same time shouting at the kaszubs to come out of their home with their hands in the air. Adam Kaszuba saw no way out of his predicament. With his hands raised high in the air, he came out of the house, closely followed by his wife, Katarzyna.

Facing Adam Kaszuba, Corporal Kula yelled, *"You kurva, you shot my soldier."*

"It couldn't have been me. I have no rifle. I heard the shot. It came from the forest."

"You lying bastard. Shoot the son-of- a- bitch. The sukinsynu shot Lew."

Both Adam and his wife were shot several times by members of Brygada Salon.

"Set the goddamn house and barn on fire," commanded Corporal Kula.

Frightened and crying with fear, two little infants suddenly emerged from the burning home. Sofija and Franek, the two infant children of Adam and Katarzyna Kaszuba had been hiding in the cellar of the home. At first, they refused to come out of their hiding place. However, the heat and smoke from the fire soon convinced them that they should immediately come out of hiding. Even as infants, they must have known that something terrible was unfolding. Sofija was just four years of age. The younger Franek, less than two years of age, screamed in pain, only to be quieted by his older sister.

"You bastards," screamed Bronislawa Zaborniak, the grand-daughter of Johannes Kaszuba, *"why did you have to shoot Adam and his wife? Is it necessary to shoot innocent people? Didn't you hear my cousin Adam Kaszuba say that he did not have a rifle?"*

"Shoot innocent people? Are you crazy? That lying son-of-a-bitch shot a member of our troop. If not him, then it was one of his murdering friends hiding out in the forest."

"You stupid bastards, Adam is my cousin. You just shot them for no reason, you piece of shit. If I had a rifle I would shoot all of you."

*Adam and Katarzyna Kaszuba, birth parents of
Franek and Sofija Zaborniak, 1938.*

"*Whose children are these?*" asked Corporal Kula.

"*Good Lord,*" sobbed Bronislawa, "*these are the children of Adam and Katarzyna Kaszuba.*"

At that moment, Puma raised his rifle to shoot the two infants only to be interrupted by Corporal Kula who commanded him to put down his rifle.

"*Look, babeczka,*" declared Corporal Kula, showing no interest in being formal, "*do you want to see more killing? Is that what you want our troop to do?*"

"*I beg of you, please don't shoot the children. They are innocent of any wrongdoing.*"

"*Leave them be, Puma,*" agreed Corporal Kula, "*we do not shoot children. Let the Zaborniaks look after them. They want to be friends with everybody. This is their chance to be friends with the two little children. We must look after Lew's body.*"

In the midst of all of the tears and the misery, the remaining members of Brygada Salon must have felt a considerable degree of compassion. Wilk, having discovered the identity of Tetyana Groszko, felt a twinge of guilt for allowing the troop to murder her. Surrounded by death and destruction, Brygada Salon decided to help the Zaborniaks with the burial of Lew, Adam, and Katarzyna.

If Kula had hoped for any kind of a funeral ceremony, he would have been disappointed. Considering their circumstance, it was neither possible to mourn the dead nor a time to evaluate the life of those left behind, even though the Catholic faith would have demanded just that. In times of peace, a funeral would have given the priest sufficient time to celebrate the passage of the deceased, to rebuke the living for their sins, and to call upon the living to lead a better life. In this case, there was no such opportunity.

Had it not been for the death of one of their own, Brygada Salon would not have stayed behind for the burial of three individuals. With the help of Franciszek Zaborniak, the brigade put together three crude caskets and the following day commenced the graveside committal service. While throwing a handful of soil onto the caskets as each was lowered into a grave, they repeated the well-known phrase, *Dust thou art, and unto dust thou shalt return.* Brygada Salon bid farewell to a fallen comrade and the Zaborniaks said their goodbyes to Adam and Katarzyna Kaszuba. Their two tearful infants looked on.

Before leaving Ruda Różaniecka, Corporal Kula had a question of the Zaborniaks. *"What will happen to the two little infants? Who will look after them?"*

"We will look after them. These are the children of our family. Don't worry about them. We shall protect them from harm," Bronislawa Zaborniak tearfully assured Corporal Kula.

That evening, Corporal Kula said his goodbyes to Pan Kruczko and Doctor Voljanchuk. Brygada Salon's work in terrorizing the villages of Płazów and Grochi came to a sudden end. Kula well knew that there would be other marauding bands of Poles making sure that any Ukrainians left in the surrounding villages would be forced out or killed in the process. If the Polish bandits did not do their work, the Polish Home Army would finish the job.

When the smoke cleared in the village of Ruda Różaniecka, a ghastly, hair-raising scene appeared before anyone witnessing the carnage. Here and there walked ragged shadows. A woman was heard to lament, *"Why did they kill her? Why have they murdered them?"*

An elderly man who survived the attack exclaimed, *"Look at what they have done. That is my neighbour. My dead neighbour holding a child, burned to a crisp."*

An elderly resident of the community had difficulty containing his anger when he saw that the child had been bayoneted. On the other side of the street was his dead wife, with several bayonet stabs in her breast and her legs badly mutilated.

"*She is my wife,*" whispered the man, "*all have been murdered. Only I remain. Why?*"

In the Moskali mass graveyard located in the forest, several dozen bodies had already been placed in a common grave. All were horribly mutilated—men, women, children, and old people alike met the same cruel death. Near the grave there were several corpses awaiting burial. One was that of an old man who had been shot while praying. The bodies of adult males and females showed bruises from rifle butts, barbed wire, and nails with which they had been tortured before being shot.

The Polish government-in-exile was well aware of these atrocities, which is why the government's propaganda machinery quickly went to work. Spin doctors explained that those killed were members of the Ukrainian underground army, commonly known as *banderivtsi*. Obviously, this was not true. Children, infants, and old people could hardly be acccused of belonging to a secret partisan organization. The real reason that they were killed was that they were Ukrainians and simply had to be exterminated.

Villagers who had miraculously escaped the massacre slowly began to find their way to Soviet Ukraine. Despite persistent orders from the Polish puppet government in Lublin put into place by the Soviets that all Ukrainians must go east of the Curzon Line, many preferred to remain in their native land. Polish authorities were equally determined that they should not be left in peace. The Lublin government's position was supported by Moscow. Demand after demand from the Soviets urged all Ukrainians to surrender without delay and without any exception.

Just as suddenly as Brygada Salon's reign of terror began in their target villages, it seemed to come to a screeching halt. Their unit was one of several such units operating in this region of Poland. In many cases, the same village was attacked and pillaged by more than one unit. No one knew for certain which unit was specifically responsible for which burnt-out village. No one stopped to count the dead. It is without question that the nationalistic Polish units did their dirty work with the full knowledge and support of Lublin. This is not to say that UPA and OUN did not also contribute to the destruction.

Brygada Salon's mission of forcibly removing, through coersion or at the point of a rifle, every Ukrainian from the villages assigned to them did come to an end. However, for those Ukrainians who survived the onslaught of Brygada Salon and who were now fleeing from their burnt out homes and villages, their challenge was just beginning.

By prior rumour and whispered agreement, each survivor first had to find their way to Płazów and the Ukrainian Greek Catholic Church. Once in the presumed safety of the church, the families would have to rely on the sanctity of the church to survive any further attacks by Poles before charting their route to Soviet Ukraine. Although Soviet and Polish authorities guaranteed safe passage for those who would sign up for transfer, did not mean much in the face of reality. After all, the sign-up location for transfer to Ukraine was not in the village of Płazów, but rather in the town of Jaroslaw, more than sixty kilometres distance. With so many other roving Polish bands still bent on killing Ukrainians, how would one be able to find safe passage to Jaroslaw?

It was also a time for Brygada Salon to return to Narol and discuss, with Kapitan Kon, their next mission. In the meantime, Wilk had a special mission of his own. First and foremost, he wanted to find this girl named Anna. *But how to find her? Where was she?*

Wilk recalled the brief conversation that Kula, the leader of their brigade, purportedly had with her in Bełzec. According to Corporal Kula, Anna informed him that she had just returned from Germany and was replaced by a young Ukrainian girl by the name of Tanja. This revelation convinced Wilk that Anna might be able to provide him with additional information. *Where*, in Germany, *had Anna worked?* If she was a Zivilarbeiter, *what was the name of the German family for whom she slaved? Would he be able to contact this German family? How?*

Suddenly, the challenge ahead for Wilk was far more than simply one of hastening the removal of all Ukrainians from Polish soil. His feelings of love for a Ukrainian girl were far stronger than was his goal of removing Ukrainians from Polish soil. By this time, Wilk was convinced that Anna was in possession of information about his sweetheart, information that he desperately needed. Yet, in the midst of so many conflicts, how was it possible to find Anna?

Wilk realized that members of clan kaszub were in hiding trying to find safe passage from Płazów to Jaroslaw. This could only mean that Anna would keep a low profile with members of clan kaszub in order to avoid contact with Polish nationalistic units. Realizing this only added to Wilk's challenges.

14

Seeking Safe Haven

The treacherous road to a place of brutal physical and social repression

Someone once said that *good fences make good neighbours.* Perhaps the authors of the mutual agreement to transfer Poles out of Soviet Ukraine to Poland and Ukrainians out of Poland to Soviet Ukraine at the end of World War II had this thought in mind when they signed the mutual resettlement agreement.

To prevent unnecessary and continued bloodshed resulting from ethnic conflicts, the decision on mutual resettlement took place in fulfilment of the agreement between the government of the Soviet Union and the Polish Committee of National Liberation. It stipulated that the mutual resettlement had to be carried out from October 15, 1944 to February 1, 1945. Officially, the resettlement was stipulated as being voluntary. On paper, the agreement looked rather generous, specifying that settlers who were moved into their country of birth would receive the sum of 5,000 roubles or the equivalent in Polish zloty. Each evacuee would be permitted to take their livestock, agricultural equipment, up to two tons of food and property, and up to 1,000 roubles.

In theory, transferees were also to be offered compensation for the loss of their residential and farm buildings. In the Polish-inhabited regions of Soviet Ukraine, a register of the Polish population that had to be evacuated was made up. Another list was made of those who volunteered to move. As at September 1, 1944, this list included 41,800

Poles in the Oblast of Volhynia, 50,000 in the Oblast of Rivne, and 162,229 in the Lviv region. Registration continued into 1945 at which point the Oblast of Ternopil was added. In all, 226,952 people received documents for evacuation to Poland.

In contrast and of particular interest is the number of Ukrainians residing in Poland who registered for transfer to Soviet Ukraine between 1944 and 1946. We do know that the total number of registrants at the end of this period was 492,682. However, of this number, 400,000 registered between July of 1945 and July of 1946. This means that during the initial stage of the transfer program from the fall of 1944 to July of 1945, fewer than 100,000 Ukrainians registered for transfer, constituting only 25% of the total. Little wonder that the Soviet Union was so intent upon advancing the transfer program through aggressive militant means.

In the first place, Stalin's population transfer program could not be carried out without regard for the conduct of World War II. After all, most of the able-bodied Soviet citizens were enmeshed in the war effort. For the Red Army and the NKVD, winning the war was the most important challenge. The tide in favour of the Allies began to take shape after the victory of the Red Army in the Kursk tank battle in July and August of 1943, a battle which involved 438,000 German combat troops backed by 2,816 tanks against the Red Army's 1,420,000 troops and 3,600 tanks. One final move by the Soviets in the south completed the campaign of 1943-1944 and wrapped up a Soviet advance of over 500 miles. In March, 1944, twenty German divisions were encircled and defeated in the Battle of Ternopil. Immediately following, the Soviet Union planned another major offensive.

Consisting of four Soviet army groups totalling over 120 divisions, *Operation Bagration* began on June 22, 1944, exactly three years after Hitler launched Barbarossa. More than 2.3 million Soviet troops went into action against the Nazis. The Red Army achieved a ratio of ten to one over its enemy in tanks and seven to one in aircraft. In its drive from Verbitsk to Warsaw's outskirts, the Red Army killed 381,000 Nazi soldiers and captured 160,000 more, 50 percent of this number were later murdered by the Red Army. With each increasing Soviet victory, the front line moved farther west.

Operation Bagration was immediately followed by the *Lwow-Sandomierz Offensive* on July 13, 1944. By early August of 1944, the Red Army was within striking distance of the Vistula River and the outskirts of Warsaw. Eastern Poland was completely under the control of the Soviet

Union. Stalin understood that once the war effort was over, he would have more military personnel at his disposal for the population transfer initiative.

Many German and Soviet accounts agree that Operation Bagration was Hitler's worst military setback. For the Soviet Union, Operation Bagration ensured that the former Soviet republics, from the Baltic Sea to Crimea, would return to the Communist fold. It set the stage for Soviet domination of much of Eastern Europe for the next 40 years.

Recognizing that the Red Army had its hands full defeating the Nazis throughout 1944, it was clear that the completion of the resettlement set for February 1, 1945 was impossible. Therefore, the deadline was extended to May 1, 1945. A new proposal further extended the deadline to January 15, 1946. By this time, a total of 789,982 Poles were evacuated from Western Ukraine to Poland. Though the vast majority of these numbers were ethnic Poles, more than 30,000 Jews were also included.

The Poles were heavily influenced by broadcasts from the London government which led them to believe that after the defeat of the Axis powers the Polish state would be restored according to its pre-September, 1939, borders. In response, the Polish underground movement in Lviv planned to establish its authority once the Germans retreated and before the arrival of the Red Army. Therefore, one week before Soviet troops entered Lviv on July 27, 1944 Armija Krajowa occupied major buildings and schools in Lviv and raised the Polish flag on them.

This led to a treaty between the Polish Committee of National Liberation and the Soviet Union granting the Soviets full control over civilians in liberated areas. By August of 1944, the Soviets captured all of Belarus and Ukraine, and advanced well beyond Lublin. However, the Ukrainian Insurgent Army (UPA) would not only continue to wage a guerrilla war against the Soviets but also continue its skirmishes against the Poles.

As the autumn days of 1944 turned into the colder days of late fall, Brygada Salon had to admit that their mission to hasten the exit of all ethnic Ukrainians from the villages assigned to them was coming to a successful conclusion. However, according to Kapitan Kon, there remained many other villages in Gmina Narol that had not been cleansed of all Ukrainians.

"I am able to confirm this for you, Corporal Kula," reported Kapitan Kon, *"that Gmina Narol contains eighteen villages. Brygada Salon has cleansed only four of them. Armija Krajowa will inform me next week which of the remaining fourteen require attention."*

"I read you, Kapitan. However, I am heartbroken about the loss of Lew. Worse yet, I am now convinced that Lew was not murdered by the kaszubs but by the UPA. We grieve the loss of a dear friend and an excellent soldier."

"I will discuss all of this with Armija Krajowa. Tragedies happen. It could have been much worse. You will soon be assigned another mission. I want to remind you, Corporal Kula, the new treaty between the Soviets and Poland to hasten the removal of Ukrainians has been extended. This will give Brygada Salon additional time to give Ukrainians the Polish boot."

Even in advance of any formal agreement between the Soviet Union and Poland, roving nationalistic Polish bands increased their attacks, working hard to rid the countryside of all Ukrainians. In the opinion of Josef Stalin, however, population exchanges during 1944 were not advancing as quickly as hoped. As a result, the Soviet Union put forth a more formal agreement to deal with the matter. Coming into effect on September 9, 1944, the new agreement on population exchanges was about to have a most deleterious impact upon stubborn Ukrainians who resisted all efforts at being transferred. The situation for them would soon become worse, much worse.

Hundreds of Ukrainians living in Gmina Narol refused to register for deportation to Soviet Ukraine. Their determination not to leave their ancestral lands developed to such a degree that towards the end of the war the Ukrainian underground resistance movement numbered in excess of 100,000 well equipped and highly disciplined fighting men. Entire districts and towns were in their hands. The authority of the Ukrainian Insurgent Army was felt not only in the Carpathian Mountains, but as far as the woody and marshy regions of Volhynia. When units of Marshal Malinovsky's Second Army were returning eastward from the war in Germany, thousands of Ukrainians serving in the ranks seized the opportunity to desert the Soviet ranks to join the Ukrainian nationalist partisans who fought not only against Stalin's regime but also against their Polish henchmen. The desertion of Ukrainians from the Red Army did not sit well with Malinovsky who spearheaded the defeat of Nazi forces at the Battles of Stalingrad and Budapest; a man regarded as one of the most important military leaders in the history of Russia.

As the kaszubs planned their trek from Płazów to Jaroslaw, word out of Lublin was that strongly armed bands of Ukrainian nationalists were terrorizing southeastern Poland, crossing the demarcation line from the Russian side of the frontier and burning villages, carrying off livestock, and leaving thousands of Polish peasants homeless and destitute. The wave of terror, extending southeast from Rzeszow along the San River, was fought by several divisions of Polish militia. Many Ukrainians insisted upon their right to remain on Polish soil, at the same time demanding that Ukraine be made an independent state. In particular, Poles living in homes once occupied by Ukrainians were targeted by UPA. This situation, unfortunately, did not necessarily help the kaszubs in their effort to reach Jaroslaw in safety.

The actions of UPA resulted in a drastic decision by the Soviet Union. When Ukrainians west of the Curzon Line did not respond to Soviet and Polish appeals to join their Ukrainian brothers in *"...the happiest country in the world,"* the Soviet government adopted the drastic policy of *forcibly* deporting all Ukrainians from Poland. To accomplish this, the Polish government in Lublin was told by Stalin to muster the entire Polish Army, the Citizens' Militia, and the Corps of Internal Security.

In several localities, men, women and children were murdered in order to terrorize the rest of the population into leaving for the Russian-occupied Soviet Ukraine. Those who were compelled to go were given only two hours time to make their departure. Generally, only a few personal belongings were allowed to be taken. Thousands of Ukrainians were then forced to a railroad station under armed escort and shipped to the Soviet Union.

The plan to exterminate those Ukrainians who refused to be sent to the Soviet Union originated in the Kremlin. Stalin could not tolerate a Ukrainian-conscious minority, particularly outside the Soviet Union. From the time of the establishment of the Soviet-Polish frontier on the Curzon Line, the Soviets had waged ceaseless efforts to persuade the remaining Ukrainians to go to the Soviet Union. Toward that end, they had sent several repatriation commissions which began functioning in Przemysl, Sanok, and Jaroslaw. With the help of Polish authorities, the Soviets held several propaganda meetings at which time they strove to convince Ukrainians to go east of the Curzon Line.

The Repatriation Commission in Jaroslaw experienced limited success. Ukrainians stubbornly refused to move from the localities in which they had been living for centuries. As a consequence, Poles arrested and summarily executed several Ukrainians in Jaroslaw. Polish groups began to terrorize the Ukrainian population and loot their homes. Other Ukrainians were kidnapped and turned over to the NKVD. Ukrainian houses were set ablaze. Furniture, kitchen utensils, and paintings were all thrown out of their homes. Determined Polish partisans roamed about, shooting wildly at random. There were instances where struggling women and girls were dragged out of their homes. The children wept, calling out for their parents. The dead bodies in the streets bore signs of brutality and rape. No one cared for the wounded.

Events in Poland turned tragic when a Polish army unit entered a village near Przemysl. Armed with machine and field guns, they carried out the registration of the villagers for deportation to what some facetiously referred to as Stalin's Paradise. The UPA discovered these plans and attacked a Polish garrison. Over 250 houses were burned during a battle that lasted throughout the night. In the morning, the UPA troops and villagers began retreating into the forest. Some were saved by a Polish Major who supplied them with travel documents destined for Soviet Ukraine.

To protect themselves from random Polish assaults, Ukrainians created a self-defence group made up of 50 men in the village of Sahryn. Polish bands attacked the group and began to massacre the villagers. Old people, women, and children were killed. One girl was reportedly pierced with a pitchfork and some 600 Ukrainians were killed. Countless Ukrainians lost their lives, not at the hands of the Nazis, but at the behest of Polish citizens who decided to build a national state by eliminating those who stood in their way.

In contrast, the situation in the province of Volhynia was somewhat different. During the same period of time and under the threat UPA and local Ukrainians, thousands of Poles had already left the provinces of Volhynia and Eastern Galicia in favour of Poland. In all, the number of Ukrainians who registered in the border counties of Poland for transfer to Soviet Ukraine reached less than 500,000, far short of the target number. Many Ukrainians continued to resist transfer. They were not overly thrilled with the prospects of life in a Soviet Bloc country.

In light of these political developments, the work of Brygada Salon was about to take on a new meaning and increased significance. The Soviet-Polish agreement enabled units under the direction of Armija Krajowa to be more forceful in removing Ukrainians from Poland. Resulting from the loss of Lew in Ruda Różaniecka, Corporal Kula asked Karabin to remain with the unit. Karabin's return to his Armija Krajowa unit in Tomaszów Lubelski would have to wait. Now composed of only four members, Corporal Kula contacted Kapitan Kon with the hopes of clarifying their future missions. Kapitan Kon informed Kula that additional district commissions were set up in several centers to deal with the transfer of stubborn Ukrainians. With the signing of a new transfer agreement, Ukrainians had no choice but to register with a Commission for resettlement in one of the nine centers set up for this purpose near the Polish-Soviet Ukraine border.

Most Ukrainians from Gmina Narol were directed to a district commission located in Jaroslaw. Unfortunately, being directed to Jaroslaw was one thing, arriving there in one piece was quite another. The biggest obstacle to registration with a commission came from Polish paramilitary units who were intent upon murdering reluctant transferees before they could reach their point of registration and departure. The situation for Ukrainians who possessed horses and horse-drawn wagons was somewhat more favourable; they were permitted to exit Poland via Lubaczow or Rawa Ruska.

Although most Ukrainians did not want to abandon their ancestral lands and resettle in Soviet Ukraine, they well understood that Polish and Soviet security forces would soon be deployed. Polish authorities began to conduct mass arrests of local Ukrainian elites and applied a variety of coercive measures to pressure families and individuals to relocate.

Even as Polish bandits accelerated their efforts to force all Ukrainians to leave Poland, Wilk became more and more preoccupied with his own misfortunes. His thoughts frequently turned to his sister Monika who was serving the Nazi regime somewhere in Germany. At other times, he entertained daydreams about his teenage sweetheart, Tanja Konenko. Despite the difficulties between the Ukrainian and Polish communities, Wilk could not get out of his mind that his love for Tanja had little regard for artificial boundaries imposed by fellow man.

The function of the commissions, staffed with both Polish communists and Soviet personnel, was to register, co-ordinate, and facilitate the transportation of individuals and families to Soviet Ukraine. In addition, the commissions had the responsibility of conducting propaganda work among the target population. Because of the propaganda, which falsely promised Ukrainians better living conditions in Soviet Ukraine, there was some initial success; however, the number of applications for resettlement soon tapered off when word concerning the actual conditions in Soviet Ukraine began to spread.

No matter the form into which Brygada Salon morphed, their murderous work was very much dependent upon the conduct of the war. In fact, any initiative by the Polish nationalistic units was entirely tied to the belief that war's end would allow Poland to regain her lands and once again realize her important stature in the international community.

Much of the hate that was previously directed by Poles at Germans was now directed at Ukrainians. The conduct on the part of a number of individuals can only be described as brutal. Ethnic cleansing certainly did not make them tender or caring for their fellow man. Disturbingly, the war changed many of the perpetrators and made them seek revenge. There was no military reason for some of the atrocities. Valuable food, household goods, blankets, and clothing were lost in the homes which were burned to the ground. Worse yet, not only did residents have to deal with the senseless destruction of their homes but also with the rape of so many young women and girls.

As the Nazi troops retreated from Ukraine and Belarus in 1944, they requisitioned food for their armies and fodder for their draft horses. Many local residents in Gmina Narol refused to help the Nazis. As a result, many were executed by the Nazis and many others died from starvation. While retreating, the Germans systematically applied a scorched earth policy, burning towns and cities, destroying infrastructure, and leaving civilians to starve or die of exposure. In many towns, the battles were fought within towns and cities, with trapped civilians caught in the middle.

The Nazi ideology of mistreating the local population and Soviet prisoners of war encouraged partisans who were fighting behind the front. Even more significant, it motivated anti-communists to ally with the Soviets in an effort to defeat the Nazis.

By June of 1944, the Soviets had pushed back the Nazis beyond the Dniepr River at which time Stalin ordered the liberation of Ukraine. The objective of the offensive was to liberate Lviv, clear the German troops from Ukraine, and capture a series of bridgeheads on the Vistula River. The Soviet Union, with over one million troops at her disposal, was upbeat after recent victories in Eastern Ukraine. The attack on Nazi forces was two-pronged, one towards Rawa Ruska and the second one towards Lviv. Gmina Narol, situated between these two forks in a heavily-forested region, enabled its citizens to escape the full force of the military onslaught. As a result, residents of Gmina Narol were able to survive the most ferocious of battles and minimize their losses.

The situation for Ukrainians might have been much worse had it not been for the difficulty experienced by Poles in forming paramilitary units. As it turned out, the members of the nationalistic bands had to be drawn from the pool of Poles not already committed to the military of the Soviet Union or Poland's Armija Krajowa. Further to this, many young Poles were already working in Germany as Ostarbeiters, while many others were in concentration camps in Germany or labour camps in Siberia.

On the day that the village of Grochi was destroyed, the kaszubs, one by one, emerged from the pine forest and sought safety in the Ukrainian Greek Catholic Church in Płazów. However, to approach the church as one large group was completely out of question. For reasons of safety, family members took differing routes through the forest. Near the Greek Catholic Church, the youthful Mikhailo Kaszuba tried to assist a young woman, hysterical beyond description. She was holding the hand of a young girl with blond pigtails. Both were crying.

"What happened? Why are you crying?" enquired Misha.

"That roving pack of Poles kicked us out of our home. They beat us. They raped us. My daughter is only thirteen. Two of them did it to her. And several raped me as well. I don't know what happened to my little boy."

While ensconced in the church, strange things began to happen. First of all, the local Polish residents were unlikely to allow roving Polish bandits to attack any Ukrainian in a house of worship. The local residents were empathetic to the plight of Ukrainians. Many provided food and clothing to those inside the church. Secondly, the Polish bandits also exercised some care in their attacks on Ukrainians in and near Płazów for fear of retribution from well-armed members of UPA, who were also operating in the region.

Those inside the church planned to leave the church, one by one, or in very small groups during the night, travel through forested areas, and meet once again in a village of Gorajec, twelve kilometres from Płazów. Word had reached them that safe haven would be provided in Gorajec, a region under the protection of the UPA and armed Ukrainians.

With this plan in mind, several members of clan kaszub made a decision to leave the Greek Catholic Church in the dead of night and seek refuge with a local Polish family who was sympathetic to the plight of Ukrainians. With this information in mind, Mikhailo approached a Polish family by the name of Machaiym. Making certain that no one followed him, Mikhailo discreetly knocked on Pani Machaiym's door.

"Who is it? What do you want?"

"This is your neighbour, Mikhailo Kaszuba. I need your help."

"Come in, but I shall not light my coal oil lamp. I don't want to bring attention to us."

At first, Pani Machaiym expressed some reluctance to offering safe haven for eleven members of clan kaszub—Mikhailo's family of six, Dmetro's family of four, and 20-year-old Anna. But, after a brief discussion, she consented to harbour the kaszubs until such time that they could find safe passage to Gorajec. Hidden in the cellar of the Machaiym home, the family felt relatively safe. However, after only one day in hiding, Brygada Salon discovered that Pani Machaiym was harbouring a Ukrainian family. The brigade was about to decide what to do about the situation.

"I believe," declared Corporal Kula, *"that we should attack that double-crossing Machaiym family and burn their house down. They are traitors to our cause. What do you think, Wilk?"*

Wilk did not answer for the longest time. He must have been thinking about his sister and his Ukrainian sweetheart. In the end, he decided that he would have to take a position on the matter without revealing his reasons.

"Corporal Kula," asserted Wilk, *"I do not feel comfortable about killing a Polish family or burning their home. Our work is to make sure the Ukrainians leave and not punish, in the process, a Polish family. Why kill any Poles? Why burn their homes?"*

"I respect your judgment, Wilk. Tomorrow, if those stubborn Ukrainians are still at the Machaiyms, then we will kill all of them."

That evening, the three members of Brygada Salon returned to their place of temporary residence in Narol. Once Wilk was certain that Kula, Puma, and Karabin were asleep, he returned to Płazów with the hopes of approaching the Machaiym family. Alone so as not to attract the attention of any Polish or Ukrainian units, Wilk quietly knocked on the Machaiym family home. Upon hearing the knock, Pani Machaiym didn't know what to do. Not to answer the door might bring the wrath of hell upon her family and those she was harbouring. On the other hand, to answer the door might well lead to a positive result.

"Who is it? What do you want?"

"My name is Wilk. I am serving with Brygada Salon. I have come in peace."

"Are you a member of any military unit? Are you a Polish nationalist?"

"Yes, I am a member of a brigade. But that is not my mission tonight. I need your help."

"Why, then, are you here if not to kill harmless Ukrainians?"

"I heard that you are harbouring a Ukrainian family. Is that true?"

Once again, Pani Machaiym was at a complete loss for words. How did this nationalist find out about the particular Ukrainian family she was harbouring? She could do little else but reveal the truth even if that meant that she would bring a problem to her door. To do otherwise might well result in her death and that of the entire kaszub family.

"So, if I have a Ukrainian family with me, what is it that you want with them?"

"Some time ago, our brigade was in Bełzec. Corporal Kula, our leader, met a young woman named Anna. We learned that this Anna is with the family you are harbouring."

"What would all of this have to do with Anna?"

"Anna served as a slave in Germany. When she was released from slavery by the Gestapo, she was replaced by another Eastern Worker. This Anna might have some information about her replacement and about my sister, Monika, who is also slaving away in Germany. Please, can you help me?"

"Leave your carbine and ammunition with me and wait outside in the front yard. I will see if I can help you."

Perhaps against her better judgement, Pani Machaiym found her way into the cellar.

"Anna, I am so sorry to bother you and your family. Did you and your family hear what this bandit said to me?"

"Yes, Pani Machaiym, I heard the whole conversation."

"Do you recall meeting a Polish soldier when you were in Bełzec?"

"Yes, I did meet a band of Polish nationalists but I do not know the name of the soldier who spoke to me."

"Do you want to talk to this soldier named Wilk? I have his rifle in my possession. I think you can trust him."

"I will meet him if you allow me to do so but only in the barn. Not in the house."

By this time, the neighbourhood was in complete darkness. All was quiet and no one was in sight. Discreetly, Anna made her way to the barn. Exchanging greetings with Wilk, Anna was surprised to note that Wilk was fluent in both Ukrainian and Polish.

"Do not worry, Anna," explained Wilk. *"I worked very hard to find you. I have this feeling that God has made it possible for us to meet."*

"How can I trust a murderer? Why would your God send a murderer to talk to me?"

"I promise that I shall do my best that no harm will come to you."

In the darkness of the barn with no more than a few beams of moonlight shining upon them, Wilk decided to get to the purpose of his visit.

"Anna, you said that you worked in Germany."

"It is quite obvious that you already know my name. You also know that I am from Płazów and that I worked in Germany. What more do you want to know?"

"I talked to Corporal Kula about your conversation with him. Corporal Kula told me that he talked to you in Bełzec. Unfortunately, he did not raise any questions about your time in Germany as a slave. Can you tell me something about your time in Germany?"

"Why should I trust you with this information? What if you are a spy?"

"You can trust me. I gave up my weapon."

"I was taken by the Gestapo in 1940 when I was fifteen. I worked as a Zivilarbeiter on a large dairy farm near the German city of Hamburg. I also worked in a sugar refinery."

"And you returned to Poland after three years in Germany?"

"Yes, I pleaded with the German family to release me so that I could be with my parents. They needed my help."

"They released you from bondage? Why? How did that happen?"

"I believe that it was God's will. I am convinced that Frau Neumann is a true Christian. She told me that the authorities would find another worker to help her with her dairy farm."

"Did you happen to meet the girl that was to replace you?"

"I met her but only for a moment as I was leaving to catch a train to Bełzec."

"Corporal Kula told me that you mentioned her name. Is that true?"

"I don't recall her family name but I do remember her Christen name. Her name was Tanja, a very pretty Ukrainian girl."

Staring at Anna, Wilk sat on a milk stool without saying a word. Finally, it was Anna who broke the silence.

"What's wrong, Wilk? Why are you suddenly so sad?"

"It's a long story. At times I feel very ashamed of what I am doing. My sister Monika was captured by the Gestapo and taken to Germany. So was Tanja, my girlfriend."

"Tanja was your girlfriend? And you say that you are ashamed? Are you ashamed of Tanja? Why would you be ashamed of Tanja?"

"I cannot tell you. I must keep that secret to myself. What about Tanja? What did she look like?"

"At first, I thought that she was a Polish girl. She first spoke to me in Polish but I could see that her first language was Ukrainian. She looked very normal to me. Yes, a normal-looking teenager. I remember that she had short blondish hair and blue eyes."

"Did she say where she was from?" pursued Wilk.

"No, except that Frau Neumann, in discussing the matter with her children, said that the girl was from Volyn."

"Tanja was from Volhynia? That is a big oblast. Did they mention a city or a village?"

"I heard them talking about Lutsk."

The very mention of this particular Tanja being from Lutsk brought back a flood of memories to Wilk. Feeling somewhat more at ease with Wilk, Anna went on to briefly tell him about her time working in a sugar processing factory in the small German town of Wedel, located just twenty kilometres west of the city of Hamburg.

"Wedel," Anna explained, *"is situated on the banks of the Elbe River. It has a long and proud history. But, during the war, it also had its darker side. Aside from being in the cross-hairs of the Royal Air Force, it was home of the Neuengamme Concentration Camp."*

"You know all of this, Anna?"

"Yes, I know all of this. The Neumanns treated me like family. They wanted me to come back to Germany after the war. As for the concentration camp, I know nothing about it. I was lucky to leave the region just after most of it was destroyed by the Allies in 1943."

"Were you in Wedel when it was bombed?"

"Yes, I was there but the railway station and the sugar processing plant were spared."

"Anna, if I were to contact this Neumann family, how could I do it?"

"Why would you want to contact the Neumanns? That would be very difficult. The war is not over. But you can try to contact Frau Neumann. That is all I know."

"Thank you, Anna. I will do what I can to make certain that you have safe passage to Gorajec."

To Anna's surprise, Wilk slowly approached her and gave her a warm hug. Just like that, he disappeared into the night without even bothering to collect his rifle or the ammunition. At this point, Pani Machaiym was well aware that she had been discovered by a Polish nationalistic unit. As a consequence, she urged the kaszubs to immediately leave her home. As the kaszubs were ready to leave, she had a few words of advice for the family.

"Mikhailo, you needn't worry too much about being attacked by Polish bandits. I have the assurance of their leader that they will not attack your family."

Taking their most precious possessions, the kaszubs set out on their trek through the forests and fields in the direction of *Łowcza,* about five kilometres southeast of Płazów. Once again in possession of secretive information about the names of Polish families prepared to help Ukrainians exit Poland, Mikhailo was assured by Pani Machaiym that they would be safe in *Łowcza* with a Polish family by the name of Mikhailo Koriya.

"The Koriyas, I can assure you," promised Pani Machaiym, *"are friends of the Ukrainian community. They will feed and protect you. In Łowcza, the Ukrainian presence is quite noticeable and local Ukrainians are protected by an armed brigade."*

The kaszubs were most thankful for the assistance received from Pani Machaiym. Before leaving, each member of the family hugged her and said their goodbyes. Anna was the last one to leave.

"Anna, I want you to take this carbine and the ammunition left behind by Wilk. You may have some use for it in the coming days. Your journey will be very dangerous."

"Thank you, Pani Machaiym. May God always be in your thoughts and in your heart."

It did not take the kaszubs long to find their way to *Łowcza* and meet up with the Mikhailo Koriya family. To their surprise, just two days later, the senior Andriy and Maria Kaszuba also arrived in *Łowcza.* Unfortunately, it was here that Maria Kaszuba, my paternal grandmother, took ill. Perhaps the stress of having to leave Poland was too much for her. Sadly, her life ended in *Łowcza.* The next day, Maria was laid to rest in the local cemetery.

For the kaszubs, more bad news would soon follow. While in *Łowcza,* they were told that the members of the local Ukrainian bands had left the region. No longer with the added protection of a UPA unit, Mikhailo Koriya suggested that the twelve remaining kaszubs vacate *Łowcza* in favour of the safety of Gorajec.

Leaving *Łowcza* in the darkness of night and sending Mikhailo in advance of the others to scout for any potential danger, the family was able to arrive in Gorajec by daybreak. During the trek and even during the darkness of night, they came across no fewer than 120 dead bodies, mostly males, moot testimony to the rumour that the UPA was no longer in complete control of the region.

By a strange quirk of fate, a tragic event was about to unfold, not for clan kaszub but for Brygada Salon. Just a few days earlier, it was Pani Nadia Kostritsky's husband who was murdered by members of Brygada Salon in the village of Płazów. Unfortunately for the four remaining members of Brygada Salon, Nadia Kostritsky promised her dead husband that she would move heaven and earth to get revenge. Through her network of contacts, Nadia was able to get word to her brother, Ivan Maczaj, the underground leader of a UPA unit in the region. In a clandestine meeting with Ivan, she tearfully described how her husband was murdered and begged that something be done by way of retribution.

Not only was Nadia's brother made aware of the tragic murder of her husband but word got back to Mykola Lebed, the leader of OUN-B, the militaristic wing of OUN. He took it upon himself to investigate further. Through his network of informants, he discovered that Brygada Salon was planning to attack the village of Gorajec.

Meanwhile, gathered in a secret hiding place just five kilometres north of Gorajec, Brygada Salon was planning its next attack on the Ukrainian community. To accomplish its mission, Wilk volunteered to approach the starosta in the village of Gorajec with an ultimatum: leave by noon of the following day or plan to be annihilated and the village burned to the ground. In the process, Wilk's mission was undertaken with the belief that UPA units were no longer operating in the region. This turned out to be a tragic miscalculation.

With an intimate knowledge of the region and having access to a number of informants, not only did Mykola Lebed learn of the hiding place of Brygada Salon but also of their plans. Events unfolded quickly. In fact, Wilk did not even get an opportunity to complete his reconaissance mission at Gorajec. No sooner had he left the hiding place of his unit than all hell broke loose behind him. Corporal Kula, Puma, and Karabin found themselves in a firefight with a UPA unit. Quickly returning to see what all of the shooting was about, a scene of horror unfolded before Wilk. The UPA unit was long gone. So were Brygada Salon's military-trained horses. Left behind as a reminder of the work of UPA were the dead bodies of Kula, Karabin, and Puma. Just like that, the wish of Nadia Kostritsky was fulfilled and the fate of Brygada Salon was forever sealed. To mourn the loss of the unit was the sole survivor, Wilk. Soon, Kapitan Kon would learn of the tragic event.

During that same evening, the kaszubs, en route to Gorajec, listened intently to the explosive firefight as the UPA unit ambushed Brygada

Salon. They didn't know what to make of the skirmish. None was aware that a UPA unit had come to the area with a mission, and that was to destroy the Polish paramilitary unit who murdered Nadia's husband and raised havoc in other villages in Gmina Narol. Neither were they aware that Wilk was the only survivor of Brygada Salon, now trying to find his way back to Narol on foot. Yet, to no one's surprise, other Polish bands were present.

Just as the sun rose that morning, the kaszubs were attacked by a group of Polish bandits. Luckily, it was not their intent to kill anyone but rather to rob them and hasten their exit. Mikhailo and Dmetro, in particular, were severely beaten for the second time. Had they retaliated, both would likely have been shot by the heavily-armed bandits. What the bandits did not know is that Anna was about to get her hands on the carbine left behind by Wilk and shoot a couple of them. However, the confrontation was suddenly brought to a peaceful conclusion when a senior Polish officer appeared out of nowhere, identified himself, and forbade the bandits from inflicting any further harm on the kaszubs. With the help of the Polish officer, they eventually arrived at Gorajec and the safety of the Greek Catholic Church in the village. The dead bodies along the route were later loaded onto wagons by Poles for burial in a mass grave.

"My dear father," a tearful and shocked Anna declared, *"it was like running a gauntlet, all the while hoping that someone would not pummel us to death!"*

Once again in a region under the protection of Ukrainian units and the UPA, the twelve members of clan kaszub went into hiding in Gorajec. Here, they spent two weeks planning how they might find safe passage to the small village of Nowe Sioło, a distance of only seven kilometers. To improve their chances of arriving safely in Nowe Sioło, the kaszubs split up. Their de facto leader, Mikhailo Kaszuba and his family, along with the Stupak, Zhukiv, and Grokh families took different routes through forested areas. The others waited one day before following similar routes to Nowe Sioło. All arrived safely at their planned destination.

In Nowe Sioło, the kaszubs sought safe harbour with Polish families prepared to help them. Andriy Kaszuba, now in the company of his daughter, Anna, met up with a woman by the name of Oksana Petelai. In the sparsely populated area near the village of Nowe Sioło, Oksana Petelai consented to harbour and protect Andriy and Anna Kaszuba. The others in the group found safe haven with other Polish families. In order to survive, the kaszubs were able to find piecemeal work with sympathetic Polish farmers in the immediate area.

Andriy Kaszuba, now a widower, lost much of his zest for living. Perhaps this contributed to his coming down with a serious case of asthma. Much like my paternal grandmother, my grandfather soon succumbed to his condition and died. The local people and members of the family buried him in a cemetery near Nowe Sioło.

With the loss of her father, Anna decided to join her brother Mikhailo and his family in the nearby village of Dachnow, about four kilometers to the southwest of Nowe Sioło. Good fortune followed Anna and Mikhailo. Becoming aware of the difficulties encountered by Ukrainians in their attempt to reach Jaroslaw in safety, a senior Soviet official came to Dachnow, registered the kaszubs, and promised them safe passage to Jaroslaw. He assured them that Polish military guards would offer security and assistance.

But what kind of safe passage would the Polish guards provide? During the forced march from Dachnow to Jaroslaw, Ukrainians were molested and even beaten by the escorting Polish guards who were armed with rifles and pistols. No medical attention was permitted and any Ukrainian who fell ill or ran out of energy was, as a rule, shot on the spot. As a result of such actions, a number of innocent Ukrainians met an untimely death, even though they were supposed to be under the protection of Soviet and Polish security troops.

Despite the difficulties and the loss of several Ukrainians in the group who were murdered by overly-zealous Polish guards, the kaszubs, after a two-day march from Dachnow, did arrive safely in Jaroslaw. Once in Jaroslaw, their registration papers, completed earlier, were checked by the Soviet NKVD and any necessary corrections or changes made. The kaszubs, now under the direction of the NKVD, were ready for transport to Lviv. Depending upon the availability of space on a train, some went right away while others left Jaroslaw by later transport.

When one considers what happened to so many others during the historic trek from the burnt-out village of Grochi to Jaroslaw, the kaszubs were the lucky ones. Although it is true that during the stressful journey, both my grandmother and grandfather succumbed to their weakened physical and mental conditions, eleven kaszubs did arrive safely in Jaroslaw. It would not be until days later in Soviet Ukraine that they would learn what happened to Feodor Kaszuba, one of the other kaszub siblings. They would also learn as to what happened to Oksana Kaszuba-Dutkiewycz and her two young boys.

Heartbroken and in tears, the kaszubs were forced to say goodbye to the land of their ancestors. They could do little else but look forward with fear and trepidation to Soviet Ukraine and Stalin's *land of paradise*.

Once in Soviet Ukraine, the kaszubs learned that many other Ukrainians refused to be transferred to Stalin's *land of milk and honey*. Those who managed to hide out or were a part of UPA operations, later came under the purview of Operation Vistula.

As Ukrainians from Gmina Narol boarded a train that would take them from Jaroslaw to Lviv, they must have felt quite optimistic. After all, they had survived the onslaught of Polish bandits who were determined to remove them from Polish lands and kill those who refused to leave. But, to no one's surprise, Stalin's land of milk and honey would bring little joy to anyone.

PART 7

COMMUNISM, THE EQUAL SHARING OF MISERY

15

Welcome To Stalin's Paradise

"You cannot make a revolution with silk gloves,"
Josef Stalin

P acked like sardines into train carriages at a railway siding in Jaroslaw bound for the city of Lviv, a distance of 150 kilometers, it was not unusual for transferees to suddenly recognize a relative or a neighbour. Several realized that they were in the company of members of their own extended family or in the presence of friends or neighbours from Gmina Narol whom they had not seen for some time. As victims of the tentacles of the Soviet population transfer program, all felt lucky to survive the war and the incessant attacks from marauding Polish nationalistic units.

As each train arrived in Lviv, no one knew for certain who was in what carriage. Only the Soviet officials who registered them in Poland had that answer. Disembarking in Lviv, the transferees were directed to a large detention compound near the station especially put into place as a clearinghouse. Each transferee was checked against the list prepared in Jaroslaw and then entered into a logbook along with a note as to what belongings each family brought with them. Once processed, these official transfer documents were left in the care of the State Archives in Lviv.[2]

---

2   The transfer document for Mikhailo Kaszuba obtained from the State Archives in Lviv is presented in Ukrainian in Appendix A. An English translation follows.

Members of clan kaszub did not arrive in the same carriage or at the same time. All that mattered was that most arrived safely and could now count on each other for moral support. Other families were not so lucky. Several families became separated from their children, not knowing of their whereabouts or whether they had survived the journey in the first place.

During their brief detention in the refugee camp in Lviv, Anna and Mikhailo Kaszuba attained some level of comfort knowing that they were in the company of the Stupak and Zhukiv families from the village of Grochi. It was also an opportune time to mingle with other transferees and share stories of conflict and survival. Since Lviv, also known as Lemberg during the Austrian Empire, was the centre of the historical region of Galicia, refugees had much to talk about. It was also during one of these informal conversations that a transferee approached Anna.

"Hello, Hanka, you may not remember me but my name is Grokh, Misha Grokh. I am from the village of Grochi. We are both from the same village."

"Yes, of course, I remember you. I remember you from grade school in Płazów. I am glad you introduced yourself. You look a mess! It's no wonder I didn't recognize you!"

"This has been a difficult journey for me, much like hell on earth. Not only that, but I have been in hiding for a long time trying to avoid service in the German or Russian armies. I have not had a bath or a shave for weeks. No wonder I look a mess! What about you, Hanka?"

"Thanks to the Nazis, I have been away from Grochi since 1940. With the Nazi and Soviet armies constantly at our doorstep, just staying alive was a minor miracle, not to mention the Polish bandits who were bent on robbing and killing all of us."

Being mindful of the shabby clothes that she was wearing, Anna was suddenly overcome with an attack of self-consciousness. Misha Grokh, in noting her shyness, made every attempt to put her at ease.

"Don't worry about the manner of your dress. We are all in the same boat. You look just fine to me. I can see that you are no longer a little school girl!"

"Oh, Misha, your words of encouragement mean a lot to me!"

"You're so pretty I completely forgot what else I was going to say."

During their time in the refugee camp in Lviv, the names and destinations of all those in the compound were posted by Soviet authorities. Mikhailo Kaszuba noted that the kaszubs were scheduled to leave Lviv for the city of Ternopil the following Monday.

"Mikhailo," asked an anxious Anna, *"you saw the list of families going to Ternopil? Was my name on that list?"*

1995: Mikhailo Grokh and Aunt Anna Kaszuba-Grokh.

"Good fortune, Hanka! Along with my family, you are on that list."
"What about the Grokh family? Are they on the list?"
"Yes, they are on the list, but why do you ask about them?"

If Anna heard the question, she elected not to answer. In tears with the good news, she could only embrace her brother and whisper *thank God*. At first glance, it may sound strange that transferees knew so little about other deportees. After all, those earmarked for transfer had little opportunity to get together in Poland for fear of attack by nationalistic bandits. To travel as one large group would have been quite dangerous. As a result, families frequently split up, each being responsible for him or herself. It would not be until they arrived in the city of Ternopil that a true picture would emerge of the final destination of the transferees.

While awaiting instructions for their passage to Ternopil, members of clan kaszub were able to get together for the very first time in many months. Not surprisingly, much of the talk centred round the family of Dmetro and Mariia Kaszuba, not so much about their four-year-old son Dima but rather about their infant son, Ivan, born just two months earlier while hiding out in the forest near Grochi.

There was one other important question on everyone's mind, *what happened to Anna's older sister, Oksana?* The family was aware that she had married Ivan Dutkiewycz in the mid-1930s and that they had two boys, Ivan and Jaroslaw. They also knew that Oksana left Płazów in 1938 with the hopes of finding work in France. *Was she still in France? Had she survived the war? What of her husband Ivan and their two little boys? Where were they?*

As for the other members of clan kaszub, all were accounted for with the exception of Feodor Kaszuba and his family. Although not certain, they suspected that Feodor, his wife Marika, and their children, seven-year-old Zenoviy, six-year-old Jaroslaw, and three-year-old Marika were still hiding out in the village of Stary Lubliniec or Stary Dzików, a short distance west of Grochi. They must have been aware of the dangers associated with the trek to Jaroslaw and preferred to hide out until such time that they could safely exit Poland by way of Rawa Ruska.

Although weary, hungry, tired, and in need of a bath, there was also an air of optimism. All were surprised at the hustle and bustle evident at the Ternopil train station. In particular, the locals wanted to share their stories about the fierce fighting that took place between Soviet and German forces in the Ternopil region, both wanting to capture a city important for its rail transportation system. After the Nazis were routed in the fall of 1944, the Soviets deported all Poles to the Wroclaw (*Breslau*) region of what today is part of Western Poland, imprisoned all Ukrainian nationalists, and deported to Kazakhstan the former state administration, police, and business owners. During the early stages of the war, when Ukraine was under German control, the Jews in the region had been rounded up and sent to the Bełżec extermination camp.

For members of clan kaszub, their time in Ternopil was just long enough to receive their deployment orders from the Soviet Transfer Commission. As might be expected, they knew little about the rich history of Ternopil. In learning more about the region, they were somewhat relieved when told that their final destination would be to villages in the Oblast of Ternopil, and that other transferees in their detention compound would also be travelling to these villages. During their time in Ternopil, they listened with a great deal of interest and anticipation to stories about the richness of Ukrainian culture and customs.

At the time of their transfer, the Oblast of Ternopil was composed of seventeen administrative districts, sixteen cities, nineteen urban-type settlements, and hundreds of small villages. With the large number of small villages in the oblast, it became abundantly clear that the Soviet authorities would have little difficulty in placing all transferees. The oblast had a well-developed agricultural and industrial base, requiring considerable manpower in the food, sugar, alcohol, canned vegetable, and fruit processing industries. Its favourable geographic position, climate, fertile soil, and convenient transport routes served by two river systems, the Dniester and Seret, made the oblast a good antidote to the region the family left behind.

According to a notice posted at the train station in Ternopil, Dmetro Kaszuba noted that his family was assigned to the village of Yabluniv, while Mikhailo's family, including Anna, were destined for the village of Loshniv. With 64 percent of the land mass in the Oblast of Ternopil dedicated to agriculture, Dmetro and Mikhailo felt certain that they would have no alternative but to be assigned to work on state-operated agricultural kolkhozes.

Arriving at their final destinations, Dmetro, Mikhailo, and their families were in a state of shock. Everywhere they looked there was evidence of the destruction of war. The Poles who had previously occupied the various homes were long gone. The war had destroyed many homes while others were in a state of disrepair. What had previously been bustling villages—home to Poles, Ukrainians, and Jews—were now virtually deserted.

Before being forced to leave Poland, Ukrainians were assured that they could bring with them all of their belongings. However, this was an impossible dream, nothing more than communist propaganda. Roving Polish bands first robbed them of their land, cattle, and household goods, while other nationalistic bands followed on their heels by burning their homes and villages. A lack of safe transportation and the short notice given them before being kicked out of Poland only added to their problems.

In an attempt to boost the morale of the kaszubs, Mikhailo Kaszuba tried to make a fundamental point. *"You know, brothers, maybe this is God's will. Ukrainians have long fought for independence. Maybe, all of this will result in a free and independent Ukraine."*

"I will believe it when I see it," replied Dmetro, *"I heard that Stalin is a butcher and a murderer. He has other ideas and they sure as hell are not meant to help us."*

"Shush, Dima! The Soviets do not take kindly to criticism. I hate the very thought of being shipped off to a labour camp in Siberia because of a careless remark."

Silence, no one had an answer to Mikhailo's words of caution.

Now safely in the Oblast of Ternopil and even though gossip was discouraged, the transferees did not hesitate to talk about what they knew of the forcible transfer program imposed upon them by the Soviets. All agreed that the hell that Ukrainians underwent on both sides of the Curzon Line was indescribable. Their repatriation to what the Soviets called the *Soviet Fatherland* was forcible and certainly not voluntary resettlement as portrayed in Soviet propaganda. Ukrainians who did not want to go voluntarily to Soviet Ukraine were forcibly expelled by Stalin's Polish lackeys. Many fought with the greatest of stubbornness and determination against expulsion from their ancestral lands. However, their efforts were futile. Those who had somehow escaped deportation to Siberia were later rounded up and re-located to Northern Poland.

Making matters worse, those earmarked for deportation were terrorized to such a degree that no one knew what to do or where to go for help. There was no one to protect them. Some villages had organized impromptu defences. In cases where the Polish bandits approached at night, the church bells would begin to ring and the people would run for their lives. Occasionally, the UPA did come to their defence, but they were not able to protect all the villages or to destroy all the armed bands sent by the Polish government.

Mikhailo Kaszuba was of the opinion that what the Poles did to them was far worse than any crime committed in the times of the Mongolian invasions of Ukraine. In particular, he could not get out of his mind the image of a Polish government order emblazoned on huge posters in Poland, *"Musimy wysiedlic wszystkich Ukraincow do jednego, we must resettle every last one of those Ukrainians."* These huge posters, exhorting all Ukrainians to go voluntarily to the east, were widely distributed.

By organizing armed bands of civilians and sending them into Ukrainian villages, the Poles devised a very ingenious method to get rid of Ukrainians. By day and night, Poles raided Ukrainian villages. Their priests and teachers were the first to fall victim to this unbounded Polish bestiality. Promptly arrested, they were forcibly deported east of the Curzon Line. UPA, the Ukrainian resistance organization, fought these inhuman deportations, but eventually the Poles brought up several army divisions and expelled great numbers of Ukrainians.

The kaszubs had plenty of time to reflect upon what had just happened to them. The family survived the horrors of three battles when three major fronts moved through Gmina Narol. Yet, they had to admit that living through the war was safer and easier than was their life during the period of ethnic cleansing. Looking around at their current situation, it appeared as though they had fallen from the frying pan into the fire.

"So this is Stalin's Paradise," they were heard to say, *"what kind of paradise is it far from our ancestral village of Grochi and with very little prospect of personal freedoms under government policies that embrace slave labour for all?"*

Political changes abounded everywhere. Unfortunately, none was democratic. Since the Oblast of Ternopil had been under Polish rule from 1919 to 1939, those Ukrainians who remained behind in the region at the end of the war were not subject to deportation to Poland. They were already in *Stalin's Paradise*. Those arriving from Poland had to have regard for how and why the Soviet Union came into being. The first important step taken by Russia following the Bolshevik Revolution of 1917 was to nationalize the land and eliminate the class of *gentry landlords*. In order to carry out their agrarian program, organize the village poor to fight against the kulaks, and to build a new life in each village, the Bolsheviks sent their representatives to each village.

With Stalin's first Five-Year Plan in 1929, the massive kolkhoz movement began. This meant that the kulaks were liquidated as a class to make way for collectivization. Progressive workers and experienced Communists commissioned by the party to the village played an enormous part in the formation and consolidation of the kolkhozes. According to the Communists, *"...collectivization delivered the countryside from kulak bondage, class differentiation, ruin, and poverty."* They were of the opinion that the collectivization of agriculture and the industrialization of the country created the prerequisites for applying the principles of planning and construction to all rural-populated areas.

The soviet village and the kolkhoz system withstood the harsh trials of the Great Patriotic War. During the war, the Nazis burned and destroyed thousands of rural populated areas in the territory, along with thousands of soviet kolkhozes. In 1945, the number of able-bodied men on the kolkhozes was 60% below the prewar figure. After the war, full reconstruction and further development of the villages demanded enormous efforts by the entire country. Taking into account these circumstances, Soviet officials had little difficulty in finding a home and work for Ukrainians arriving in the Oblast of Ternopil from Poland.

Shortly after their arrival in Loshniv, the deportees had an opportunity to meet in the community centre and to listen to Soviet administrators who painted a very rosy picture for the new arrivals. However, for those who had arrived earlier and had attended similar meetings, the propaganda was met with a considerable amount of skepticism.

"Those damned Bolsheviks," was the way that Mikhailo Kaszuba spoke, in private, of the Soviet officials, *"sure they told us that they would soon issue passports for each of us. They promised that we would soon see the benefits of a communist way of life. What kind of smelly manure is this?*

Equality for everyone, they said. My royal pissed-off ass there is equality! And those so-called passports they issued for each of us? They are for travel within this oblast only. To go to another oblast is impossible."

"You mean," asked Anna, *"that we will not be able to visit our brother, Fedjko, if he ends up in another oblast?"*

"Sure looks like it. We are now prisoners in this forlorn land. The Soviets call this Stalin's Paradise? What kind of horseshit is this? My pigs lived better in Poland."

As time went on, news filtered back to the transferees that the Poles had burned hundreds of Ukrainian villages in Poland, along with hundreds of farm buildings. At the same time, it was learned that the UPA had destroyed hundreds of farms in Poland, two railway stations, six bridges, six oil wells and over seventy Polish villages. Eight trains were dispatched by the Soviets to transport the re-settlers to Soviet Ukraine. To add to the horrors of deportation, several trains were ambushed, either by nationalistic Poles or by members of the UPA. In all, 163 carriages were destroyed and 22 rail lines cut. It took a considerable amount of good luck to survive ethnic cleansings in Poland, even before boarding a train bound for Soviet Ukraine. As the kaszubs settled into their new homes, a strange sort of peace enveloped them and the countryside.

In the Oblast of Ternopil, agriculture quickly became the primary source of employment. Village communities were organized around the economic institution of the collective farm. Most collective farms became known as *kolkhozes,* while state farms became known as *sovkhozes.* In the meantime, villages were operated as *village soviets.* These administrative organizations employed the elite of rural society, nearly all of whose members were men.

What the Soviet government saw in the Oblast of Ternopil, required attention. Soviet planners saw the need for extensive construction of production and public buildings and housing in the countryside. They foresaw that many of the rural settlements would be built according to standard or specially developed master plans. Public centres required administrative buildings, libraries, clubs, schools, athletic facilities, stores, consumer service enterprises, post offices, and telegraph and telephone offices. They saw the need for the construction of buildings using brick and stone as well as other modern building materials. Most of all, the Soviet lackeys wanted to consolidate smaller kolkhozes and merge several small populated areas into larger administrative units in order to improve villages and better the lives of the soviet.

These were the fundamental changes envisioned for the culture of the soviet village. There was a need for schools so that illiteracy could be eliminated. Various clubs had to be organized, libraries built, books and magazines procured, and film projectors acquired. The growth of culture and scientific propaganda for atheism caused a retreat from religion by the rural population and a decrease in the number of believers. Moscow started preparing to liquidate the Greek Catholic Church after the Soviets came back to Western Ukraine in the summer of 1944. In 1945, Stalin personally approved written proposals to liquidate the Ukrainian Greek Catholic Church by putting it under the jurisdiction of the Moscow Patriarchate. The presumed purchasing power of rural residents had to be addressed as well. This meant that the soviet government would have to address the need for modern furniture and clothing, bicycles and motorcycles, and radios for everyday use.

Yes, this was the type of propaganda put out by the Soviet government. However, this did not decrease in any way the suffering confronting those who found their way to Loshniv and Yabluniv. There were no economic and cultural ties between the socialist village and the socialist city. The city of Ternopil was not that interested in supplying the villages with farm machinery. Nor were they interested in supplying agronomists, physicians, teachers, engineers, and technicians to the small rural communities. Sure, they talked about an increase in agricultural production, the amelioration of the village, and a higher cultural level among its rural population—but it was simply propaganda.

Those arriving in the small villages began to ask questions, *"When would electricity arrive in the villages? What about the rumour of those well-organized buildings to bring consumer services, domestic enterprises, cultural, and medical institutions to the villages? When would these come?"*

1938: Oksana Kaszuba-Dutkiewicz and Ivan Dutkiewicz.
Oksana perished in France when the war broke out. In 1998,
we located their two sons, Jaroslaw and Ivan.

Soon, the kaszubs learned that in the soviet state there was no place for freedom of speech or press for the foes of socialism. The test in the totalitarian state was not whether the publication was treasonable or seditious but whether it tended to advance official ideology. They realized that the true meaning of Communism denoted a system of social organization based upon common property and an equal distribution of income and wealth. The system of soviet control quickly became evident in the villages. Organization of the Communist party became the norm everywhere with the primary or lowest level of organization at the village level. Information moved always upwards with no direct election of representatives to the supreme congress being provided. At the bottom, membership was grouped in primary party organizations, sometimes known as cells. These cells were organized in factories, villages, collective farms, and educational institutions.

Soviet propaganda about collective farming:
"We will keep the kulaks away from our collective farms."

The important functions of local government were carried out through an extensive network of soviets, the elected local or district councils. This entailed wide participation by the population in the work of the party and government at all levels. Each soviet elected its own chairman, deputy chairman, and secretary who formed the executive responsible to the local soviet and to the next superior local soviet. These soviets directed the work of those reporting to them to ensure the maintenance of public order, the observance of the laws, the protection of the rights of its citizens, and to direct the local economic and cultural affairs. They were responsible for the operation of public housing, local transportation and industry, schools, and health facilities. They approved economic plans and budgets. No critical debate or adverse votes occurred because deputies were largely Communist Party members bound to resolve disputes privately.

Taking stock of the hardships encountered by the kaszubs while being transferred to Soviet Ukraine, perhaps Dmetro encountered the greatest of challenges. Married to Mariya Litkovich just as the war broke out, the arrival of their second child could not have been more bizarre. It happened at a time when Brygada Salon attacked the village of Grochi. Located near his father's home, Dmetro had just completed the construction of his home when Brygada Salon attacked. Dmetro and his pregnant wife barely escaped with their lives into the adjacent forest. While hiding out in the forest with their four-year old son, Mariya gave birth to Ivan.

A short time after his arrival at the small village of Sukhostav, Dmetro elected to supplement his meager income on a collective farm by undertaking piece-meal work in the logging camp in the Transcarpathian region. He survived the hardships of the war, the attacks by nationalistic Poles, and the transfer to Soviet Ukraine, only to lose his life while providing security service for a state logging operation. Here is how it happened.

1999: Ivan Kaszuba came to Soviet Ukraine in 1945 as a youngster and worked on a kolkhoz at Sahustav, Ukraine, for most of his adult life.

One day, a security guard at the logging camp asked Dmetro to take his night shift in protecting the government's stockpile of timber. The security guard wanted an evening off for personal reasons and those personal reasons had to do with his love for the wife of a fellow security guard. Somehow, the love triangle was discovered by the woman's husband. Mad as hell, the jealous husband took matters into his own hands. That evening, in a rage of anger, he shot what he believed to be his unfaithful wife's lover. Shot to death, unfortunately, was the security guard's replacement, Dmetro Kaszuba.

Unlike other members of his family, Fedjko Kaszuba, married to Mariya Klymus in 1937, did not leave Poland until the spring of 1945. Hiding out with a Polish family first in Stary Dzików, just a short distance from Cieszanow, and later in the nearby village of Stary Lubliniec, he had no intention of leaving Poland. However, with increased pressure from the Soviet Transfer Commission, he at last consented to leave Poland in the spring of 1945. By this time, his wife Mariya had given birth to Yaroslav in 1938 and Maria in 1940. With two horses hitched to a wagon and tugging one cow behind, their exodus from Poland to Buzk via Rawa Ruska took more than three weeks to complete. Eight months pregnant by the time they arrived at their destination, Mariya gave birth to their second son, Zenovij, in the village of Buzk.

Of the twenty kaszubs forcibly driven from Poland in 1944 and 1945, eighteen arrived safely. Regrettably, my paternal grandparents, Andriy and Maria Kaszuba, perished during the initial stage of the stressful journey.

In Poland, the transfer commissions were composed of Polish Communists and Soviet personnel. In Soviet Ukraine, the transfer commissions were composed of Soviet NKVD. The prime purpose of the population transfer program was ethnic consolidation. Eligibility for forced transfer was determined by ethnicity and not by country of birth. Members of clan kaszub who belonged to the Ukrainian Greek Catholic Church and whose mother-tongue was Ukrainian were earmarked for transfer to Soviet Ukraine. Left behind within my extended family were those who identified themselves as being ethnic Poles.

In contrast to members of clan kaszub, the families of my maternal grandparents met differing fates. Long before the outbreak of the war, several members of the Ivan Groszko family had already left Poland in favour of United States, Canada, and Latvia. As a result, the forced transfer of ethnic Ukrainians to Soviet Ukraine had a lesser impact upon them. This coupled with the fact that the extended Groszko family encompassed both Ukrainian and ethnic Poles meant that those identified as ethnic Poles were not subject to transfer. As a consequence, only the families of Stefan, Vasyl, and Oksana Groszko were subject to forcible transfer from Poland to Soviet Ukraine.

In the spring of 1945, eleven members of the Groszko family left Poland via Rawa Ruska for Soviet Ukraine, some by horse-drawn wagons, others on foot. Vasyl Groszko, his wife Parashka, and their two children,

Olha and Bogdan, ended up in the town of Buzk. Stefan and Anastasia Groszko and their children, Vasyl and Stefania, were directed to the city of Lviv. Volodymyr and Oksana Groszko, and their infant daughter, Marika, were destined for the town of Kamianka-Buzka in the Oblast of Lviv.

Once in Soviet Ukraine, stories of the survival of Ukrainians while in Poland began to emerge; stories of genocide characterized by torture and barbarity. The methods in use involved the hacking of Ukrainians with axes, throwing wounded victims into wells, sawing and dismembering them, horse dragging their victims, eye gouging and the pulling out of tongues, and other unspeakable atrocities. Facing threats of physical harm and even death, most Ukrainians elected to abandon their homes as quickly as possible. No one could guarantee their safety if they decided to remain behind. Running away and hiding was considered to be a treasonous act against the Poles. Ukrainians were well aware of what awaited them if they hunkered down in their own homes.

Special mention must be made of the viciously criminal stance taken in cases of mixed Ukrainian-Polish marriages. In such cases, the Polish assassins often murdered, wherever possible, whole families including the children or at least the Ukrainian partner. In addition, there were instances where a Polish husband was forced to kill his Ukrainian partner with his own hands. The same guideline applied in cases where a Polish woman was married to a Ukrainian partner.

Ethnic cleansings of Ukrainians were usually accompanied by barbaric scorched-earth policies. After being robbed of their property and livestock, their houses and other buildings were burnt to the ground. There was also total destruction of a large number of historical Ukrainian country houses along with their farm buildings and gardens. Sadly, many Greek Catholic Churches and Chapels were also destroyed.

Armija Krajowa, created in 1942, condoned the use of self defence units to assist in the genocide against Ukrainians. Added to this were bandits armed with axes and pitchforks, often composed of neighbours who formed a kind of a mobilization of Polish masses. All unmarried able-bodied men were requisitioned for this purpose. Accompanied by women, youths, and even children, these bands busied themselves with looting, arson, and finishing off disabled or wounded Ukrainians. All of this took place despite years of supposed mutual friendship or bonds of gratitude that had existed towards Ukrainians. Imbued with spiritual wellness and believing in God did not help those who were victimized.

Yet, it is doubtful that the kaszubs would have survived their journey to Soviet Ukraine without specific assistance from Poles. One must remember that in 1944, Polish nationalistic bands attacked Ukrainian villages in earnest. It would not be until 1945, however, that Ukrainians had officially registered for transfer to Soviet Ukraine. Based upon this timeline, *how is it that so many Ukrainians survived during that one year of terror?* Were it not for Poles harbouring Ukrainians, *how many of them would have survived?*

The answer to these questions is obvious. There were dozens of Polish families in Eastern Poland who aided Ukrainians by warning and hiding them, feeding them, and transporting them to the nearest centre for deportation to Soviet Ukraine.

We now know and accept that the kaszubs would not have survived their time in Poland from 1944 to 1945 had it not been for assistance from unexpected sources. That unexpected source came from Polish families. The Jews like to refer to those who helped members of their community survive the atrocities of World War II as *The Righteous Among The Nations,* a special honour bestowed upon them by the Jewish State. In fact, research shows us that several residents of Gmina Narol received this recognition from Israel. Perhaps a similar honour should have been extended to hundreds of Polish families who helped Ukrainian families survive their time in Poland in advance of their forced transfer to Soviet Ukraine.

As Ukrainians in Eastern Poland were being deprived of their prewar means of livelihood—expelled from their farms, factories, businesses, offices, and homes—along came sympathetic Polish families. Dozens of Polish families came to their rescue. They were under no obligation to risk their own lives and even more, those of their families and neighbours. The helping hand they extended to Ukrainians often lasted not only for a couple of days and nights but weeks and even many months; always in secret and always risking discovery.

In late summer 1945, Polish authorities officially renounced the *legal fiction* of the voluntary character of repatriation. In September, Polish authorities ordered three infantry divisions to forcibly resettle all remaining Ukrainians to the Soviet Union. The ranks of two divisions composed of ethnic Poles from Volhynia, some of whom now exploited their positions as soldiers of the state to extract personal revenge on Ukrainians. Polish soldiers killed hundreds of Ukrainian civilians as they forced 23,000 Ukrainians to evacuate Poland.

In April 1946, Polish authorities organized three infantry divisions into *Operational Group Rzeszow,* tasked to complete the expulsion of Ukrainians from Poland. Villages that had earlier resisted expulsion were now violently pacified. The troops moved from village to village, forcing inhabitants into convoys bound for Soviet Ukraine. Between April and June of 1946, an additional 252,000 Ukrainians were deported. During the entire period of repatriations between October 1944 and June 1946, 482,000 Ukrainians departed Poland for the Soviet Union, most by coercion and only a small number of their own free will.

Now working on Soviet kolkhozes, the attitude of the kaszubs towards the kolkhoz system was, not surprisingly, negative rather than positive. The workers were particularly hostile towards soviet management during the initial period of collective farms when kolkhozes had no assets of their own and the possessions of people were collectivized or taxed. The public opinion became somewhat more lenient when kolkhozes had secured their position. The workers were paid wages, especially in cases where manual labour substituted machine-operated work.

Most every person assigned to a collective farm soon faced feelings of anxiety and despair. Their presence on a kolkhoz was not a matter of choice. Those who refused to work on the kolkhoz had to pay high kulak taxes and live in danger of repression. Yet, entering a kolkhoz gave people a vague sense of security and hope that they would not be deported to Siberia. Times were rough and nobody joked about it. The worst ordeal that people had to go through was giving up their possessions, domestic animals, farm tools, and foodstuff. This had a destructive effect on both the emotional and economic life of the people.

Life in the small village of Loshniv was not without its lighter moments. Shortly after getting settled into the daily routine of life on a kolkhoz, Misha Grokh wanted to spill the beans, as it were, to Anna Kaszuba, shocking her with a confession, *"I knew the moment I saw you in Lviv that there was something about you I needed. Turns out it wasn't something about you at all. It was you. Will you marry me?"*

At first, a shocked Anna, caught off guard, didn't know what to say. Recovering quickly, her response was, *"Yes, yes, I accept your proposal. Before I met you in Lviv, I never knew what it was like to smile for no reason!"*

So many years later, in discussing this phase of her life, my Aunt Anna Grokh seemed to be imbued with that infectious smile, perhaps remembering the moment that Misha proposed to her. *"Sometimes,"* recalled an emotional Aunt Anna, *"someone comes into your life, my life in this case, who changes everything. Misha made me laugh and made me feel like me. It was something that I cannot put into words."*

In discussing the many challenges on the kolkhoz, Anna Kaszuba-Grokh had often turned to her husband for support.

"I hate the Bolsheviks," was the way Anna characterized the kolkhoz, *"look at all of the injustices and at the top of the heap is the kolkhoz foreman."*

"Oh, Hanka, you are so right," Misha Grokh would say, *"I am amazed how the Soviet people overcame the hardships they created for themselves."*

Given the opportunity, Anna would express the opinion that the kolkhoz workers would have deserted the villages and the injustices confronting them if they had the opportunity to do so. Each knew that work on kolkhozes was not very prestigious. The general view was that those who worked on the collective farm were never given a choice. Over time, most adopted and then adapted to the new regime. Those who managed to escape the kolkhoz had a certain advantage over all the others. They did not have to suffer the hardships experienced by those who stayed. Nevertheless, those who stayed did not necessarily support the kolkhoz; they were unfortunate victims of fate.

"One thing is for certain," Anna confessed, *"the kolkhoz taught people how to steal. People adjusted to the collective farm without any difficulty. If they were not paid for their services, they took to stealing. People did not feel proud about it but stealing did become the norm."*

Jaroslaw Kaszuba was in agreement with this assessment, adding, *"The attitude towards stealing was in a sense also connected to the question of ownership. After all, before entering the kolkhoz, the Bolsheviks stole all of our belongings. Despite all of this, our family kept on working with their own horses and with state-owned machines. Stealing from the kolkhoz was not like stealing the property of another person."*

Competition among and between the kolkhozes soon reached a fever pitch. As a result, the workers looked upon their labour as leading to increased productivity on the collective farms. Those who refused to contribute to the welfare of the kolkhoz were frequently shipped off to Siberia for re-education. With time, the situation improved and kolkhoz workers were paid in the currency of the day. As a result, people began to look more optimistically to the future. Collective activities and parties became increasingly popular. Soon, life on the collective farms in the villages of Loshniv, Sukhostav, and Yabluniv was determined by two main factors, the personality of the kolkhoz foreman and relationships between kolkhoz workers.

While serving on collective farms the kaszubs saw themselves as being ruled by a foreign power in Moscow. *"They,"* as Mikhailo Kaszuba was heard to say, *"represent the foreign power. They represent nothing good."*

This prejudice towards the ruling class in Moscow was held by all kolkhoz workers and explains why the kolkhoz foreman played such an important role as mediator and a link between *us* and *them.* The kaszubs, however, rarely talked about the situation for fear of retribution. Infrequently, a Communist stranger would come to the kolkhoz on his motorcycle, leather boots, and riding breeches with leather patches. He would sneakily warn everyone, *"He who will not enter the kolkhoz willingly and contribute to its success will be shipped off to Siberia."*

Of course, everyone was afraid of him. No one wanted to go to Siberia. Everyone was cautious of spies, all kinds of investigators, and party officials. When a stranger came to a kolkhoz, word would spread quickly and the workers learned to keep out of his way. Mysterious strangers, who appeared from out of the blue sky, caused the most fear.

One day, while working in the family garden weeding a bed of beetroots, Anna Grokh was approached by a tall woman dressed in flapping clothes. The woman was stamping restlessly, hiding one hand behind her back.

"What do you want," asked Anna suspiciously.

"Can I have some water," asked the woman in a most husky voice.

Anna tried to oblige only to have the woman tell her that she wanted to drink the water from a proper cup and not from a common water-dipper at the well. The woman wanted to drink from a glass inside the house. Not wishing to stop work, Anna told the woman that she had no intention of obliging. Looking up the narrow road leading to the house, she saw a man approaching.

"Just a moment," said Anna, *"here comes my brother. I will get my brother to get you some water from the house."*

The thirsty woman suddenly left in a hurry along the path towards the woods. She didn't even look back. When she was gone, Anna, frightened and pale, told her brother about the tall woman with hairy legs, a dark moustache line under her nose, and a leather sheath which held a knife at her side.

"I am sure," stuttered Anna, *"that this brute, dressed as a bitch, would have killed me if I had let that suka into the house."*

When Anna and Mikhailo reported this intrusion to the kolkhoz foreman, he was most sympathetic. After the incident, however, the kolkhoz workers took it upon themselves to be more vigilant and to report any future incidents to the kolkhoz hierarchy. Some went so far as to arm themselves while working in the fields.

Despite the hardships on the collective farm, the kaszubs recognized and accepted that the foreman stood between the two character groups of *we* and *they*. They did not belong to either group, even though they did serve on various committees. The most serious problem in establishing kolkhozes was that of finding qualified administrators. Candidates were required to have management skills, be familiar with local problems, and be respected by the kolkhoz workers, while at the same time being loyal to the Soviet regime elsewhere. Since few people met these requirements, conflicts frequently occurred.

In the end, no matter how the Communist leaders tried to leave the impression about the glow of Communism, the experiences of those transferred from Poland to Soviet Ukraine saw it quite differently.

"Sure," they would say, *"there is always a touch of positive in negative things; however, nothing good every came from collectivization."*

Each day on the kolkhoz was filled with hard work and household tasks, made more tiring because *theirs* was a world with a minimum of artifacts. Most of the household objects were made by peasants from local materials: wood, linen, hemp, leather, and plant roots which were commonly used as soap or onion skin to dye cloth. Still, the workers were thankful for their own large gardens, and for the pigs and cows that provided for their sustenance. Like so many farmers the world over, each looked forward to a brighter future.

This restricted and tiring daily life became a basis for reconstruction. National attachment to Ukrainian culture and customs was maintained by taking part in festivals and religious rites, the language spoken at home, traditional songs, and some article kept or copied. These activities, along with exchanges of services and skills, shared leisure and social events, all enhanced local integration. Daily life was an area where different worlds of collective work and private activities could meet. It was here that various traditions imposed by the soviet world lived alongside the local world.

Living on or near the collective farms, various members of clan kaszub were sorted into work brigades where the state dictated what, where, and how much to plant. Most agricultural collective land was cultivated to grow low-value staples such as grain, cotton, flax, forage, and seed. All produce had to be sold to the state at set prices. As a result, rural enterprise was now out of the hands of the rural people. As Mikhailo defined it, "*...the very lives of the peasants were now virtually owned by the state.*" A system of internal passports meant they could not leave their farms. If they were born there, they would have to toil their lives away there, a continuation of the slave serfdom the peasants had experienced under the Tsars and Polish Counts. Their *landlord* had merely changed from a local landowner to the state.

The result of these measures was catastrophic. Productivity and efficiency plummeted as the inefficiencies of a centrally-planned system took their toll. Mass starvation swept the countryside as harvest and livestock yields dropped. It would not be until Josef Stalin passed away in 1953 that conditions would begin to improve.

This was how most kaszubs, under duress, found themselves to be working on Soviet state farms in Soviet Ukraine. The situation, however, for those captured by the Gestapo for work in Germany or those arrested by the NKVD and then deported to Siberia was far more complex and more dangerous. Here are their stories.

16

Siberia And Amnesty

"Pack lightly, where you are going we have everything you will need."

The shocking story of what happened to members of the Wozniak and Konenko families immediately after the outbreak of World War II can be laid at the feet of those who signed the infamous Molotov-Ribbentrop Pact. Had it not been for this particular alliance, it is doubtful that these tragedies would have occurred.

Shortly after occupying Volhynia in 1939, the Soviets arrested and deported to Siberia thousands of Volhynian residents. The Soviets ceased to recognize the Polish state and immediately set out to destroy the Polish people and their culture. At first, many Polish citizens and Ukrainian peasants perceived the Soviet entry into Poland as an opportunity to take part in communist activities. However, their enthusiasm for communism quickly faded.

To the shock and disbelief of the Wozniak family, as if it wasn't enough to have the Red Army occupy Volhynia, the NKVD arrested Filip Wozniak and their teenage son, Donek. For some inexplicable reason, the NKVD did not arrest Marta Wozniak or their daughters, Monika and Agatha. Arriving moments later at the nearby Konenko residence, the NKVD arrested Jan Konenko and their teenage son, Janko. As was the case with the Wozniak family, the NKVD neither arrested Danuta Konenko nor their daughter Tanja. Under NKVD guard, Filip, Donek, Jan, and Janko were escorted to a railway siding in Lutsk and loaded onto unheated cattle cars. In a couple of days, the cattle train would leave for Siberia.

The neutrality pact between Germany and the Union of Soviet Socialist Republics sounded the death knell for the Republic of Poland and led to the arrests of thousands of her citizens. Germany was in full control of western Poland while the Soviets controlled eastern Poland. Josef Stalin, visualizing what the future might hold for an expanded Soviet Union and wanting to neuter any potential opposition to his rule, elected to deport all potential political dissidents in the newly-acquired region.

When the Russians invaded eastern Poland, they already had a plan in mind. It was their objective to impose a new political and economic order. Soviet authorities began to introduce drastic political, socioeconomic, and demographic changes in the region under their control. In order to accomplish this goal, the Soviets planned to deport to the northern parts of the Soviet Union all those they suspected might be in opposition to their grandiose plan.

By this time, Poland had already lost its war against Germany and the Polish government was about to abandon western Poland. To Poles, however, the Soviet attack on eastern Poland came as a surprise. To justify the attack, the Soviets stated that the purpose of the invasion was to protect the minority groups living in Volhynia, particularly the Ukrainians.

As the Red Army marched through hamlets and villages, they dropped leaflets explaining that the Army was assisting Poland in her fight against Germany. At the same time, leaflets urged Belorussian and Ukrainian peasants to grab pitchforks, axes, saws, and scythes and overwhelm their Polish landlords. Appeals were made to Red Army soldiers to turn their guns on the Polish officers who made them fight an unjust war. As the Red Army moved through the countryside and villages, political commissars and soldiers told the local peasants to take all they wanted from Polish landlords and rich farmers. Much blood was shed without the Soviet Army having to fire a single shot.

When Galicia was ceded to Poland after WWI, the tensions between Ukrainians and Poles escalated. The Polish government brought the so-called *military colonists* from Poland to the Kresy region and selected the majority of the local administrators from this group to carry out Poland's prejudicial policies. However, after the incorporation of Kresy into the Soviet Union in 1939, the political landscape changed yet once again. The military colonists (referred to as the *osadniks* by the Soviets) were branded as *kulaks* and *enemies of the people.* As a target of Soviet propaganda, the *osadniks* became one of the *categories* of crimes within the Soviet penal system.

The Wozniak and Konenko families did not always reside in the Lutsk region. At the end of World War I, those who had served in the Polish military were invited to leave the over-developed and over-populated region of Poland in favour of Volhynia. Since both Filip Wozniak and Jan Konenko had served in the Polish Home Army, they were eligible to be classified as military colonists. This enabled them and their families to move from the County of Tomaszów Lubelski to the less populated and under-developed region of the new and expanded Polish state and take up residence in the small village of Polonka.

Although the Konenkos and Wozniaks were on friendly terms, this did not mean that all Ukrainians living in Volhynia had the same respect for Poles. When the Soviets came to Volhynia, the gap between most Poles and Ukrainians had widened into an abyss. Subjugated by the Poles for so many years, Ukrainians saw this as an opportunity to join the Soviets in opposition to the ruling Poles. Even before the Soviets entered Volhynia, Ukrainian committees spontaneously formed in many places to replace the local Polish administration.

"You'll get used to it or you will croak," the Soviets used to say to the Poles, not maliciously but merely summing up the commonsense wisdom life had taught them. As an afterthought the Soviets added, *"There are three categories of people in the Soviet Union, those who were in jail, those who are in jail, and those who will be in jail."* They did not mean this in a vindictive way but rather because this was the story of their own lives.

The initial regulations issued by the occupying authorities were essentially the same throughout the entire territory. People were required to register their radios and turn in their weapons, refuse shelter to Polish Officers and policemen, refrain from gathering in groups, and remove all Polish state symbols and official portraits. Freedom of travel without official authorization was denied and confiscation of landed estates and larger industrial property was initiated. Zealous Soviet committees issued ordinances forbidding people to speak Polish.

Barely one month after the Soviet Army crossed the Polish frontier they organized a plebiscite in what was then eastern Poland. The entire population was called out to vote for candidates to the national people's assemblies of Volhynia. The enormous effort that went into this election required manpower and an organizational network capable of contacting and bringing to the ballot box every individual in the conquered territory.

From the beginning, the purpose of the new administration was not to restore peace and order but to prepare the region for incorporation into the Soviet Union.

After invading Volhynia, the Red Army's challenge was not only to put into place a legitimate process for incorporating Volhynia into the Soviet Union but also the enormous challenge of feeding her soldiers. As a result, farmers in the Lutsk region were ordered to give up their grain for this purpose.

"If you don't give us your grain," warned an NKVD operative, *"we will burn your home and your barn. In fact, we may elect to burn your whole village."*

The Russians also warned every family to hang out a Russian flag. Those residents who did not, *"...will be executed and the whole family arrested and thrown into prison."*

October 22, 1939, would turn out to be a day that the Wozniak and Konenko farming families would never forget. Young Wiktor Wozniak happened to be in the city of Lutsk looking at the possibility of attending a post-secondary school institution. His sister, Monika, was visiting a close friend over the weekend. The other members of the Wozniak family were fast asleep at home, not knowing that calamity was about to descend upon them in the middle of the night. Similarly, all of the four members of the Konenko family were tucked away fast asleep in their beds. Tomorrow, they would take in the last vestiges of their family garden.

Unfortunately, it was a time when the Moskali were everywhere. They would enter a business establishment, robbing and arresting Poles. They were closing churches, demolishing Polish schools, establishing kolkhozes, and instilling communism on all those who would listen. Everyone was hiding in cellars and in other secluded places. When the Moskali entered a store, they would stuff themselves with baker's yeast and with everything else their eyes saw. They would stuff their pockets with sausages and when they didn't have a place to stuff them, they would put the sausages in their bootlegs and around their necks, barely being able to move when they left a store.

Exactly at the moment when the sun was about to rise, three Soviet military soldiers entered the Wozniak farmyard. They didn't politely knock on the front door of the family home, they kicked it right off its hinges. Once inside the house, their command was unequivocal, *"This is the military police. Everyone in this house, get your asses down here immediately or we will kill all of you and set the house on fire."*

Frightened out of their wits, Filip, Marta, Donek, and Agata were all in the living room in a moment. They did not even have time to do anything else but get downstairs in their night clothes. Pointing a rifle directly at Filip, an NKVD operative yelled, *"No one leaves this house without my permission. Try it, you thieving, slovenly, synowie suk, sons of bitches, and you will be shot on the spot! Rooki vyerh! Put your hands up and sit down in this chair. Bring all members of your family to the living room. Wieprzowy. Pigs."*

Once this was accomplished, the NKVD made a complete search of the home. Satisfied that the family did not possess any weapons, the NKVD began their interrogation.

"Who lives here?" was the first question from the NKVD.

"My wife and my children," stammered Filip Wozniak.

"Don't give us that arrogant bullshit. What are their names? Give me their names."

"My wife, Marta, and my children, Wiktor, Donek, Monika, and Agata live here."

"In that case," demanded the NKVD official, *"get all of them down here immediately."*

"They are all down here now," sheepishly responded Filip.

"What the hell is going on here," demanded the officer, *"you said that you have four children. You are some kind of a stupid bastard. Can't you count? There are only two children here. Where are the other two?"*

Thinking quickly, Filip decided to withhold the truth as to their whereabouts, *"...both Wiktor and Monika are attending university in Lutsk,"* responded Filip.

After a moment's thought, the leader of the NKVD troop had a decision, *"You, Pan Wozniak and your son have exactly one hour to pack."*

At that moment, Filip Wozniak realized what the future held for him. It was obvious that the NKVD had already determined that he was a military colonist belonging to prosperous group of farmers called the *kulaks.* Unfortunately for Filip, the Soviets planned to confiscate and collectivize all agricultural land in Volhynia. In order to accomplish this, all kulaks, including Filip Wozniak, had to be separated from their land and deported to Siberia.

"Pack up, you dogs," was the NKVD command, *"we are taking you to another oblast."*

"To which oblast are you taking us?"

"Don't worry," responded an agent of the NKVD, *"it is near here."*

"What shall we take?" asked Filip.

"Take whatever you can carry on your back. Where you are going, we have everything."

At gunpoint, Filip and Donek were escorted to the Konenko family home. Joined by three other NKVD agents, they did not waste any time knocking down the front door and arresting everyone inside. Earlier, they had determined that Jan Konenko was a Ukrainian nationalist who exhibited anti-communist sentiments. As was the case with the Wozniaks, the NKVD police only arrested the two male members of the family, Jan Konenko and his sixteen-year-old son, Janko.

"Get dressed you two thieving Ukrainian dogs. Skurwysyny, we are taking you to another oblast where you will be taught the principles of communism."

Scantily dressed and each carrying a sack of clothing and some food, the four captors were taken to Lutsk and loaded onto a cattle car at the railway station. During the loading process, several of the prisoners started running away through the windows and hiding in the forests. During these attempted escapes, the NKVD shot to kill. Several met an untimely death.

Filip, Donek, Jan, and Janko soon joined hundreds of other deportees in crowded railway carriages. In their carriage were several families with young children. At nightfall, some of the prisoners spread themselves on plank beds. Unfortunately, others, while covered over with blankets, had to try to get some sleep in a sitting position. The train was supposed to start the next night, but was delayed. Locked in the stuffy cattle car overnight on a cold evening in mid-October, several infants nearly froze to death. To relieve themselves, the deportees had to do so through an opening in the middle of the carriage. Most everyone in the car was crying in despair, not knowing what to do.

Before the deportation train was ready to leave Lutsk, the deportees realized that these would be their final moments in their Fatherland, a time for reflection. Everyone knew that they were about to be deported deep into Russian Siberia. Most were of the opinion that they would ever see their beloved homeland again. Finally, after three days at the Lutsk railway station, the 70-carriage train was fully loaded and ready for its journey to the *Russian Hell*.

Three days into the journey, hunger began to set in for those deportees who did not bring sufficient food with them. Initially, the Russian guards did not give the deportees any food or water. Starving for food and drink, several deportees took to sucking on frozen screws in the cattle car. Into the fourth day of travel, each carriage was given two kilograms of bread for the whole day, a pail of watery oat soup, and 200 grams of flour per person. The further the train travelled into Russia, the less were the rations. When the train reached the Ural Mountains, an armed guard declared, *"Budit vam kharasho budietie mielie vsiho mnoha, everything will be fine for you, you will have a lot of everything."*

Throughout the three-week journey to a lumber camp near Omsk, Filip had little to say. Neither did Jan. Looking at other Poles and Ukrainians in the carriage, Filip could find no answer as to why only two members of his family were deported. Others were not so lucky. There were a number of children in the carriage, some as young as one year of age.

"You know what, Janko," observed Donek, *"it seems to me as though our carriage has lost a couple of victims each day. When we left Lutsk, I counted fifty-eight. Now there are only fifty of us. Those Soviet murdering bastards are trying to kill everyone before we reach Siberia."*

"How cruel can these Russian thugs be? Those who died during our journey," responded Janko, *"were simply thrown out of the carriage. Not one had a decent burial."*

At a railway siding near Omsk, an NKVD official announced the names of twelve deportees and ordered them out of their cattle car. Among that group were Filip, Donek, Jan, and Janko. In a few moments, they were loaded onto a horse-drawn sleigh for transport to a logging camp. After one day's rest in a logging camp barrack, everyone was put to work. Even two teenage girls, merely thirteen years of age, were forced to carry boards from the saw mill to a stockpile, a total of one hundred metres distance. Thick and heavy, the boards were twelve metres long and five centimetres thick, causing the girls to frequently stumble and fall. Weakened by hunger and cold and working under extreme temperatures, the two teenage girls became the first casualties of those who arrived in the logging camp from Lutsk. Both came down with typhus and soon died. They were laid to rest in a primitive gravesite in the nearby forest.

Filip Wozniak did not fare much better. He, too, came down with typhus and couldn't go to work. To make matters worse, those who worked, got 700 grams of bread. Those who did not work received only 300 grams of bread. This rationing of food did not help Filip. A so-called medical doctor from Omsk visited the logging camp twice monthly. On one such visit he declared that Filip had lied about coming down with typhus. *"He should be working,"* declared the doctor. Forced to work, Filip succumbed to his condition in less than three weeks.

From time to time, a Soviet official would address the logging camp workers. The message seemed always to be the same. *"There is no such creature as God and any prayer to such a person is strictly prohibited. Anyone caught praying will be put into an isolation cell for two weeks with little food."* In several cases, a slave labourer confined to an isolation cell for praying to God did not last very long.

For months on end, no one in the barrack was able to escape their worst nightmare. Relentlessly, the bed bugs tortured everybody. Yet the work of cutting down the forest and rafting the logs down the river to a saw mill continued without interruption. The work was hard and the prisoners worked from dawn to dusk. Most every meal consisted of thin cabbage soup without any fat. Sometimes, along with a couple of mushrooms, a few grits would be thrown into the watery soup-mix. If a worker met his production quota, he was given four roubles a day. If not, his food rations would be decreased and his pay cut to zilch.

The logging operation required that the tops of the healthiest and tallest pine trees be trimmed. One day through the obvious carelessness of workers nearby, Jan Konenko was struck by the top of a falling pine tree. The force of the tree broke his back. Try as he might and in the absence of proper medical care, Jan was not able to recover.

Just like that, both Donek Wozniak and Janko Konenko were left without fathers. The simple task of survival took on a new meaning. Yet, all was not doom and gloom. In the spring of 1940, Donek and Janko were transferred to an agricultural kolkhoz in Kazakhstan. Their destination followed the pattern of the existing labour settlements where the NKVD was in charge of arranging their housing, providing employment in agriculture, and ensuring that each slave labourer was provided with the barest of necessities. The economic objective pursued by the Soviets included the expansion of areas used for the production of sugar beets and tobacco harvesting.

Donek and Janko joined other Ukrainian and Polish *osadniki* or *special re-settlers*. Included in this group were police officers, state employees, kulaks, teachers, petty traders, prostitutes, land proprietors, industrialists, and members of insurgent organizations who were assigned the category of *administratively-exiled*. It was the intent of Josef Stalin to augment the agricultural labour force to a level necessary so as to improve the economic profile of the newly adopted lands in Kazakhstan.

En route to the kolkhoz in Kazakhstan, Donek and Janko traversed some of the most barren land that they had ever witnessed before arriving in the Central Asian steppe and the village of Spaask, just south of the city of Karaghanda. Described as *zsylni* or *exiles,* they were issued Soviet *internal* passports which were valid for five years. Spaask operated as a division of the Gulag forced-labour camp system known as the Karlag. In addition to agriculture, the labour camp was becoming famous for the extraction of copper from nearby mineral deposits. In an attempt to collectivize agriculture, the kolkhoz system was established some ten years earlier in order to industrialize a largely agrarian country and to transform an entire people's culture.

After their arrival in Spaask, Donek and Janko didn't even get one day's rest before being forced into the labour pool. They soon discovered that all of the labourers faced constant hunger and high death rates in an oppressive atmosphere of violence and freezing cold temperatures. The boorish farmers behaved coarsely in a foreign and hostile environment, always spitting, cursing, and screaming at the boys. When entering the local village, Donek and Janko were received in a most unfriendly manner. Locals considered the two boys to come from Polish nobility, opposed to hard work. Being envious of these things, the local people tried to take advantage of the boys in every possible way, demanding the boys' belongings in exchange for food products and housing.

In an attempt to educate the newcomers in the ideals of communism, Soviet officials bombarded the labourers with propaganda and rumour. Those identified by the NKVD as *incorrigible enemies of the state* were executed outright. The others in the kolkhoz were kept alive by virtue of their capacity to contribute their labour to the cause of socialism. If a prisoner refused correction, the brutality of the labour camp would lead to an inevitable death. In the end, the communists were not humanitarians. If mistakes were made, they accepted that it was better to kill too many than too few.

Living with other people in clay huts, Donek and Janko went to work in the fields where they were paid one rouble, eight kopecks per day. To a large extent, this meagre salary was spent on food. Neither boy was able to buy sugar or soap. In addition to living on boiled flour, each worker was given 700 grams of bread at the end of each work day. In the mess hall of the barrack, one litre of the so-called cooked *caudal* soup, made from the tail end of some sort of animal, could be purchased for one rouble. The soup had the appearance of murky water with a few kernels of crushed grain swimming on top. Additional roubles were given to those labourers who were able to fulfil a norm. Once fulfilled, a labourer would get additional roubles. However, rarely did any labourer meet the norm.

Snowstorms raged constantly and winds blew without mercy. In the winter months, it was not unusual to reach temperatures of -50 degrees Centigrade. Polish and Ukrainian children would go around begging. As a consequence, the exiles protected one another. There was no medical aid and it was difficult to afford any type of a medicine other than a few drops or ointments for colds.

There was only one store in the entire settlement in which one could buy bread, but only in exchange for food coupons. Merchandise such as shoes, coats, and cloth were available once a month. Without meeting the norm, Donek and Janko were not in a position to buy any merchandise in the store. There was also a school where the Russian language and the basics of communism were taught. Although the two boys did not want to attend the school, they were signed up by the NKVD anyway. It appeared as though the school's main objective was to teach that there was no God and that Stalin gives everything whereas God gives nothing. However, Donek and Janko fervently believed in God. They were not persuaded. The school, however, wanted to break the spirit of the boys and turn them into communists.

Labouring at the kolkhoz from dawn until dusk, time passed quickly. On July 30, 1942, those deported to Siberia as citizens of Poland got the surprise of their lives. Nazi Germany had attacked the Soviet Union in 1941 and Josef Stalin now desperately needed those Poles who were deported to Siberia to fight on the side of the Allies in an effort to defeat the enemy. As a result, the Polish-Soviet Pact was signed and Poles were granted general amnesty, even though no one could explain the crime they had committed in the first place.

Two waves of groups received amnesty, the first wave being the masses of prisoners released from concentration camps. They would wander around, travelling aimlessly. Ragged, wasted, and swollen, they travelled around not knowing what to look for. As a result, chaos prevailed on the railroads. At the same time, rumour had it that a Polish army was being formed somewhere in the Middle East. As a result, Polish and Ukrainian prisoners released from slave labour had an option of either joining the Red Army or the Polish Army.

As citizens of the former Polish province of Volhynia, Donek and Janko were issued documents of Polish citizenship by the NKVD and were told that they were free to join the Polish Army. As it turned out, it was a good thing that the NKVD did not determine that Janko was an ethnic Ukrainian and therefore not eligible for amnesty.

1942: Polish refugees leaving Siberia
after being granted amnesty by the Soviets.

A representative from the Polish Army under the leadership of General Wladyslaw Anders helped them find their way south to G'uzor, Uzbekistan. Wladyslaw Anders, whose father was an ethnic German, was born in a Polish village, then part of the Russian Empire. During World War I, Anders served as a junior officer with a Russian Lancers Regiment. After the Polish independence, Anders joined the Polish Army as a cavalry officer and later led a cavalry brigade near Tomaszów Lubelski. Intercepted by Soviet forces, Anders was jailed in Lviv before being transferred to Moscow's notorious Lubyanka Prison.

The long and arduous escape route taken by Poles and Ukrainians through Perm, Karaghanda, Guzar, Krasnovodsk, and Anzali en route to Italy. Many, like Janek and Donek Wozniak, joined Anders Army and fought on the side of the Allies in Italy.

When Germany attacked the Soviet Union in 1941, Josef Stalin sorely needed the leadership of General Anders. Released from prison in 1942 on the condition that he would form a Polish Army to fight against the Germans alongside the Red Army, Anders was able to agitate for the release of Polish nationals still in Siberia. It was his plan to form Anders Army by enlisting Polish civilians who had been deported to Siberia from Soviet-occupied Poland.

With this plan in mind, General Anders created several locations where recruits could be accepted into the Polish Army. Instead of fighting on the side of the Russians, however, Anders led his men to the Middle East and formed the Polish 2nd Corps. This is how the Persian Corridor became the conduit for Polish deportees into Iran, Iraq, and Palestine. In 1943, the Polish 2nd Corps was sent by the Western Allies to Italy where Anders' soldiers were instrumental in the Battle of Monte Cassino.

For Donek and Janko, the trip by train from Karaghanda, Kazakhstan, to G'uzor, Uzbekistan, turned out to be another nightmare.

First of all, the two boys came down with dysentery and malaria. Tired and ill, they boarded, as stowaways, a night train after bribing a railroad employee. They were forced to spend several nights at various railway stations hoping not to be discovered. Having recovered from their illness, they were finally able to join other able-bodied Poles in an effort to arrive at the Polish Army recruitment station in G'uzor.

The biggest challenge in their journey to G'uzor was to avoid arrest by the NKVD. Thankfully, at a critical point in their escape from Siberia, the boys received the guidance and protection of a senior Polish soldier. This assistance proved to be important because Polish-Soviet relations continued to be uncertain and strained. The Bolsheviks did not agree to let a large number of civilians go or to let the Polish Army continue forming there. Neither did they agree to let Jews and Ukrainians from Poland go, considering them to be their own citizens.

From G'uzor, a group of young Poles was told to find their own way to Krasnovotsk, Turkmenistan. From Krasnovotsk, Donek and Janko continued their journey across the Caspian Sea to Iran by boat. Crossing the Caspian Sea in an oil tanker turned out to be another form of torment. Dust storms, heat, and heavy labour took their toll. Finally, Donek and Janko let out a sigh of relief when they arrived in the Persian city of Anzali, vowing never to go back to Russia ever again!

Enlisted in Anders Army, Donek and Janko did not have the luxury of any extensive formal military training. Assigned to the 22nd Artillery Supply Company of the Polish 2nd Corps, they would see their first action as part of Operation Diadem. It was on April 24, 1944, that General Anders would relieve the British 78th Division in the mountains behind Cassino, Italy. Their objective was to preserve the treasured artifacts stored in the abbey of Monte Cassino and open up a safe access to Rome. The richness of the abbey's archives, library, and gallery included papal documents, manuscripts on parchment, prints, and separate collections.

The large troop movements required two months to execute and the first assault on Monte Cassino took place on May 11, 1944. For three days, Polish attacks and German counterattacks brought heavy losses to both sides. On May 17, Polish 2nd Corps launched their second attack on Monte Cassino. On May 18, the Germans retreated. However, the Polish offensive was so battered that it took some time to find men with enough strength to raise a Polish flag over the ruins. Sadly, Janko Konenko lost his life in the battle for Monte Cassino. His heart broken with the loss of

Janko, Donek Wozniak spent three days at the gravesite, mourning the loss of his best friend.

1942: General Wladyslaw Albert Anders: Granted amnesty in Siberia, many civilians crossed different countries in the Middle East, joined Anders Army, and fought on the side of the Allies in Italy.

As the war came to a close, the soldiers who served in Italy under General Anders were offered special treatment by the High Command of the United Kingdom and invited to take up residence in Great Britain. Despite the invitation, most of the soldiers wanted to return to a free and independent Poland after the war. This, however, was not to be.

Roosevelt and Churchill had agreed that tens of thousands of veteran Polish troops under British command should lose their Kresy homes to the Soviet Union with the implication that their relatives, including wives and children, would be at the mercy of the NKVD. In reaction, thirty officers and men from the Polish 2nd Corps committed suicide. When the war ended, a communist government was installed in Poland. Most Poles felt betrayed by their wartime allies and refused to return to Communist Poland because of the Soviet repressions of Polish citizens from 1939 to 1946. Most of those who served under General Anders elected to travel to the United Kingdom. Eventually, Britain passed the Polish Resettlement Act in 1947, the United Kingdom's first mass immigration law.

Donek Wozniak, his family decimated, took up residence in London. He soon married an expatriate Polish girl and felt right at home living near a Polish Catholic Church where Polish clubs, organizations, cultural centres, and the Polish Scouting movement sprang up. The original aim of these Polish organizations was to ensure a continuation of the Polish language, culture, and heritage for the children of those who so valiantly served the Allies. Nevertheless, Donek did not forget his friend Janko Konenko. Out of respect, he joined the Association of Ukrainians in Great Britain, founded in 1945 by Ukrainians who came to Great Britain at the end of the war. Included in the association were over six thousand ethnic Ukrainians who served General Anders and another eight thousand from the Galician Division who came to Britain from POW camps.

Donek Wozniak refused to entertain the idea of returning to Poland, a communist country after the war. Perhaps Donek took his cue from Lieutenant General Anders[3] who chose to live in the United Kingdom instead of Poland, as Poland was now essentially a puppet state of the Soviet Union. By 1948, only about half the Polish soldiers opted to return to Poland. Many immigrated to the United States and Canada. Some found a new life in Australia, New Zealand, and Mexico.

Since Poland is now a member of the European Union, it is possible for Poles to leave Poland for visits to their families in London. In fact, exiled Poles living in England are encouraged to return home to live or make a visit. However, the Polish community is split between those who visit Poland and those who do not. For ethnic Ukrainians who served in Anders Army, a very different situation exists. Since Ukraine is not a member of the European Union, the relationship between Ukrainians living in England and those living in Ukraine is far more distant.

The Polish government sought ways to persuade the Poles in exile to return home. They were told that they were not considered political exiles but emigrant workers whose real home was Poland. The overtures, however, have met with little response. Those Poles who have British passports and travel to Poland tend to return to Britain feeling more Polish than those who have not changed their nationality.

Today, Izabela Wozniak, the granddaughter of Donek Wozniak, is of the view that young ethnic Poles naturally want to merge into their British background. Yet many as they grow through adolescence begin to

---

3   General Anders served as the Inspector General of the Polish forces-in-exile. He passed away in 1970 and was buried at the Polish War Cemetery at Monte Cassino. For many Poles and Ukrainians, he continues to be the greatest personality among the descendants of soldiers who served under him.

realize the importance of their heritage. For this reason they are stirred by a desire to learn their native language and their own literature and history. They begin to find a pride in being Polish.

We can blame the secret pact between Germany and the Soviet Union for driving Donek and Wiktor Wozniak in very different directions. After the war, Wiktor sought happiness in his native Poland while Donek elected to remain in England. They were blood brothers, yet there was as much to keep them apart as there was to bring them together.

We now turn our thoughts to Tanja Konenko. She was one of thousands of young people arrested by the Gestapo and shipped off to Germany as a slave labourer. At the end of the war, all forced labourers were to be repatriated to their country of birth. Many refused to be returned to the Soviet Union. One of those was Tanja Konenko.

What follows is the story of Tanja's dangerous journey to freedom.

17

The Repatriation Of Tanja

"I will not let the NKVD repatriate me to the Soviet Union…"

T he use of forced labour in Nazi Germany during World War II took place on an unprecedented scale. It was a vital part of the German economic exploitation of conquered territories. At its peak, over five million forced labourers worked in Germany, comprising twenty percent of the German work force.

Hitler declared that Germany required thousands of women and girls from Ukraine and Poland to free German women from housekeeping. The Nazi regime realized that most husbands of German women were serving in the military and that many were killed or missing in action. Even though Hitler harboured some reservation about the competence of East European women, this did not stop his regime from forcibly recruiting them. Hitler also believed, resulting from earlier German settlements in Slavic countries, that there may well be a Germanic strain in many of the young people being arrested in Ukraine and shipped off to Germany as labourers.

Appointed by Hitler, it was the responsibility of Nazi Gauleiter Fritz Sauckel to recruit workers from Eastern Europe, mostly by the Gestapo and mostly against their will. In his memoirs Sauckel stated that, *"In order to provide the German housewife, above all mothers of many children, with tangible relief from her burdens, the Fuhrer has commissioned me to bring into the Reich from eastern territories some four to five hundred thousand select, healthy, and strong girls."*

History shows us that Sauckel exceeded all expectations. During the war, his propaganda machine stated that, *"Millions of citizens of enemy states are now working satisfactorily in Germany."*

Captured by the Gestapo in 1943, Tanja Konenko and Monika Wozniak travelled under guard from their village of Polonka to Germany. As it turned out, what happened to each of the two teenagers while in Germany and immediately after the war was a matter of good luck or bad luck, depending upon one's point of view. By an odd quirk of fate, Tanja Konenko, classified as a Zivilarbeiter, ended up in Hamburg, Germany. At the Hamburg Bahnhof, Frau Neumann selected Tanja to replace Anna Kaszuba for work in agriculture and housekeeping. In contrast, Monika Wozniak was brought to Leipzig, Germany, classified as an Ostarbeiter, and forced to work, under constant guard, in a German munitions plant protected by a perimeter barb wire fence. Their shocking stories unfolded as follows.

Residing in the German town of Wedel, thirty kilometres west of Hamburg, the Neumanns were successful farmers. With two small children at home and her husband, Hans, serving in Hitler's Wehrmacht, Helga Neumann desperately needed the help of a Zivilarbeiter. In selecting Tanja Konenko to replace Anna Kaszuba, Frau Neumann could not help but reflect upon what happened in 1940. It was on that day that she first drove to the Bahnhof in Hamburg and selected 15 year-old Anna Kaszuba to serve as her domestic servant. Here it was 1943, and Frau Neumann was in Hamburg once again. Only this time, the purpose of her trip was to select a replacement for Anna who was released to her family in Poland for compassionate reasons. It was Helga's hope that she would find a worker as competent as was Anna.

Just two weeks earlier, the Gestapo had arrested Tanja Konenko in the village of Polonka and transported her to Northern Germany. Although Tanja was born in the Polish province of Volhynia in 1928, the Gestapo listed her as coming from *Reichskommissariat Ukraine*. This change in Tanja's place of residence came about because Germany conquered Volhynia in 1941, and then absorbed the territory into the newly-formed Reichskommissariat Ukraine. By 1943, Volhynia was completely under the control of Germany and Frau Neumann desperately needed a replacement for Anna.

Germany's need for foreign workers was felt soon after the Nazis attacked Poland in 1939 and reached a critical stage when the Nazis conquered eastern Poland in 1941. As early as 1940, the Nazis began to round up Polish slave labourers from German-occupied territory. Germany decided that it needed thousands of foreign workers to man its factories, mines, and agricultural communities. When Germany occupied eastern Poland, the villages of Grochi and Płazów became a part of territories of Poland occupied by the German Third Reich and re-named as the *General Government* region. This meant that all of the residents of Gmina Narol, including those in the village of Grochi, fell under the purview of Nazi Germany.

When the Germans first occupied Gmina Narol, rumours spread throughout the county that young people were at risk of arrest and transport to Germany as Ostarbeiters. To no one's surprise, a heavily armed Gestapo unit did show up in Grochi wanting to know the names of all unattached female teenagers living in the village. Anna Kaszuba would always remember the first words that she heard from a German Gestapo Officer.

"Guten tag Ihnen. Good day to you, Wie lautet dein Name? What is your name, junge Frau?"

"My name is Anna Kaszuba," quietly responded a terrified teenager.

"Speak up, junge Frau. Don't act so timid and stupid. How old are you?"

"I am fifteen years of age," politely replied Anna.

It did not take the Gestapo long to determine that Anna was the oldest unattached sibling in the Kaszuba household. In accordance with Nazi policy, she was immediately arrested, and shipped off to Germany to work as a Zivilarbeiter.

For three full years, Anna slaved away on the Neumann farm. On days not required by Frau Neumann, she worked at a nearby sugar refinery. At the sugar factory, she heard stories about the rampant sexual abuse of Polish and Soviet female Ostarbeiters at the hands of their overseers, stories about the rape of young girls and the newborns secretly euthanized in Nazi birthing centres. Although slave labourers were to be recruited in equal numbers of men and women so that brothels would not be needed, this was not always the case. Despite warnings from the Gestapo, many female workers did become pregnant. On occasion, a female worker and the baby's father were deemed to be of good blood. In such cases, the child proved to be racially valuable and removed from the mother for Germanization.

Confronting Frau Neumann with these rumours, Anna wanted some assurance that she would be safe while undertaking her duties on the farm.

"You are safe on this farm. You will notice that I am always armed with a German Luger. I would not hesitate to shoot an intruder. Tell me, did someone attack you at the sugar refinery? You're not pregnant, are you?"

"No, Frau Neumann, I am not pregnant. I stay away from German men."

"I am happy to hear that you stay away from German men. There are precious few young ones left in this town. All are serving our Fatherland in the Wehrmacht. But please be comforted by the fact that if you were to have a child, I would care for it."

Frau Neumann treated Anna like a member of the family, going so far as to allow her to write the occasional postcard to her parents in Grochi, even though there was little assurance that the postcard would actually find its intended destination. Despite the hard work in Germany, Anna was mindful of the fact that life for a teenager living in Grochi was no picnic either. In her third year with the Neumanns, Anna received a postcard from her mother.

"My dear Hanka, моя дорога дочка, please ask Pani Neumann if she could release you from your work. Your father and I are in poor health and desperately need you at home."

Realizing that her parents were ailing at home, Anna pleaded with Frau Neumann to be released from bondage. Understanding the urgency of Anna's request, Frau Neumann approached the Gestapo, hoping to gain Anna's release from her work in Germany. However, and even though Sauckel was of the view that, *"…every civilian worker must be fed, sheltered, and treated in such a way as to exploit them to the highest possible extent at the lowest degree of expenditure,"* his office did approve Anna's release but not until a replacement was found.

In the fall of 1943, the Gestapo informed Frau Neumann that a trainload of Eastern Workers would soon arrive in Hamburg from *Reichskommissariat Ukraine*. As a result, Frau Neumann once again drove to the Bahnhof in Hamburg with the hopes of recruiting a farm labourer to replace Anna. With the help of the Gestapo, Frau Neumann selected a teenager by the name of Tanja Konenko. Anna was overjoyed to learn that Tanja Konenko was fluent in Polish and Ukrainian.

"You are very lucky, Anna," commented Tanja, *"to be returning to Poland. You must have a good reason to return."*

"I got word from my parents in Grochi that they needed me. Both my father and my mother are very ill. It must be as a result of this stupid war," explained Anna.

"You were able to communicate with your parents?"

"Yes, I did get a postcard from my mother. She said that she desperately needed me. And now you will be the lucky one. Frau Neumann is actually a fine human being. She made me feel that I was a part of her family. When not busy in her home, I spent two or three days a week working in the sugar refinery near Wedel."

"And during your time here, Anna, you became fluent in the German language?"

"Yes, I did. Learning German was not easy but Frau Neumann was most helpful. I am sure that you will want to learn the German language as well."

"I want to say goodbye to you, Anna. May God always be with you."

"Thank you, Tanja. I look forward to being in Płazów once again."

"You are going to Płazów and not Grochi? This is a surprise to me. Where are these two villages? Are they in the same gmina?"

"The two villages are very close together. Why are you surprised?"

"I am surprised because I have a great Aunt who lives in Płazów."

"What is your Aunt's name?"

"Her name is Tetyana Groszko. My grandmother and Tetyana Groszko are sisters. We have not been in touch with family in Gmina Narol for many years."

"Do you remember your grandmother's family name?"

"Yes, my grandmother's family name is Klymus."

Not only was Anna surprised to learn that Tanja Konenko was related to a family living in Płazów, but especially to discover that they were related through marriage.

"What a shock, Tanja, we are both connected to the Klymus family! My oldest brother, Andrij, married Ewa Groszko. Ewa's mother was a Klymus, Tetyana Klymus. Andrij and Ewa were married in Płazów in 1924. They now live in Canada!"

Anna spent one week helping Tanja get used to her domestic duties. During their time together, the two teenagers talked about their families, their capture by the Gestapo, their work, and the conduct of the war. At the end of the week, Frau Neumann drove Anna to Hamburg so that she might catch a military supply train scheduled to deport to Bełżec and rejoin her family in the nearby village of Grochi.

With Anna back in Poland, Tanja toiled for two years putting in long days as a domestic for Frau Neumann and also as an employee of the sugar refining factory. During this period, several major battles took place in various regions of Europe, including Northern Germany. Just to survive required considerable luck. In 1943, the City of Hamburg was carpet bombed by the Allies. Fires raged in the streets, devouring every trace of oxygen. Sixty thousand citizens perished in Hamburg while 900,000 fled to the surrounding countryside.

Without exception, Tanja continued to fulfil her duties diligently. In early May, 1945, however, Frau Neumann approached Tanja in tears, *"My dear Tanja, mein Herz is gebrochen! My heart is broken."*

"Your heart is broken," asked a very surprised Tanja, *"what happened? Is it something that I did? Or is it perhaps something that I didn't do?"*

"No, my dear child, it is nothing you did. I just heard that the war is over. The Nazis have surrendered."

"Does that break your heart, Frau Neumann?"

"No, my heart is not broken because the war is over. It is broken because I will lose you. I have been informed that all Zivilarbeiters and Ostarbeiters will soon be returned to their homeland."

The unconditional surrender of Germany in 1945 would soon free upwards to 5.5 million Eastern Workers from bondage, three million of whom laboured in German factories. During 1944, most foreign workers arriving in Germany were under the age of sixteen. Those males older than 16 were already conscripted and serving in the Wehrmacht. Thirty percent were as young as 12-14 years of age when they were taken from their homes. Some were even as young as 10 years of age. Since about half of the adolescents were female, Ostarbeiters were often the victims of rape and tens of thousands of pregnancies occurred.

"Sie erkennen, Tanja," noted Frau Neumann, *"you have been with our family for nearly two years. I feel so blessed. At first it was Anna who was such an angel to us, now it is you, du bist ein Schatz!"*

"Danke, Frau Neumann. What will happen to me now?"

"I don't know. I will check with the Gestapo. Maybe I can get you to stay longer."

Tanja had served the domestic needs of Frau Neumann during the final two years of the war. As early as the summer of 1944, most of those living in Wedel were aware that Allied troops had invaded France. By the end of July, the Red Army had taken Brest-Litovsk in Belarus; Belgium in September. For Germany, more bad news followed. By March of 1945, the Germans were in general retreat throughout all of Germany.

As difficult and tiring as was the work, Tanja learned a lot about Germany, sugar processing, and farming. Most of all, she became proficient in the German language. This is why the sudden shock of learning that all of this would come to a screeching halt unnerved her. Although her wage was one-half the gross earnings paid to German workers, it was far more than she might have received for her labour in Soviet Ukraine. Tanja was aware that other Ostarbeiters working in Wedel attempted to send money home to their family. Unfortunately, she was not able to do so. A short time before her capture by the Gestapo, the Konenko family home was torched by the UPA, and her parents murdered. Tanja had no one to whom she could have sent the funds even if she wanted to. Most of the money she earned went toward the purchase of food, clothing, and board.

Classified by the Nazis as *Untermenschen*, Tanja was restricted to her place of residence by German law and told that her masters could *kick, beat, terrorize and even kill her for the slightest transgression*. Any Ostarbeiter who tried to escape from factories enclosed by barbed wire, were often hanged. This immediately put a damper on other Ostarbeiters harbouring any idea of escape. To leave without authorization or to try to escape was punishable by death. Even though Tanja did have some freedom of movement on the Neumann farm, she also realized that she had to abide by the most stringent of rules established by the Nazis.

Unlike most other Ostarbeiters who lived in private camps owned and managed by large companies or in special camps guarded by privately paid police services, Tanja Konenko lived in the Neumann family home. Towards the end of the war, many Ostarbeiters in the Hamburg region died when Allied bombing raids targeted the factories where they worked. Others perished because the German authorities ordered that, *"...they should be worked to death."* Fortunately, Tanja was treated differently. Unlike other German families who tried to enforce total separation, she was permitted to eat at the same table as Frau Neumann and her two young sons. Throughout the war, German workers became supervisors over forced labour in factories and, as such, no solidarity developed between foreign and German workers. Tanja became accustomed to these inequalities. As time went on, Tanja became indifferent to her plight.

One day, seemingly out of nowhere, Frau Neumann shocked Tanja.

"I should have told you this earlier. Today, I feel badly that I did not. Ich habe einige Informationen für Sie."

"You have some special information for me, Frau Neumann?"

"What I did not tell you is that I got a short postcard from a person by the name of Wiktor, a Wiktor Wozniak. He said that he knew you."

Tanja could scarcely believe what she was hearing. After regaining her composure, Tanja was full of questions.

"Frau Neumann, you heard from Wiktor? How was that possible during the war?"

"Yes, I did hear from him. In the postcard, he said that he loved you. He also said that he moved from Volyn to Poland and now lives in the Polish town of Zamosc. But I did not want to trouble you with news that would make your life more miserable."

It took Tanja the longest time to digest what she had heard from Frau Neumann. *Why had she not told her about Wiktor earlier? Why did she withhold this information?*

Earlier, German authorities had informed Frau Neumann that all Zivilarbeiters would be placed in Displacement Person (*DP*) camps in Germany from which they would be moved to Kempten, Germany, for processing before being returned to their country of origin. Unfortunately, most Ostarbeiters and Zivilarbeiters shuddered at the thought of forceful return to the Soviet Union. As Germany's concentration camp gates creaked open, thousands of workers mobilized for the war effort would soon be returned to their homeland, many against their will, thus creating many difficult problems.

Post-Nazi Germany, 1945-49, showing the British, French, American, and Soviet Zones. Berlin became a quadripartite occupation area and Bremen consisted of two American enclaves within the British Sector.

Interestingly, Hamburg was the last defense for the Germans in the north. On May 7, 1945, Germany capitulated, surrendering unconditionally. As war activities began to wind down, refugees were assembled into DP camps, and the Soviets began to use special Agitprop brigades to convince all Eastern Workers to willingly return to the Soviet Union, their homeland. At the same time, Agitprop disseminated the basics of communism, including explanations about the policy of the Communist Party and the Soviet State.

Many Eastern Workers were still children or young teenagers when they were taken away from their homes. As a result, many of them wanted to return home to their parents. However, this was not the case with Tanja. In a discussion with Frau Neumann, Tanja suspected that she would be forcibly returned to Soviet Ukraine, a place reflecting an oppressive environment. If this were to happen, she realized that she would never get to see Wiktor ever again. Worse yet, in the event that Soviet authorities felt that she embraced western ideas, she could well end up in Siberia for what the Soviets called a *re-education to the ideals of communism.*

Frau Neumann soon learned that during the initial stages of the Soviet repatriation program, Stalin treated many eastern workers as traitors. Those identified as traitors were expelled to remote locations in Russia, denied basic rights, and not given any opportunity for further education. Nearly 80 percent of Russian workers and prisoners of war returning from Germany were sent to forced-labour camps in Siberia. Some were given fifteen to twenty-five years of corrective labour while others were sent off to hard labour. All were categorized as being socially dangerous. *What, then, was their crime?* The answer was quite simple, while serving the Nazis in Germany they had been exposed to western ideas.

Having considerable knowledge about the plight of DPs, Frau Neumann had a plan and decided to approach Herr Eisenberg at the sugar factory in Wedel with a special request.

"Herr Eisenberg, I want you to make a change in the passport of one of my workers."

"You want my office, Frau Neumann, to change the place of Tanja Konenko's birth from the province of Wołyń in Poland to that of Gmina Zamosc, Poland? That's a crazy idea. Why would you want me to list the town of Zamosc as her home town? Why would that matter to anyone?"

"Yes, Herr Eisenberg, this small change would help Tanja immensely. Her passport must not show that she was born in Wołyń but that she was born in Zamosc, Poland. I want to help Tanja find her childhood sweetheart who now lives in Poland."

At first, Eisenberg refused to help Frau Neumann. It took Frau Neumann the longest time to convince him that the war was over and that the least they could do was help Tanja return to her family.

"Frau Neumann, you must be out of your mind helping a slave. What does it matter to you if she returns to her lover? Those damn Poles are still our enemies."

"They may be our enemies but that is all in the past. These people are human beings."

"All right, I will do this but only for you. Do not come here asking for any more favours and do not tell anyone about this. My print shop will make the necessary changes."

It is interesting to note that so much human kindness was frequently shown in Germany when the Nazi forces capitulated. A revised passport in hand, Tanja took some comfort in knowing that she would not be one of those Poles or Ukrainians who eventually ended up in Soviet hands to face a fate worse than death. Many resisted repatriation by all means, including suicide. The Soviet representatives were very disturbed when they learned that so many citizens of the Soviet Union refused to return to their homeland. Soviet officials claimed that their resistance to deportation to the Soviet Union violated the Yalta agreement.

By August of 1945, the Soviets anticipated this problem and issued a policy for the forcible repatriation of its citizens. All persons proven to be Soviet citizens before boards of United States Officers were designated for transfer to camps under Soviet administration. In these camps, the Soviet officials became responsible for putting the repatriates aboard trucks and trains bound for the east. As citizens of the Soviet Union, they were given no options.

These adamant demands by the Soviets for the return of every one of her citizens in Western Europe stemmed from a variety of motives. Among the reasons was a collective vindictiveness seemingly endemic to the system of government. Soviet authorities wanted to make sure that all Eastern Workers would be returned to the Soviet Union. Soviet statutes defined treason broadly enough to include not only military collaborators but also POWs and forced labourers who had worked in Germany. Those associated with Germans in any way during the war, rightly or wrongly, faced severe punishment.

With the help of Britain and the United States, thousands of those who had fled Russia after the Bolshevik Revolution were now forcibly returned to the USSR. Many other people of Russian descent who had never lived within the borders of Russia were also expelled to the Soviet Union. In 1944, a United Kingdom legal adviser declared that, *"In due course all those with whom the Soviet authorities desire to deal must be handed over to them. We are not concerned with the fact that they may be shot or otherwise more harshly dealt with than they might be under English law."*

The agreed-upon definition of a Soviet citizen was *a person born or resident within the pre-September 1, 1939, boundaries of Russia.* Clearly, a citizen living in the village of Polonka, located in the Polish Oblast of Volhynia before September 1, 1939, would not be classified as a citizen of Russia but rather as a citizen of Poland. In other words, Tanja Konenko should not have worried about repatriation to the Soviet Union after the war. However, this analogy was disregarded by the NKVD. In their mind, the Oblast of Volhynia became a part of Soviet Ukraine in 1939. That was good enough for them. They considered Tanja to be a citizen of Russia.

Military officers ordered to enforce repatriation were often surprised at the alarm expressed by the refugees when the refugees learned that they were to be shipped eastward. Many Ukrainian and Polish Ostarbeiters begged to be allowed to stay in Germany. They knew that the conditions in Germany were far better than those back home. Even the Commander of the 2nd Polish Corps, General Anders, complained that the Soviets were trying to kidnap Polish citizens. Pope Pius XII, the Catholic Pope, sent a plea to the British Foreign Office that Ukrainians, *"...should not be sent back to the Soviet Union after the war."* Yet, Foreign Office officials held that Stalin's intentions towards the West were beneficent and that to work in cooperation with him was essential to British interests.

"The fate of those Russians whose return they would enforce," stated the *communiqué* from the British Foreign Office, *"is an unfortunate but unavoidable sacrifice to the greater aim."*

With a new passport in hand showing that she was born in Zamosc, Poland, Tanja Konenko felt quite optimistic. She knew that her fate would now rest with British officials who controlled the Hamburg region of a defeated Germany. After some more paperwork, Tanja was cleared and placed on a secure train bound for Kempten, West Germany. Once in Kempten, Tanja would have to seek approval for the next leg of her repatriation journey to Zamosc, Poland, from American officials.

Once again, luck was on Tanja's side because she was not compelled to travel through the Soviet-controlled eastern region of Germany. Had she travelled through East Germany, she would have been intercepted by the Soviets and immediately deported to Siberia. Wrapping what personal belongings she could fit into a bundle, Tanja set out for Kempten. A new life was about to unfold for her. Entering the accommodations of an old stone building in Kempten, Tanja would now have to await clearance for her final destination.

At Kempten, it was the responsibility of American officials to clarify the eligibility criteria for the immediate repatriation of Eastern Workers and refugees. Tanja soon learned that those DPs and refugees who had resided outside the Soviet Union in September 1939 were considered ineligible for involuntary repatriation to the Soviet Union. This policy protected from repatriation Baltic citizens, Poles, and Ukrainians who lived outside the Soviet Union. *However, this still allowed for the forced repatriation of all Soviet Ukrainians.* Born in Volhynia, Tanja realized that she would have risked being identified as a Soviet Ukrainian in contravention of the history of the region. After all, the Oblast of Volhynia did form up a part of Poland until the Molotov-Ribbentrop Pact changed the borders.

Confusion was widespread and American officers held different conceptions of their responsibility and orders. A USA Army Lieutenant stationed in Passau, Germany, wrote to her Commanding Officer stating that Ukrainians were, *"...being sent to the Soviet Occupation Zone against their own free will and therefore had been used against all orders given previously."*

To avoid repatriation to the Soviet Union, Tanja was horrified to learn that several refugees went so far as to self-inflict wounds. In one particular case, three refugees committed suicide rather than face repatriation to the Soviet Union. This was why some officers refused to carry out repatriation orders.

An absence of effective communication caused many problems. Western authorities had never been informed about national and political repressions in the Soviet Union. On the local level, many American soldiers were not sympathetic to the plight of DPs. Care and supervision of the DPs and refugees, while the war with Japan was still being fought, was considered to be excessively burdensome. Many solders wanted to return home to the United States as soon as possible. The German population charged with providing housing and clothing to the DPs and refugees resented them and influenced the decision-making process undertaken by American officials. To make matters worse for refugees when determining their nationality, many United States officers tended to listen to Russian soldiers.

In May and June of 1945, Ukrainian DPs formed committees so that their concerns would be heard. Some survived by living outside their camp while others roamed to other DP camps thereby becoming easy prey for Soviet officials bent upon returning just about every Ukrainian-speaking refugee to the Soviet Union. The United Nations Relief and Rehabilitation Administration was not in favour of this kind of behaviour on the part of the refugees, but decided not to take any immediate action.

When it came time for Tanja Konenko to be interviewed by an American officer, she already had had a brief conversation, in German, with two German nationals who did the initial screening. Consequently, it did not take the American officials long to confirm that Tanja was born in and should be repatriated to Zamosc, Poland. Her passage to Zamosc, however, did not occur overnight. It took two more months for a sufficient number of Poles to be cleared for repatriation to Eastern Poland and fill, to capacity, one train set aside for this purpose.

While being transferred to Zamosc, Tanja attempted to avoid any difficulties by not entering into conversation with strangers. All around her were recriminations, comments, and discussions about the events that occurred during the war and the difficulties confronting all refugees en route to Eastern Poland. In one such conversation, a young but outspoken Polish woman caught Tanja completely off guard.

"I think that you are a Russian spy. If not, you are then a Ukrainian nationalist who should have been sent to the Gulag."

"You are wrong, very wrong. Look at my passport, you dumb suka. I was born in Zamosc, you dumb stupid bitch. Sure, some of my family might have been Ukrainians. So what if they were, you dumb whore?"

"Don't call me a dumb bitch. You are a dumb Ukrainian whore, a traitor. You know that Stalin hates Ukrainians who collaborated with the Germans during the war. He wants to repatriate all of them to the Soviet Union. He wants to send many of them to labour camps in Siberia. You should be going to Siberia."

Tanja remained silent. Thankfully, the repatriation train finally arrived in Zamosc. By this time, the train contained only four carriages filled with refugees. When Tanja detrained, she found herself in the company of a large number of other refugees who seemed at a loss as to what to do with themselves. Few, if any, had family to meet them. How could they? The countryside showed the devastation and scars of the war. Many buildings in the town had sustained considerable damage. Befriended by another female refugee, it was time to come to grips with reality.

"Is it true Tanja that you were born in Zamosc," asked a woman who also got off the train in Zamosc, *"or were you born in a village near Zamosc?"*

Thinking about the difficulties she would experience in the event that she revealed the truth, Tanja decided to avoid saying anything that would incriminate her. *Perhaps,* she thought, *if I redirect her question, she will not pursue the matter of my place of birth.*

"Yes, I was born near here, in a small village near here. But, I believe that the war has destroyed the village. I am looking for my friend, Wiktor Wozniak. He now lives in Zamosc. Do you know the family name?"

"No, I must say that I have never heard of the name."

With her new friend in tow, Tanja decided to take her advice and seek the help of Father Henry, the local Roman Catholic Parish Priest. Upon meeting Father Henry, Tanja told him that she wanted to share a secret with him. Father Henry was full of curiosity.

"You are telling me, młoda kobieta, young woman, that you are from Volhynia and that you have a close friend by the name of Wiktor Wozniak?"

"Yes, Ojciec, my German Hausherrin, Frau Neumann, heard from Wiktor. Wiktor told Frau Neumann that he was now living in Zamosc."

"Why don't you stay with my family until we can find this Wiktor Wozniak?"

"Thank you, Ojciec. Can I do that?"

"Yes, of course. I will get the word out to our parish and invite Wiktor to attend Sunday Mass. Hopefully, he will respond and meet you on Sunday."

Father Henry escorted Tanja to the parish residence to meet his wife and two children. The fact that Father Henry was married with family, made their relationship more meaningful. Much as was the case of all Greek Catholic Priests, since 1921 Roman Catholic Priests were also permitted to marry and raise a family. Tanja, now under the care of Pani Gayda, was provided with a modest change of clothes.

By Sunday, after her ordeal in Germany, Tanja looked surprisingly refreshed. During the Eucharistic liturgical service, Father Henry announced to his congregation that he wanted to meet, if possible, a Wiktor Wozniak. After the Holy Communion, a time during the Christian worship when bread and wine are consecrated and shared, the priest's assistant, Deacon Antoni, was receiving confessions from penitents. To his surprise, a young man entered the confessional and declared that his name was Wiktor Wozniak.

"Thank you, young man, for coming into the confessional and telling me that your name is Wiktor Wozniak. Please identify yourself to Fr. Henry when he is finished his duties."

Immediately after Fr. Henry finished his duties he was approached by a stranger, *"Ojciec Henry, my name is Wozniak. Wiktor Wozniak. You wanted to see me after the Mass?"*

"Thank you, Lord. Thank you, Wiktor, for coming forward. You wait here. I want you to meet someone."

Father Henry knew where to find Tanja. He had asked her to join the Sunday Church Choir as a guest, even though he was aware that she would not be prepared to do so.

"Tanja, I have found Wiktor Wozniak. Please come with me."

As Father Henry approached Wiktor with Tanja on his arm, he noticed that Wiktor was in a state of shock. Embracing Tanja, both suddenly broke into tears. Tanja, in particular, had difficulty in stopping the flow of tears. Neither said a word. Father Henry excused himself with an invitation, *"Tanja, please bring Wiktor to our home for dinner."*

Following a traditional blessing at the home of Father Henry before sitting down to dinner, Wiktor and Tanja had much to discuss.

"Wiktor," enquired Tanja, *"what about your sister, Monika? Have you heard from her?"*

"Yes, Tanja, I did get a letter from my sister. Actually, it was not me that got the letter but my uncle who lives here. Uncle Tomas turned the letter over to me. The letter came from Leipzig, Germany."

"What did she say in her letter? Is she safe?"

"Unfortunately, the Leipzig region of Germany is under the control of the Soviet Union. That is the problem. I heard that the Soviets are not too kind to refugees in their zone of control. Stalin is shipping most of them to Siberia for hard labour. He wants to re-educate all of them in the image of a good soviet."

"Let us pray," interjected Father Henry, *"that your sister, Monika, will be returned safely to us."*

It would not be until some time in the future that Wiktor would learn as to what happened to his sister, Monika. What mattered most was that Tanja was safely in his arms.

18

The Re-Education Of Monika

From optimism to pessimism and back to optimism again

World War II, *The Great Patriotic War* as the Russians called it, was over but the suffering for many was just beginning. As Monika Wozniak sat in the solitary confinement cubicle in a food processing plant at the outskirts of Karaghanda, Kazakhstan, she had plenty of time to think about the war and her current predicament. This was her third day of punishment with little else to do but meditate and fight those ever-present hunger pangs. *Those godless NKVD bastards,* thought Monika, *I would like to beat the shit out of each one of those ugly Mongolian Bolshevik buffoons.*

Trying to force down some cabbage soup watered down with some sort of a dark-coloured herbal brew made by a Russian lackey resulted in a most unpleasant experience. Her broken arm still encased in a crudely made brace coupled with a splitting headache made getting around extremely difficult, even in the confined space of her cell. The only bit of satisfaction that Monika had was the realization that the NKVD operative who was hell-bent on raping her was now nursing a severely damaged eye, perhaps an eye that would never fully heal or properly function again.

It all began to unravel for Monika just a few days earlier when she was approached by an NKVD officer while attending an obligatory evening class. The Soviets liked to refer to the evening class as providing for the *re-education of those exhibiting anti-soviet characteristics.* According to the Soviets, Monika had been exposed to western ideas while working as an Ostarbeiter in Leipzig, Germany, and did fit this category.

Entering the small evening classroom without announcement on that fateful evening, NKVD agent Igor Kuznetsov addressed the instructor in a most authoritative and rude manner. Stocky of build and with the appearance of a wrestler who had taken enormous punishment to the head and facial features over the years, Igor projected the image of being a mean son-of-a-bitch. He did not disappoint.

"Comrade Lyudmila Petrova, do you have a student in your class by the name of Wozniak? Monika Wozniak?"

"Yes, Comrade, Monika Wozniak is in my class. What do you want with her?"

"Comrade Petrova, I hereby order you to release that suka to my care immediately. I want to ask that bitch some questions."

Seated in a dimly lit room adjacent to the classroom, Monika knew that the interrogation would not bring her any joy. She had heard about other prisoners being punished for some trumped-up charge. *One did not have to be a mental giant,* thought Monika, *to conclude that something terrible was about to unfold.*

"Monika Wozniak, I have a letter in my possession that was written by you."

"You have a letter that I wrote? How could that be? Where is this letter?"

"Here is the letter, written by you to a Roman Catholic Ojciec in Polonka, Soviet Ukraine. I want you to examine the letter. Did you or did you not write the letter?"

After examining the letter, Monika saw no alternative but to respond honestly, *"Yes, I did write the letter. I wrote the letter to my religious adviser in my home village."*

"Why did you write the letter?"

"I wanted to assure our Catholic Priest that I am still a firm believer in God despite the tragedy that has come to visit upon me. My three years of re-education will be up soon and I must decide what to do with my life. Fr. Ogrodski will be able to help me."

"You wrote this letter to a Priest? You are one stupid bitch. You kurva, you know that there is no such thing as God. What does God give you? What does He do for you? As stupid as you are, you must know that all good things come from our supreme leader, Josef Stalin."

"I know that my teacher, Pani Petrova, told me that there is no God. For me, there is a God. In the letter, I asked Ojciec Ogrodski if he knew the whereabouts of my brother, Wiktor."

For whatever reason, the interrogation went on and on, taking much longer than it should have. Perhaps it was the intent of Officer Kuznetsov to provide some re-education for Monika during the interrogation process. Maybe he was formulating a devious plan in his mind while at the same time wanting to impress upon Monika that she was in a Soviet labour camp for three reasons, *cooperation with Nazi intelligence, espionage, and embracing western ideas.* Whatever Officer Kuznetsov's plan, his interrogation of Monika went on long enough to bring to an end Pani Petrova's evening class. Except for Petrova, the students disappeared into the night. Monika fidgeted nervously.

Impatiently pulling out a watch out of a pocket of his Soviet Union uniform, Officer Kuznetsov had a decision for Monika Wozniak.

"Molodaya zhenshchina, Pani Monika, your term of re-education was set at three years by Soviet authorities. I shall lay no further charges against you for writing that stupid letter. Do you understand my decision and my generosity? I only ask a favour of you. I have this great sexual desire."

"What do you mean, you have a sexual desire?"

"I am not asking you if you are willing to have some raspushchennost; a bit of hanky-panky. I am simply telling you that I want to seduce you right here."

"You want some raspushchennost? Well, I don't."

Igor Kuznetsov was no shrinking violet. Fully aroused sexually by this time and suddenly acting like a raging bull, he immediately turned to violence. His sexual desires would not be denied.

"I order you to take off your panties or I will rip them off. You can see that I already have an enormous erection, a bol'shoy petukh."

To his astonishment, Monika would have none of it. In an attempt to beat Monika into submission, Igor seized her around the neck with what he liked to call a *Ruski submission chokehold.* To his surprise, Monika not only resisted any overtures to his sex-crazed advances, but she went on the offensive, attacking Igor with a vigour that he had never before experienced or witnessed in a woman. Yelling and kicking at Igor's most vulnerable parts, Monika was in no mood for sex or blackmail.

"Get off me, you ugly Mongolian beast," she screamed as she struck Kuznetsov over his left eye with a pencil she had been using in her evening class. To her surprise, the pencil broke into two pieces with one piece deeply submerged in the socket of Kuznetsov's left eye. Blood emanating from the wound formed a rivulet down his cheek. Extracting

a broken pencil from his eye and noticing the blood on his hand seemed only enraged Kuznetsov even more.

The fight did not last long. Although Kuznetsov lost his chokehold on Monika, he had the good fortune to hang onto her arm with the intent of dislodging it from its mooring. In a moment, Monika lay on the floor, her left arm broken, twisted under her back. Igor Kuznetsov, bleeding profusely from his left eye, was staring at Monika in disbelief. He seemed not to notice that his pants had fallen to the floor exposing his family jewels. He had his hands full trying to stop the flow of blood from his eye while at the same time hanging onto Monika's broken arm. Upon hearing the commotion, Pani Petrova burst into the interview room.

"Dammit, Comrade," she shouted, *"what the hell is going on here?"*

From the scene that unfolded before her, the question Petrova raised seemed out of place, almost rhetorical in tone. Monika, now standing up awkwardly with her left arm dangling at her side, said nothing. Backing away from Monika, his pants tangled around his ankles and now clutching at his genitals, Igor could do little to hide his pain and embarrassment.

"Pani Petrova, you can see for yourself what happened. This NKVD beast attacked me. He is a sex maniac," declared a defiant Monika.

"Comrade Kuznetsov, you maniac, you can put your pants back on and get the hell out of my school. I shall take this matter up with the authorities tomorrow."

Once again recalling that tragic event, Monika had to admit that the penalty served up by a three-member NKVD Tribunal could have been worse. It was most unfortunate that her letter to Fr. Ogrodski never reached its destination. Worse yet, it was returned to the NKVD office in Karaghanda by Soviet Post. It was obvious that the NKVD had opened and read her letter and must have concluded that her sentence of three years in a work camp in Kazakhstan was fair and just. Like so many before her, the Soviets felt confident that their re-education program would convince Monika that there was no such creature as God. After all, according to Soviet doctrine, God did not exist. To believe otherwise was punishable under Soviet law.

In examining the particulars of the case, the NKVD Troika gave little credence to the statement of Pani Petrova in which she stated that Officer Kuznetsov had attacked Monika. In fact, the Troika seemed to have complete disregard for the facts of the sexual confrontation, preferring to accept the written submission made by NKVD Officer Kuznetsov.

"*Pani Wozniak, please stand up and face the Troika as I read your sentence.*"

"*Your Honour, I am not too steady on my feet. Can I support myself against the table?*"

"*Yes, molodaya zhenshchina, young lady. Stand up straight and don't act stupid.*"

"*Thank you, Sir, I shall do my best.*"

"*It is the decision of this Troika that you attacked a Soviet agent without provocation. You forced Agent Kuznetsov to defend himself. This is why your arm was broken.*"

"*Your honour, the NKVD agent attacked me. That sex-crazed maniac wanted to rape me. I did my very best to resist his attack.*"

"*Pani, I am not asking you what you believe happened. We have a written statement from Comrade Kuznetsov. You severely damaged his left eye.*"

"*Yes your Honour.*"

"*All of this occurred when our Officer was in the process of examining the letter you wrote to Ojciec Ogrodski in Soviet Ukraine.*"

"*Your Honour, was it not wrong for the Soviet authorities to open my letter?*"

"*It is you on trial, not the Soviet police. You should have known that there is no God. In the process of his investigation, you attacked Officer Kuznetsov. In defending himself, he broke your arm. You severely damaged his left eye. He still has trouble seeing out of his eye.*"

"*Yes, your Honour, I did defend myself as best I could.*"

"*Since it is reported that you are a good worker and now studying the Russian language and the principles of communism, your three-year sentence will not increase. You are not to write any more letters in which you disagree with communist doctrine. As punishment, you will be confined for seven days to solitary confinement for attacking Comrade Kuznetsov.*"

Time passed quickly and Monika soon completed her time in solitary confinement. During her time of incarceration, she had plenty of time to think and formulate a plan as to how she might find her brother, Wiktor. However, having witnessed what had just taken place, she knew that she would have to find a way to outwit the NKVD, a challenge that would not be easy. To write a letter to a Polish family in Polonka was out of question. Most Poles who once lived in Polonka were either butchered by the Nazis or slaughtered by the Soviets. Those who survived likely found their way to Poland.

Relying on her mental and physical strength, Monika was not about to let the cruelty of the Soviets and time in solitary confinement deter her from pursuing her dream of finding her brother. Conjuring up various plans, Monika recalled that her brother Wiktor was in love with a girl by the name Tanja Konenko whose family lived in Polonka. She also recalled that Tanja had a great Aunt by the name of Tetyana Groszko who lived in Płazów, Poland. If nothing else, this gave her some hope. After all, if Tanja was truthful about her Aunt's family, surely one of Pani Groszko's nephews might be able to assist her.

According to Tanja, one of Pani Groszko's nephews was an organist in a Catholic Church in Cieszanow while the two other nephews were Catholic Priests, carrying out their religious duties somewhere in Poland. Monika also recalled that the family name of Pani Groszko's nephews was Mazurko. Maybe a letter to the Mazurko family would bear some fruit.

During the spring of 1948, the final year of her banishment to Karaghanda, Monika penned a short letter to the Mazurko family. In mailing the letter, she said a little prayer with the hopes that the NKVD would not open the letter before it reached its destination. Based upon an earlier experience, she now knew what not to say in the letter.

"Dear Family Mazurko: My name is Monika Wozniak. I will soon be released from my re-education program in Siberia and hope to find my brother, Wiktor, now living somewhere in Eastern Poland. Can you help me find him and his friend, Tanja Konenko? When you respond, please do not make any reference to religion or to God. As you know there is no such creature as God. Signed: Monika Wozniak."

The summer days passed quickly. Each day Monika checked with the local post office for a letter from the Mazurko family. At the same time, she hoped that her frequent visits to the post office would not arouse suspicion. All the while she hoped that the Mazurko family would disregard her comment about God in her letter. To her everlasting relief, she did receive a letter from a Jan Mazurko on September 8, 1948. However, it did not take an expert long to conclude that the letter had been opened by the NKVD.

"My dear Monika: Yes, we are related to the Konenko family of Polonka, a family destroyed by the war. I will soon be spending some time in Lublin. While there, I shall make some enquiries about your brother, Wiktor. Signed: Jan Mazurko."

Monika didn't know what to make of the letter. However, she needn't have worried. A second letter from Jan Mazurko followed on the heels of the first letter. To Monika, it was obvious that the NKVD had done its investigative work once again as evidenced by the shabby manner in which the letter was resealed. It appeared as though the NKVD had no intention of camaflouging its dirty work.

"My dear Monika: I have good news for you. I did undertake a search of your brother, Wiktor Wozniak. I invite you to come to Płazów. Once here, I will tell you how to find your brother. Signed: Jan Mazurko."

Monika was thankful that Jan Mazurko did not say any more than he had to in his letter, always mindful that the letter would be opened by Soviet officials before its release. Thinking about her brother and her release date, Monika promised herself that she would work hard to meet the daily work quota at the food processing plant and fulfill her re-education requirements. Only then would she be assured of being repatriated to Poland.

Monika felt a surge of optimism when on September 21, 1948, she received an official letter from the NKVD detachment in Karaghanda.

"Pani Wozniak, this is your notice to appear before an NKVD Troika on September 27. The Troika wants to determine your eligibility for repatriation to Poland. Signed: Mikhail Egerov, NKVD Director."

Trembling with the anticipation of her release from captivity and forced labour, Monika was ushered into an interrogation room by an armed NKVD guard. Looking at the composition of the three-member Board, Monika nearly fainted. Flanked by an NKVD agent on his left and an agent on his right, with a big black patch over his left eye was none other than NKVD Officer Igor Kuznetsov. It took Monika the longest time to regain her composure. Suddenly, she realized that her release from forced labour was no longer a sure thing. Her fears were borne out when the decision of the tribunal was rendered by Officer Kuznetsov.

"It is the decision of this Troika that your education in the ideals of communism and the importance of labour is not complete. You are required to serve an additional year of education and labour. Only then will you be eligible for repatriation to Poland."

As Monika considered the NKVD decision, she was struck with the thought that their decision was in stark contrast to her work ethic and ability to meet the Soviet daily work quota. In view of this, Monika had to admit that Igor Kuznetsov was the most vindictive son of a bitch she had ever met. Monika, however, persevered and as the spring days of 1949 got longer, she heard about a rumour circulating among forced labourers that NKVD Officer Kuznetsov had been transferred to Omsk. This gave her some hope of a successful meeting with the foreman of the food processing plant.

"Comrade Popov, is it true that I can make a request of your office? Is it possible to seek an early release? I heard that it is possible to seek one day credit for two days of work over the past year?"

"Where the hell did you hear of such a rumour? I have not heard of any such policy."

Thinking quickly and not wishing to jeopardize her chances of an early release, Monika decided to pull out all stops. After all, how would Foreman Popov know if she were telling the truth?

"Comrade Popov, this is not a rumour. Before his transfer, NKVD Officer Kuznetsov told me that this was a guideline recently put into place by Soviet authorities."

"Let me check out the latest communique from the NKVD office. I will let you know next week if there has been any change in the guidelines for an early release."

The winter of 1948-49 was among the coldest ever in Karaghanda. Monika worked hard to meet her daily work quota while at the same time reading about the history of Russia, embellished by the Soviets, while studying the Russian language. On April 1, 1949, she received a message that the Chief of the NKVD Directorate in Karaghanda.

"Pani Wozniak, you are hereby ordered to appear before the local NKVD Troika on April 7, 1949. Signed: Mikhail Sokolov, Chief, NKVD Directorate."

Appearing at the local office of the NKVD police, Monika was at a loss as to the purpose of the meeting. However, she was not kept in the dark for very long. After brief introductions by the NKVD Troika lead officer, the Troika Courts Martial had a decision for her.

"Pani Wozniak, stand at attention and face the Troika. I will read the decision of the Courts Martial. Based upon the report and request of your food processing factory foreman, you are hereby granted one day early release time for every two days of work since the revision of your sentence last September. This means that you will be repatriated to Poland on April 30."

Monika Wozniak was overjoyed in hearing the decision of the NKVD Troika. She knew that had Officer Igor Kuznetsov been presiding over the Troika, there was no way in hell that she would have been released from bondage. With her release papers in hand and railway passage to Lubaczow, Poland, the closest railway station to the village of

Płazów, Monika was about to taste her first days of freedom since her capture by the Gestapo in Polonka, Volhynia, in 1943. Her six years of hell was about to come to a screeching halt.

As Monika reflected upon her time in Karaghanda, she was left with the feeling that every Ostarbeiter now in Siberia being re-educated had a unique experience. She shuddered as she recalled the day when in 1943 she was forced into a waiting truck by the Gestapo. Only fifteen years of age at the time, she had to admit that the past six years had provided her with plenty of time to mature and see the world through a different set of eyes, thanks to the horrors of the war and slave labour in Kazakhstan while being re-educated.

Six years earlier, Monika had joined thousands of other young Poles, arrested by the Gestapo in the County of Lutsk, for slave labour in Germany. Cold and hungry during the seven-day train journey to somewhere in Germany, she could do little else but cry and think about her friends and the family she had left behind. It all sounded like a nightmare, now no more than a distant memory. To her surprise, when she had arrived in Leipzig, Germany, she encountered a Nazi soldier who was fluent in both German and Polish. This facilitated communication when he addressed the new arrivals from Poland and Soviet Ukraine. Speaking to a carriage-load of Poles and Ukrainians disembarking at a railway siding just outside the city of Leipzig, what he had to say was most revealing.

"Each of you will soon be working for the great nation of Germany. Our plan is to destroy those damn Godless Bolshevik bastards from Russia. Most of you are teenagers with little formal education. What you do know about the Soviets is a lot of communist bullshit. You will be enrolled in a German school where you Untermensch will be re-educated according to Nazi values."

As fortune would have it, Monika was able to attend class with another teenager from the County of Lutsk, a boy by the name of Danylo Antonenko. However, there was one significant difference between the two. While Monika was a Pole, Danylo was an ethnic Ukrainian. That, however, seemed not to matter; Danylo was conversant in both languages.

If Monika and Danylo were of the opinion that their re-education program would last indefinitely, they would have been dreadfully wrong. After only one week of schooling, Monika was assigned the position of *Kinderzimmer* in a nursery. As was the case with so many German families, Frau Fischer had three young children between the ages of two and six who required plenty of supervision. Her husband, Helmut, was serving in Hitler's Wehrmacht.

In contrast, Danylo was not so lucky. He was assigned to a munitions factory that required heavy police surveillance. Living in a barrack near a factory, Danylo joined hundreds of other Ostarbeiters slaving for HASAG, the Hugo Schneider Metallwarenfabrik. The munitions produced by the factory were critical to the success of the German military. Much as Danylo disliked the thought of helping the Nazis in their war effort, he was left without any other options.

Time had passed quickly for Monika as she continued with her child-care and domestic duties. Becoming more and more proficient in the German language made her tasks seem less strenuous. Yet, it seemed as though Frau Fischer looked upon her as embodying the soul of the enemy. *Maybe,* reasoned Monika, *her disposition has a lot to do with Hitler's attack on Poland and recent reports that the war was not going well for the Germans.*

Unfortunately, much of Frau Fischer's anger was taken out on Monika. One day she instructed Monika to look after her children as well as the two children of her neighbour, Frau Mueller. Despite the heavy workload, Monika was comforted by the words spoken to her by Danylo. On the last evening of their German orientation class, Danylo embraced her, whispering, *"Kocham Cię,"* in her ear. How could Monika forget those words? After all, it was the very first time that any boy had smothered her with the words, *"Kocham Cię, I love you!"*

Although Frau Fischer took it upon herself to inform Monika about the conduct of the war, her demeanour suddenly changed for the worse during the winter months of 1944. The first shock came to her when she learned of the loss of her husband while he was serving the Nazis. To add to her state of mind, as early as the fall of 1943, the war effort for the Nazis was met with the unthinkable; the possibility of defeat. Suddenly, this and the loss of her husband, Helmut, tended to strain the relationship between the two.

With the knowledge that the war effort was not going so well, Nazi officials determined that Germany needed more foreign workers, not just for HASAG in Leipzig, but also for several more of its other one hundred munitions factories throughout Germany. On February 1, 1944, the Gestapo arrested Monika and forced her to work in the munitions factory. Engaged in arms manufacturing, Monika learned that HASAG was but one of a conglomerate of arms-manufacturing factories across German-occupied Europe using slave labour on a massive scale.

Monika did not object to the transfer from Zivilarbeiter duties to one classified as Ostarbeiter duties. Fortunately, the Gestapo was not aware that Monika would be joining her friend, Danylo Antonenko, in the manufacture of military items destined for the front. Good fortune smiled on Monika because just two months earlier, Leipzig was bombed by the Allies and hundreds of civilians perished. While working for Frau Fischer, Monika survived the attack. Danylo, working in the HASAG factory, also survived the attack. Sadly, many of their co-workers perished.

In February of 1945, the British and Americans once again attacked Leipzig, damaging several munitions factories producing war materiel. The destruction of the HASAG factory turned out to be bad luck for the Nazis but good luck for the Allies. In addition, good luck seemed to follow both Monika and Danylo; neither one was injured in the bombing attack. Although HASAG ceased to be operational, other munitions factories, badly damaged, continued to operate. More bombs were dropped on Leipzig in April, 1945, and even though the Nazis won their last major battle against the Allies in this region, Germany capitulated on May 7, 1945.

With war's end came the realization to Monika and Danylo that they would soon be repatriated to their place of birth. Finding themselves in the Soviet region of control and not the American, French, or British zones of control meant only one thing—repatriation to the Soviet Union. Regrettably, their real problems were about to unfold.

Monika, born in the Polish province of Volhynia in 1928, had no problem identifying herself as being a Pole. After all, her birth occurred during the inter-war years when Volhynia was a part of Poland. However, and thanks to the Molotov-Ribbentrop Pact, Volhynia became a part of Soviet Ukraine in 1939. From this historical fact, an important question arose, *since Monika was rounded up by the Gestapo in 1943, was she a citizen of Poland, a citizen of Germany, or a citizen of Soviet Ukraine?* In turn, this raised an important decision for the NKVD, *would they treat her as a Pole and the possibility of repatriation to Poland or as a Soviet citizen and repatriation to the Soviet Union?*

In the case of Danylo, similar questions arose. Born in 1926 in the town of Dubno, Volhynia, of Ukrainian parents, he was aware that during the inter-war years Volhynia belonged to Poland. Officially, this meant that he was born in Poland. What, then, would be his status as determined by the NKVD at war's end? *Since he was an ethnic Ukrainian born in Poland, would the NKVD treat him as a citizen of Poland or as a citizen of the Soviet Union? Unfortunately, the province of Volhynia was now an integral part of Soviet Ukraine and under the control of the Red Army. More bad news was about to unfold for Danylo.*

Unlike Italian and British deportees or POWs who had no problem returning to their place of birth after the war, Monika and Danylo heard horror stories about those returning to Stalin's *Workers' Paradise.* Although homesick for their native land and concerned over the fate of friends and family left behind, they had grave reservations about returning to the Soviet Union.

Unfortunately, neither should have worried about repatriation to Soviet Ukraine or to Russia for that matter. Appearing before an NKVD Troika, Danylo, accused of aiding and abetting the Nazis by working in a German munitions factory, was sentenced to a 3-year term of punishment in Siberia. Similarly, Monika was accused of harbouring western ideas by virtue of her work as a Kinderzimmer and later in a Nazi munitions factory, was also sentenced to a 3-year term in Siberia. Both knew that their sentences involved hard labour and re-education in the ideals of communism.

Like millions of others before them, Monika and Danylo were unceremoniously loaded onto cattle carriages and sent to Siberia for re-education.

Since the Leipzig region of Germany fell under Soviet control, the NKVD was not required, in accordance with the Yalta Agreement, to seek permission of any other Allied nation before sentencing Ostarbeiters to slave labour and re-education. It was their belief that any citizen of the Soviet Union who helped the Nazis with the war effort in any way, shape, or form, must be sentenced for treason. One of their foremost reasons was a desire to punish those who had neglected their duty to the *Soviet Homeland* and assisted the Nazis, whether as actual collaborators, prisoners of war, or forced labourers.

In 1945, the Americans understood the guidelines to be applied to DPs for repatriating them to their place of residence. To them, it was clear that *Soviet citizens* meant only those who were Soviet nationals before the outbreak of the war, and thus effectively excluded Ukrainians and Poles from the regions annexed by the Soviet Union in 1939 or later. However, this did not stop the NKVD from repatriating thousands of Ostarbeiters from regions under their control. Sadly, Monika and Danylo were included in this latter group.

As Monika faced the Troika Tribunal, the history of her arrest and work in Germany flashed instantly before her eyes. Several of her co-workers in attendance, anxiously awaited the verdict of the Tribunal. They wanted to congratulate Monika and wish her well on her journey to Poland. Yes, the verdict by the Tribunal was read; freedom for Monika. However, you could hear a pin drop after hearing what Monika had to say to the members of the tribunal. Everyone sat in stunned silence. No one had the courage to even say one word. What could they say?

"Your Honour, I thank the Tribunal for granting my release and repatriation to Poland. But, I must stay in Kazakhstan until such time that I can find my friend Danylo Antonenko. Only then will I return to Poland."

PART 8

AGAINST ALL ODDS

19

The Missing Link

Two orphans of war take their rightful place on my family tree

Deep in thought as we approached the Greek Catholic Church in Płazów, a sacred place of worship, I tried to make sense of what happened seven decades earlier. Why did Brygada Salon inflict so much pain and suffering upon innocent villagers? What crime did the Ukrainians commit? After so many years of peaceful coexistence, how was it possible for Poles to attack ethnic Ukrainians, many of whom had family members in each other's communities?

With great difficulty, I brought my thoughts back to the present. Just a few minutes earlier we had left the nearby village of Ruda Różaniecka. The words of Pani Nowak kept reverberating in my head, *"Adam and Katarzyna Kaszuba lived right over there but their home was burned to the ground in 1944. Their house was set on fire by a band of Poles. Adam and Katarzyna were murdered because they were Ukrainians. They perished but their two infant children survived."*

The answers to my questions had not come easily. Nevertheless, I now knew a lot more about who was responsible for the murder of Adam and Katarzyna Kaszuba. Most of all, Pani Nowak helped me clear up the mystery of the missing branch in my family tree. It was now time to meet Franek and Sofija Zaborniak.

The drive from Płazów to the village of Nowe Sioło, although relatively short, gave me time to visualize the exodus of ethnic Ukrainians from their ancestral lands to Soviet Ukraine. As we drove past the Dormition of Our Blessed Virgin Mary Greek Catholic Church in Płazów, I could not get out of my mind how this sacred place of worship could not save all those wanting nothing more than safe passage to their gathering place in a nearby village. Of course, the nearby national forest did provide some protection but not enough to save every person from roving bands intent upon confronting Ukrainians with deadly force.

When we arrived in Nowe Sioło, the countryside was in full bloom. We were greeted by fields of yellow canola, the rapeseed crop seemingly ready to be harvested into vegetable oil. *"Can you imagine,"* I commented in wonderment and awe to no one in particular, *"that this village which provided safe haven for members of my extended family in 1944 will soon prove to be home to a couple of long-lost cousins?"*

Although Nowe Sioło is a small village in the administrative district of Gmina Cieszanow within the County of Lubaczow, its historical importance to the survival of several members of my family during World War II cannot be overstated. The residential dwellings are fairly close to one another along a narrow country highway with barns and storage sheds facing beautiful meadows.

In many ways, the village of Nowe Sioło reflects the past where villages were a usual form of community for societies that practised subsistence agriculture. In many regions of Europe, large urban centres have eclipsed villages as units of human society and settlement. During the communist era, the NKVD classified the small successful farmers in the region as belonging to a class of kulaks, their farms were confiscated, subjected to collectivization, and their property distributed, without compensation, to others. The narrow paved highway took us through the centre of Nowe Sioło to a country-residential section and a well-groomed farmyard of what appeared to be a wealthy farmer.

"Gzien dobry," I said to the owner who ventured out of his home, *"my name is Stefan Kaszuba. I am looking for family in Nowe Sioło. Is there a family in this village by the name of Kaszuba?"*

Looking at me most intently, the farmer did not immediately answer. Perhaps his mind wandered back to Poland's recent communist history where a misspoken word could bring nothing but trouble to one's doorstep.

"Yes, I am from Canada," I assured the Polish resident. *"In Ruda Różaniecka we talked to a woman by the name of Pani Nowak. She informed*

us that two Kaszuba orphans who lived across the road from her came to live in Nowe Sioło after the war. She said that they are now the Zaborniaks."

"Yes, Pan Kaszuba," replied the farmer, pointing in a southerly direction, *"the Zaborniak family lives over there."*

A thousand thoughts raced through my mind during the short drive to the Zaborniak residence. *For certain, I wanted to meet Franek and Sofija. However, would they want to meet me or would they rather not resurrect the past? Would they have different ideas about heritage and family than I did? What would the two orphans know about their past? Would they care? Had either of the orphans made any effort to contact the family of their birth parents?*

In short order, we arrived at the Zaborniak residence. Driving into the front yard, I noted that the farmstead consisted of a family home, a large barn, a granary, and a large machine shed. Beyond the Zaborniak residence stretched agricultural land. Alerted by a barking dog, a man came out of the house to greet us.

"Cześć! My name is Stefan Kaszuba. I am a visitor from Canada."

"Witam!. Welcome to Poland. My name is Franek. Franek Zaborniak."

Even as Franek introduced himself, I could see that my family name brought a quizzical look to his face. I suspected that his mind immediately went back to the history of his family. Tanned, stocky, and healthy-looking, it struck me that somehow Franek looked familiar, like a long-lost brother. My wife, Sharon, must have had the same thoughts when she suddenly whispered to me, *"Look at his physical appearance. Look at his facial features and his cheek bones. He most definitely is a kaszub."*

Franek, not being conversant in English, would not have understood Sharon's remarks. Otherwise, he might have responded to her observations. With the introductions came that typical Polish warm embrace from Franek. The introductions out the way, I told Franek, as best I could in Polish, about the purpose of my visit. Not wanting to immediately get into our relationship, I asked Franek about his farming operation. That, obviously, made Franek seem more at ease. He was most anxious to tell me about his farming operation.

"Farming," Franek explained, *"goes a long way back and the vast majority of the people are descendants of former land owners or peasants working at these estates."*

"Yes," I enjoined Franek, *"I had heard that many changes have taken place since the end of the war. I know that my ancestors were required to work for the lords who owned the land."*

"My grandfather," nodded Franek, *"worked for a Polish Baron and in return received protection, justice, and the right to cultivate certain fields within the manor in order to maintain the life of his own family."*

Pointing in the direction of his farmland, Franek proudly explained that he grew the typical crops of canola, rye, oats, barley, and wheat—quickly adding that he also bred pigs and cows. By the presence of a modern farm tractor, I could see that his farming operation was now fully mechanized. When I asked him about horses, he said that he had put the last of his horses out to pasture some two years earlier. When I turned to the matter of Poland joining the European Union, I found that Franek was somewhat reticent to discuss politics. Perhaps this came from a realization that he still had one foot in the communist camp while the other was trying hard to get into the democratic sphere.

That fateful day upon which I met Franek for the very time marked the 75th anniversary of the German invasion of Poland and Ukraine, and the centenary of my father's service in the Austrian Infantry in World War I. Twenty-five years earlier, in 1989, the Communist Government of Poland fell, leading to democratic elections and full sovereignty for the Polish people. Two years later, in 1991, Ukraine also unshackled itself from the suffocating hold of the Russian Bear and set a course for full sovereignty.

We did not discuss family until all of the small talk was out of the way and only after he introduced us to his wife and his two grandchildren. Of course, we had already confirmed with Pani Nowak that Franek had a sister by the name of Sofija. In response to my enquiry, Franek told me that his sister lived nearby but was in poor health. Otherwise, we might have asked him to collect his sister for a visit.

Gently, so as not to overwhelm Franek with questions, we talked about World War II, the historical tensions between Ukrainians and Poles, the transfer of Ukrainians from Poland to Soviet Ukraine, and the re-location of Ukrainians from Poland's border region to Northern Poland. In reflecting upon the mores of the two ethnic groups, Franek did concede that the lines between the Poles and Ukrainians are somewhat blurred when you bring food and customs into the mix. Both groups claim perogies as their national dish, as well as borsch, cabbage soup, bigos, and beef stroganoff. When a person says that *my heritage is Polish,* is not to say that it is not also *Ukrainian.* There are numerous similarities in customs, language, and religion between the two ethnic groups. At the same time, people of Ukrainian heritage no doubt carry significant DNA from Russian, Tatar, Polish, and Hungarian ethnic groups. As well, the contributions from the Celts, Goths, Khazars, the Mongols of the Golden Horde add to the ethnic mix.

"Franek," I declared, trying to measure his reaction as to what I was about to say, *"I do believe that you are my first cousin. I have been searching for your family for a long time. I am so happy to finally find you and place you and your sister on my family tree."*

My declaration about being cousins seemed not to have the effect that I anticipated. In fact, it appeared as though Franek had anticipated what I was going to say. This immediately triggered a series of questions in my mind. *Had Pani Nowak telephoned Franek in advance of our visit? Did Pani Nowak tell me the truth about Franek, his birth parents, and his adoption? Was Franek aware of the fact that he was an orphaned child born of Ukrainian parents?*

"Franek," was my next question, *"can you tell me about your birth parents and your childhood? Can you share your thoughts with me?"*

Franek did not answer for the longest time. He must have been thinking about the horrors of war and ethnic tensions between Ukrainians and Poles.

"Yes," he finally put words to his thoughts, *"I have known for a long time about the loss of my birth parents."*

"You also know that you were adopted by Franciszek and Bronislawa Zaborniak. They were your adoptive parents and members of the Roman Catholic Church, weren't they?"

"Yes, Stefan, our family is very religious. We attend church on a regular basis."

Knowing that Franek's birth parents were ethnic Ukrainians and that he was adopted by a Polish family immediately brought to mind several important questions. However and even though any questions about his adoption and childhood might have been very sensitive, I felt duty-bound to pursue the matter further.

"This, Pan Zaborniak, is a question I must ask you. Having regard for your Ukrainian birth parents and you being brought up by a Polish family, do you consider yourself to be of Ukrainian or Polish heritage?"

Looking at Franek, I could see that he felt somewhat uneasy with my question. Perhaps he was thinking about the historical conflicts between Ukrainians and Poles.

"Well, if I were to consider myself to be an ethnic Ukrainian, how do you think my adoptive parents would feel about that? They would not feel very

good about that, would they? That is why I have always considered myself to be of Polish heritage. I owe nothing less to my parents. They brought me up as one of their own."

"Franek, would you be aware of other war orphans left without parents in Ruda Różaniecka? What about Gmina Narol?"

"Yes, in Gmina Narol, the war left behind many infants and small children. My sister and I were the lucky ones. When the Germans occupied this region, I heard that they kidnapped many children under eight years of age. Aryan-looking children were kidnapped by the Nazis and transported to Germany for the purpose of Germanization."

"Were any of your childhood friends kidnapped?"

"Yes, my uncle told me that three children from our neighbourhood were kidnapped. The family tried to find them in Germany."

"Were they successful in locating them?"

"No, they were not successful in finding them. German authorities do not like Poles who snoop around their countryside looking for kidnapped children. Maybe someday we will get more help from Germany in locating these children."

From Franek, I learned that the Nazis kidnapped the children by force, often after their parents had been murdered, were in concentration camps, or shot by partisans. These children were not permitted to remain even with other living relatives. Although some may have been from German soldiers and foreign mothers, most were Polish and Ukrainian children. Orphanages and children's homes were among the first groups to be targeted by the Nazis.

According to Franek, in order to cover their crimes, Nazi officials considered the kidnapped children to be descendants of German settlers who had emigrated to Poland. Those labeled *racially valuable* were forcibly Germanized in centres and then sent to German families. Those determined to be racially *un-German* were sent to extermination and concentration camps where they were either murdered or served as living test subjects in German medical experiments.

As early as 1939, Heinrich Himmler stated that *racially valuable* Polish children should be excluded from deportation to their place of origin but forcibly acquired for German plans and purposes. He stated that the, *"...children must not be older than eight or ten years, because only till this age can we truly change their national identification. A condition for this is complete separation from any Polish relatives. Children will be given German names, their ancestry will be led by special office."*

The aim of the plan was to destroy Polish as an ethnic group and leave within Poland a considerable slave population to be used up over the next ten years. Between 1940 and 1945, according to official Polish estimates, approximately 200,000 Polish children were abducted by the Nazis, 30,000 of them coming from Gmina Zamosc. Of this number, only 15-20 percent were ever recovered. In contrast, about 20,000 children were taken from the Soviet Union, most were ethnic Ukrainians from Soviet Ukraine.

"My parents told me," explained Franek, *"that they witnessed children being taken from their mothers, some were even torn from the breast. It was a terrible sight, seeing the mothers crying over the loss of their children."*

Sometimes, the German guards could be bribed by jewelry or gold. In other cases, Poles bought children for 40 Reichsmarks and in other places the German price for a Polish child was 25 Polish zlotys. In cases where German families adopted orphans, they were told that the children had received false Polish birth certificates in order to rob them of their German heritage. Many children were placed in special temporary camps for racial examination, then divided into three groups of *desired population growth, acceptable population growth, and undesired population growth.* These racial examinations determined the fate of children.

Once selected, the children between six and twelve were sent to special homes. Their names were altered and they were compelled to learn German. If they were not disqualified, they were placed for adoption. When adoptive parents demanded adoption certificates, such records were forged for them.

Locating these children after the war turned up their stories of forcible instruction in the German language and how failures were killed. Some children suffered emotional trauma when they were removed from their adoptive German parents. Allied forces made efforts to repatriate them. Many of the children first abducted by the Nazis in 1939 and found by the Allies after the war, declared that they were German. Even more startling was the case of Russian and Ukrainian children. When found, they confessed that they were taught to hate their native countries. Consequently, they did not want to return to Russia or Soviet Ukraine.

From 1947 to 1948, the Nuremberg Trials ruled that the abductions, exterminations, and Germanization constituted genocide. Today in Germany it is believed that hundreds of thousands of Germans might be descended from kidnapped Polish and Ukrainian children. After the war, a memorial plate was made in Lublin dedicated to railway workers who tried to save Polish children from German captivity.

Bronislawa Zaborniak, Franek's adoptive mother, must have had mixed feelings when she faced a nationalistic unit whose members came from her own ethnic community. It would have been much easier for her to face the dreaded German Gestapo. Instead, she had to face Brygada Salon. At that most critical moment and even though the Zaborniaks had four children of their own, did not stop them from adopting the two orphans. The times were tough and providing for the material and health needs of the six children was quite a challenge, especially during the war.

As hostilities wound down and in possession of two orphans, Franciszek Zaborniak wanted to know if, at birth, they had been registered with the Greek Catholic Church in Płazów. Franciszek Zaborniak was not surprised to discover that the Ukrainian Catholic Church ceased to function after the war. To further complicate matters, he also discovered that the records of the local Greek Catholic Church did not survive the war. This meant that even if the infants were registered with the church, those records no longer existed. Not only that but the civic records in Narol showed no evidence of their being registered. With this knowledge, Franciszek immediately registered the births of Franek and Sofija with the Roman Catholic Church in Płazów, not as kaszubs but as Zaborniaks.

In contrast to the manner in which I set out in search of the missing branch on my family tree, many families seek the help of the International Red Cross. But even the Red Cross readily admits that information about the plight of orphans is often hard to come by. However, thanks to the persistence of the Red Cross, many orphans after being separated from their parents during the war have been located. Following the war in Europe alone, estimates place the number of orphans ranging from one to thirteen million. The Red Cross's Information and Documentation Centre in Munich is still looking for them. When made available, the Red Cross adds any new enquiry or fact to its 37 million non-computerized cards of 21 million names.

What is of interest is that the cases of more than 99 percent of the children have been resolved. During the 1990s, the Red Cross had been able to solve about 14 cases each day. Unfortunately, today, over 400,000 cases from World War II remain. It would appear as though the time has come to consider the remaining cases as *cold cases*.

Children who have spent an extended period of time in an orphanage display deficits in all areas of development when compared to any other group, early adopted or within country adopted. This speaks to the strength in young children of overcoming tremendous adversity. However, resiliency is not something within a child but develops from particular interactions with the environment. Therefore, institutionalization represents a risk factor that initially sets a child on a less-than-optimal developmental pathway. Where a child ends up developmentally depends on what happens after the initial trauma.

Children who first experienced institutionalization and were then adopted, generally arrived in their adoptive homes in poor condition. In such cases, parents had to deal with an array of problems requiring an exceptionally high level of commitment. The fact that many parents were successful in promoting optimal developmental outcomes in their children is truly a laudable achievement. Having regard for the problems experienced by so many orphans, the adoption of Sofija and Franek was rather seamless.

Immediately after World War II, the economic prospects in Europe were dismal. The creation of the United Nations in 1945 represented the coming of age of an ideal of international cooperation and a desire to promote world peace. Millions of people were still without proper shelter, fuel, clothing, or food. Children, especially, were suffering to an extent where half of all babies were dying before their first birthday. These events propelled the United Nations to create, in 1946, the International Children's Emergency Fund. A resolution of UNICEF made it possible to support children in vanquished as well as victorious countries.

Coincidentally and almost unnoticed, the international community had also embraced the new central principle *that children were above the political divide.* As a result, the major objective of UNICEF was to help children damaged by war in accordance with its founding resolution, *"...to reach every child and ensure their well-being."* In time, UNICEF dropped the words *International* and *Emergency* from its title but retained its mission, *"...to never abandon the children of crises—those affected by war, conflict, drought, famine or any other emergency."*

Simply put, children came to be regarded as a special group, much like refugees, the elderly, or the disabled. However, these new developments redefined the plight of children who were in distress or in poverty as a result of war or ethnic conflict. Where previously they had been seen as objects of purely humanitarian and welfarist concern to be taken care or given supplementary support, they were now viewed as requiring special consideration and treatment. Unlike the homeless—who were ill-fed and always hungry, frequently sick, poorly clothed, illiterate and destitute—they were always children. Unless they were orphaned or abandoned, children could never be treated in isolation from their parents and families, and especially not from their mothers.

In many ways, Franek and Sofija Zaborniak are the lucky ones. We do know that they did not have to spend any time in an orphanage. Perhaps this is why they do not display any deficits in areas of mental or physical development. Rescued at an early age, both have displayed boundless courage and strength in overcoming tremendous adversity.

Perhaps it was Franek who expressed his feelings best about being an orphan when he said, *"Orphans are the only ones who get to choose their parents, and they love them twice as much."*

In reflecting upon Franek's choice of words, I discovered that it is not the physical pain that endangers orphans the most but rather the mental pain caused by stress from years of remembering and wondering while at the same time being thankful for not being neglected, pushed aside, disregarded, unloved, and made to feel undeserving. Franek and Sofija were not made to feel like a possession but rather as equal human beings.

This story began with the hypothesis that my family tree was not complete. The discovery of two orphans, who turned out to be my cousins, confirmed the hypothesis. In the process, I discovered that the care and love of adoptive parents was a tonic for many ills. I also found answers to another mystifying question—who murdered the parents of the two orphans?

EPILOGUE

Ethnic cleansings took place in Poland and Soviet Ukraine not only during World War II but also immediately after the end of the war. Those ethnic cleansings occurred at a time when the Soviet Union had secured victory and the postwar borders of Eastern Europe were being rearranged. In all, over twenty million people were affected by ethnic cleansings, many of which bordered on genocide, *leaving behind countless orphans*. The Soviet Union was not only concerned with punishing the Germans and preventing another war of aggression but also with reorganizing, territorially and demographically, an entire continent. The primary objective was to integrate nation-states and align state and ethnic boundaries. Bilateral settlements between Poland and the USSR were crucial for effecting Poland's shift to the west and the avoidance of endless trouble with national minorities.

Ethnic cleansings caused profound loss for individuals as well as for the states and societies that enforce them, especially with respect to the way of life in the affected regions. After World War II, cities, towns, and villages in Poland and Ukraine were radically transformed. Residents of thousands of communities spoke different languages, practiced different religions, and had different national identities from the people who once lived there. Ethnic cleansings remade the ethnic and religious map of Poland and Ukraine, erasing diversity across most of the region. Violence was not the only cause of migration—some people left their homes to find better opportunities elsewhere. Millions of others were forced out or killed.

Ethnic cleansings and related violence created new identities for victims and survivors. For many survivors, the experience of having been ethnically cleansed or transferred became the pivotal event in their lives. Some clung to their memories of the past. They never forgot their old homes; they held on to maps and photos of their lost homelands. Some even tried to obtain plants from gardens they had been forced to leave.

Many of the ethnically cleansed, as well as their descendants, retained a visceral anger and mistrust toward the perpetrators. Decades after ethnic cleansing, a sense of victimization extends even to diaspora communities whose members have moved far away from Europe.

Those who occupied the place of those expelled were frequently left with a sense of unease. Some simply insisted they have every right to their homes, but others displayed a curiosity about the past by commemorating the history of the vanished and destroyed communities. Some lived with anxiety. They feared the return, not only by invading armies but also by lawyers and real estate agents representing the previously expelled or their heirs with demands for compensation or for the return of land, buildings, and businesses. Some worried that the expelled and their descendants will simply buy up what they lost. This was particularly true of Aunt Anna Grokh whose family occupied the home of a Polish family transferred to Poland after the war. When we arrived for our first visit in 1997, my Aunt felt certain that we were the Polish owners returning to reclaim their property.

Ethnic cleansings united Ukrainians and Poles even as it drove them apart. They shared a common desire for *nation states* of their own, untarnished by the presence of large ethnic or religious minorities. These dreams of purity were in stark contrast to the nationalistic myths and stories which depicted the *other ethnic group* as traitors and enemies. In reality, these were the very same people that many residents of Europe lived comfortably alongside. The first reality was of peaceful everyday relations with neighbours or fellow citizens of a different ethnic identity. The second reality—at odds with the first—was of ethnic hatred and fear that neighbours were traitors. For many, war and history confirmed those fears. Cycles of revenge killing suggested that the worst suspicions had been correct all along—neighbours were indeed enemies, and ethnic cleansing provided a way to build a better and more secure future.

While stopping ethnic cleansing has proven difficult, repairing its damage is even more complicated. The window of action is brief. Unless refugees return very soon to their homes, they are unlikely ever to go back, except as visitors. The most promising approach to reversing ethnic cleansing combines local reconciliation projects with economic development.

In a strange way, the main culprit in this story is this matter of a people's desire to build an independent country. Unfortunately, this spectre of nationalism has its darker side, most often pursued at the expense of one or more of its minority and/or ethnic groups. Even as the first members of clan kaszub appeared in Gmina Narol during the final days of the Habsburg Monarchy, they soon had this vision of either a free and independent Poland or a free and independent Ukraine. After two world wars and a series of ethnic cleansings, we are left with an over-arching thought—*who is it that survived and who succumbed to international conflict and ethnic cleansings?* Even more important is the question, *how did anyone manage to survive this period in history?*

During World War II, life on the front lines and in the trenches was horrendous in its own right. Civilian life was not much easier. War and ethnic cleansings took a great toll on the minds and bodies of innocent people. This anticipation of future destruction is what gripped much of the civilian psyche in the midst of the constant terror. Kids had trouble falling asleep, even when cuddled next to their parents. Yet, somehow, in the face of such extraordinary hardship, many civilians managed to survive.

The Second World War would have quite an impact upon all those living in Gmina Narol and the villages of Ruda Różaniecka, Huta Różaniecka, Grochi, and Płazów. Once hostilities were over, the human toll of the war reached unimaginable numbers. It seemed that every villager lost at least one member of the family. Those who survived armed conflict had to cope with their losses.

Towards the end of the war, a wave of terror swept over the region inhabited by Ukrainians living along the border between Poland and Soviet Ukraine. Hitler's ruthlessly waged total warfare had ended, but in its place retribution was dawning everywhere. Red Army forces took revenge upon anything and anyone complicit in the killings of millions of her citizens. In turn, millions of Germans in Eastern Europe met a tragic fate, paying with life and limb for the crimes committed by the Nazis. They were hunted down, humiliated, raped, bludgeoned to death, or carted off to Siberia as slave labourers. The Red Army did not spare the Poles either, even though the Germans had already carried out the *physical destruction* of Poland with horrific zeal.

It was a time when Ukrainians living in Poland near the Soviet Ukraine border fell victim to the frenzied expulsions forced upon them by the Soviets. Trainloads of transferees en route to Soviet Ukraine faced unimaginable suffering as they chugged past destroyed towns; the rubble of war with piles of dead bodies. There were graves everywhere. The villages looked sad and desolate with furniture, smashed doors, and windows ripped from their hinges scattered about. The wind howled through open houses and buildings. Numerous trains headed toward Soviet Ukraine while other trains headed in the opposite direction. There were convoys of carts carrying displaced, half-starved people heading in all directions. Hordes of children abandoned or separated from their families languished in the forests. Hundreds of thousands of people did not survive their flight from danger, expulsion, or imprisonment. Many starved, froze to death, or succumbed to epidemics and injuries. Others died as a result of the wanton behaviour of Russian soldiers.

The thought of survival consumed the minds of those being transferred during those troubled times. Tearfully exiting their ancestral homeland in Poland, family members recalled how ordinary people were guilty of looting and committing crimes while the social structure was on a temporary pause. Some civilians went so far as to impersonate police officers in order to extort, cheat, and terrorize the hypersensitive public out of money and security. Yet, most civilians took their day-to-day activities in stride, not getting caught up too much in an uncertain future.

This story chronicles the hardships and dangers encountered by members of clan kaszub and family Groszko when they were forced to leave Poland in favour of Soviet Ukraine. For family members who survived war and ethnic conflict, their memories do not fade with age. Even decades later, wartime stressors continue to cause heart disease, and negatively affect their immune systems. One can only conclude that the scars of war and ethnic conflict are both external and internal.

Since the Soviet Union disintegrated in 1991, the very absence of individual freedoms and human rights, the hallmark of communism, became a thing of the past. During communist times, consumers faced chronic shortages of food and ever-present lines. With the fall of communism, market economy took hold and the number of family members who enjoyed a reasonable level of wealth and comfort had increased considerably. The end of communism, however, was hardly seen by family members as a reason for celebration.

The key element of this story is about the crimes committed by members of Brygada Salon, villains to some but heroes to others. Depending upon one's point of view, a case can be made for either position. In fact, Ukrainians and Poles can claim that Brygada Salon did pursue compelling objectives.

Brygada Salon consisted of five active paramilitary members and their leader, Kapitan Kawa. After the war, Kapitan Kawa, the military coordinator of the brigade, spent his years in retirement in the community of Zamosc. Adam Krawczyk was killed while undertaking the unit's dastardly deeds in Gmina Narol. Corporal Kawa, Wiktor Wozniak, Myron Mora, and Michal Komarski were ambushed and all were killed by a UPA unit. This brought to an abrupt end the mission and existence of Brygada Salon. Only Wiktor Wozniak survived.

As fate would have it, Wiktor Wozniak, the original member of Brygada Salon, fell in love with the girl next door. Through an interesting twist in life's journey, the love of his life turned out to be an ethnic Ukrainian girl while his parents were ethnic Poles. How to reconcile the tensions between the Polish and Ukrainian communities and his love for this girl was his challenge. The very resilience of his love for Tanja occurred at a time when his unit, the Brygada Salon, set out to remove all Ukrainians from Gmina Narol.

Even while carrying out the unit's dastardly deeds, Wiktor could not get out of this mind his sweetheart, Tanja Konenko. In the end, it was not Wiktor who set out in search of Tanja but the other way around. With the help of a Catholic priest in Zamosc, Tanja did find the whereabouts of Wiktor, far removed from their home village of Polonka. Despite ethnic and religious differences, love triumphed and the two were married. Their grandson, Antoni Wozniak, now living in Zamosc, Poland, thought that his grandmother, Tanja (Konenko) Wozniak, was truly a child of God.

"Look at what she went through," was the way Antoni described it, *"she lost her family in Volhynia, worked in Germany as a slave, and then set out in search of my grandfather, Wiktor Wozniak, eventually marrying him."*

Despite marrying his childhood sweetheart, all was not peaches and cream for Wiktor Wozniak. The end of the war was perhaps the most difficult time in his life. Living in Zamosc, he missed his home town of Polonka, now absorbed into Soviet Ukraine. According to Antoni, *"my grandfather was always nervous and as mean as a rattlesnake. He did not trust anybody and he didn't want to be around anybody. He couldn't stand to have people walking behind him on the street. And yet my grandmother found him to be the most loving person in the world."*

Antoni believed that it took his grandfather the longest time to turn his life around and accept Zamosc as his home town and put aside his time and murderous deeds as a member of Brygada Salon. In fact, many of those involved in ethnic conflict struggled with the new reality. Some just couldn't get started rebuilding their lives after the war while others couldn't stand the thought of leaving the military. For many soldiers, the war didn't end when World War II ended. There was still the imagery of what they had seen and what they had done to stay alive. The date in a history book might define a time for a country's surrender or victory but the personal battles continued for many people, Wiktor Wozniak among them.

Perhaps the saddest tragedy to befall any of the characters in this book belongs to Monika Wozniak. Monika had completed her three-year sentence of re-education in Siberia and was released by the NKVD for repatriation to Poland. However, she refused to be returned to Poland until such time that she could find her true love, Danylo Antonenko, also being re-educated by the Soviets. With this objective in mind, she wrote a letter to Fr. Mazurko in Lublin, Poland, telling him of her intentions. That is the last time anyone heard from Monika. We can only assume that Siberia not only took the life of Monika Wozniak but also that of her true love, Danylo Antonenko.

They were not the only victims of the Gulag. Of the main characters depicted in this story, Jan Konenko was killed by a falling pine tree in a Siberian logging camp, and his son, Janko, lost his life in Italy in the service of the Allies. Although Filip Wozniak succumbed to typhus while slaving in the Gulag, there was one ray of sunshine. His son, Donek Wozniak, after serving three years of his five-year sentence in Siberia, was granted amnesty by the NKVD and encouraged to enrol in the Red Army. In fact, all Poles, especially those of military age, were granted amnesty. But, instead of joining the Red Army, Janko Konenko and Donek Wozniak promptly joined General Anders Army and saw service with the Allies in Italy. Unfortunately, Janko Konenko lost his life in the Battle of Monte Cassino. Donek Wozniak survived the war and took up residence in London.

After their service in Anders Army and pursuant to the Polish Resettlement Act of 1947, over 200,000 Poles were offered British citizenship for their contribution to the World War II effort. They opposed the Soviet takeover of their homeland and refused to return to a Communist Poland. As a result, they accepted the offer of British citizenship, Donek Wozniak among them.

Donek's granddaughter, Krystal, living in London, described it this way, *"After my grandfather served in Anders Army, he said that he was the luckiest man in the world. Lucky, that is, until he discovered that Eastern Poland was lost to the Soviet Union after the war. He refused to return to a Communist country."*

Many ethnic Ukrainians who served in the Polish Armed Forces accepted the offer of British citizenship and formed the *Association of Ukrainian Soldiers*. At its height, AUGB had as many as 29,000 members whose initiatives focused on the provision of material assistance and moral support to various Ukrainian groups. The head office provided advice, translation, and interpreting services, and other practical assistance in connection with matters such as finding employment, applications for official documents, the resolution of issues, and bringing family members to the UK from overseas.

Especially troubling is the fate of untold millions of prisoners who were shipped off in cattle cars to the Gulag. Many slaves and prisoners were freed because they finished their sentences while others received amnesty and were encouraged to join the Red Army or General Anders Army. Some were released because they were invalids or women with small children or because they were promoted from captive to guard. Some 18 million prisoners passed through the gates of the Gulag between 1929 and the death of Stalin in 1953. Only in 1987 did Mikhail Gorbachev, himself the grandson of Gulag prisoners, convince the Soviet Union that all labour camps should be dissolved. In 1991, the Supreme Soviet of Russia officially established October 30 of each year as the *Day of Remembrance of the Victims of Political Repression*.

War has had a catastrophic effect on the health and well being of people living in Poland and Ukraine. Studies have shown that conflict situations cause more mortality and disability than any major disease. War and ethnic conflicts destroyed communities and families and disrupted the development of the social and economic fabric of Poland and Ukraine. The effects of war include long-term physical and psychological harm to orphans, children, and adults, as well as a reduction in material and human capital. Only through a greater understanding of conflicts and the myriad of mental health problems that arise from them can coherent and effective strategies for dealing with such problems be developed.

As I conclude this story, I want to reiterate that the secret pact between Stalin and Hitler, signed on August 23, 1939, did change the course of European history. Seventy-eight years later, on August 23, 2017, Justin Trudeau, the Prime Minster of Canada, issued the following statement on Black Ribbon Day, the National Day of Remembrance for the Victims of Communism and Nazism in Europe:

"Today, we join people in Canada and around the world to remember the victims and survivors of Communism and Nazism in Europe, and to

pay tribute to all those who continue to face violence, loss of dignity, and repression from totalitarian regimes.

"On Black Ribbon Day, we mark the anniversary of the Molotov-Ribbentrop Pact, which was signed in 1939 between the Soviet Union and Nazi Germany. The infamous agreement carved Eastern and Central Europe into spheres of influence of Nazi Germany and the Soviet Union, and led to one of the darkest periods in human history.

"In the years that followed, the Soviet and Nazi regimes trampled upon national and personal freedoms across Europe. They robbed millions of people of their lives and livelihoods, and subjected countless men, women, and children to untold atrocities.

"Many of those who struggled against the horrors of the Soviet and Nazi regimes came to Canada as refugees. These Canadians and their descendants continue to make remarkable contributions to our country. Their stories underscore the importance of universal human rights – and remind us of the fragility of freedom.

"On behalf of the Government of Canada, I urge Canadians to reflect on the significance of this day. We all share the responsibility to promote and protect human rights, freedom, and democracy. We must stand guard against those who seek to devalue the humanity of others, and uphold the inherent dignity of every human being."

I applaud Justin Trudeau, the Prime Minister of Canada, for recognizing the devastation of human misery left in the wake of the secret pact between Nazi Germany and the Soviet Union.

In the final analysis, a number of factors contributed to the relatively high survival rate of members of my extended family. Among the positive factors are geographic location, direct assistance from Poles and/or Ukrainians during periods of conflict, and avoiding service in the German Wehrmacht, the Red Army, or a partisan unit. Not only did most of my family members survive the war but they also survived ethnic conflicts, population transfers, and the spectre of communism. Sadly, Jan and Janko Konenko, Filip and Monika Wozniak, and Danylo Antonenko did not survive. Neither did my grandparents, Andriy and Mariia Kaszuba, who perished while attempting to find safe passage from Poland to Soviet Ukraine.

It matters little if their final resting place is in Poland, Ukraine, Germany, Siberia, or Italy, may they all rest in peace. I hope that their descendants can enjoy the fruits of their sacrifices.

APPENDIX A

Transfer Document For Mikhailo Kaszuba And Family

Appendix A: Transfer document for Mikhailo Kaszuba, 1945.

English Translation: TRANSFER DOCUMENT, MIKHAILO KASZUBA and FAMILY

SOURCE: STATE ARCHIVES OF LVIV, UKRAINE

NAMES OF THOSE TRANSFERRED:

KASZUBA, Mikhailo Andriyovycz, b. 1904
KASZUBA, Eva Mikhailivna, b. 1903
KASZUBA, Lesia Mikhailivna, b. 1936
KASZUBA, Mikhailo Mikhailovycz, b. 1938
KASZUBA, Ivanna Mikhailivna, b. 1942
KASZUBA, Maria Mikhailivna, b. 1931

Transferred in 1945, to Lviv Oblast, from Plaziv, Lubaczow Powiat, Voivodeship of Rzeszow, Poland

LEFT BEHIND IN POLAND

Home, 150 cubic meters; Barn, 120 cubic meters; Shed, 80 cubic meters; Granary, 160 cubic meters Land consisting of 15 hectares; 9 hectares being cultivated and 6 hectares for haying

TOTAL VALUE: 6,800 karbovanets

SIGNED AND SEALED: B. I. Kuchenda; E. L. Sztatman

Note: During the Nazi occupation of Ukraine, 10 Ukrainian karbovanets = 1 Reichsmark. From 1941 to 1948, 1 Reichsmark = US$2.50. Property valued at 6,800 karbovanets = 680 Reichsmarks = US$1,700.

Selected References

Applebaum, Anne. _Gulag, a History,_ Anchor Books, A Division of Random House, Inc., New York, 2003.

Babiak, Matthew. _Ethnic Cleansing or Ethnic Cleansings? The Polish-Ukrainian Civil War in Galicia-Volhynia,_ Euromaidan Press, Article uploaded on internet by Mat Babiak, 2014.

Himka, John-Paul. _Galician Villagers and the Ukrainian National Movement in the Nineteenth Century,_ St. Martin's Press, 1988.

Himka, John-Paul. _Religion and Nationality in Western Ukraine: The Greek Catholic Church and the Ruthenian National Movement in Galicia, 1867-1900,_ Montreal and Kingston: McGill-Queen's University Press, 1999.

Luciuk, Lubomyr. _Searching for Place, Ukrainian Displaced Persons, Canada, and the Migration of Memory,_ University of Toronto Press, Toronto, 2000.

Magocsi, Paul Robert. _A History of Ukraine,_ University of Toronto Press, Toronto, 1996.

Magocsi, Paul Robert. _The Roots of Ukrainian Nationalism: Galicia as Ukraine's Piedmont,_ University of Toronto Press, Toronto, 2002.

Marples, David R. _Heroes and Villains: Creating national history in contemporary Ukraine,_ Budapest: Central European University Press, 2007.

Misilo, Eugeniusz. _Operation Wisla, the forced transfer Ukrainians from the border region of eastern Poland to northern Poland after World War II,_ *documents compiled in Polish (1993) and then translated into Ukrainian by Ivanna Svarneka*, Ukrainian Archives, Warsaw, 1997.

Snyder, Timothy. *Bloodlands, Europe between Hitler and Stalin,* Basic Books, A Member of the Perseus Books Group, New York, 2010.

Snyder, Timothy. *To Resolve the Ukrainian Problem Once and for All, The Ethnic Cleansing of Ukrainians in Poland, 1943-1947,* Journal of Cold War Studies, 1999.

Snyder, Timothy. *The Causes of Ukrainian-Polish Ethnic Cleansing 1943, Past and Present,* Volume 179, Issue 1, 1 May 2002, Pages 197-234.

Subtelny, Orest. *Ukraine, A History,* Published by the University of Toronto Press in Association with the Canadian Institute of Ukrainian Studies, Toronto, 1988.

CPSIA information can be obtained
at www.ICGtesting.com
Printed in the USA
LVHW031046081019
633479LV00002B/2/P